Tasmania—A Guide

A HERITAGE FIELD GUIDE

TASMANIA—A GUIDE

Darrel and Sally Odgers

Kangaroo Press

Cover photograph of Cradle Mountain courtesy of Tourism Tasmania

Maps by Jennifer Hinch

© Sally Farrell Odgers 1989
  Darrel and Sally Odgers 1997

First published in 1989 in Kangaroo Press Pty Ltd
Second Edition published by Kangaroo Press 1997
an imprint of Simon and Schuster Australia
20 Barcoo Street (PO Box 507)
East Roseville, 2069, Australia
e.mail: kangaroo@parramatta.starway.net.au
Printed by Australian Print Group, Maryborough 3465

ISBN 0 86417 842 5

Contents

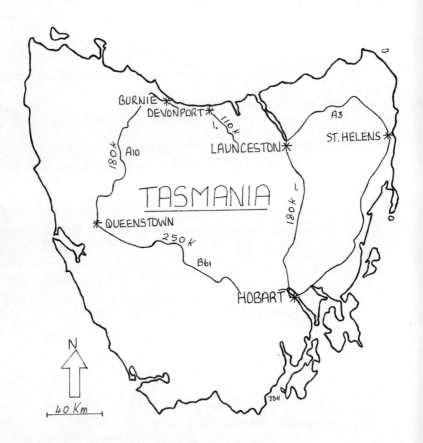

Introduction
TASMANIA—A GUIDE

The original edition of *Tasmania—A Guide* was written in 1988. Various friends and family members spent six months driving around and about in Tasmania, seeking out interesting routes and good places to go. Since the brief was to provide a friendly historical guide for travelling families, the emphasis was on country drives with historic or scenic flavours, and the result was published in 1989.

A light update was done in 1992, but by the middle of 1996 it was obvious that parts of the book were feeling their age. The social history and natural scenery sections remained relevant, but some of the routes had changed with the updating and upgrading of highways and lesser roads. A few featured buildings and tourist venues had vanished or been damaged, and some signposts had been moved or changed or obscured. Gravel roads had been sealed, large bends had been ironed out, resulting in the retreat from sight of some features which had been easily visible. It was time to redrive the routes.

This time, Darrel was major driver, joint researcher, photographer and route-finder extraordinary. We were both born and brought up in Tasmania, but we found ourselves in corners of the state we had never visited. On one trip we covered nearly 900 km, on another, longer, two-day expedition it was well over 1200.

This book is not meant to be an exhaustive history of Tasmania, nor does it pretend to cover every interesting destination. What it does set out to do is to provide an informative and (we hope) entertaining companion for your travels.

Here are a few points to remember when using *Tasmania—a Guide*.

There are 19 chapters most of which feature day trips. In at least two cases the trips would be better undertaken over two days. This presupposes that you have at least three weeks to spend.

For shorter stays, check through the opening paragraphs of each chapter for highlights of the drives concerned. Then choose the ones that appeal to you most.

Accommodation is available in most towns in Tasmania, ranging from caravan parks through budget and colonial accommodation to luxury motels.

Distances between destinations generally aren't long, but winding roads on the east and west coasts can slow you down. Food and petrol are usually easy to find; in the rare cases where this isn't so, the fact is mentioned in the chapter.

Routes suggested are seldom the only paths to the destination and are not always the fastest or major routes. What we have tried to do is to cover the greatest number of interesting features while not sacrificing a reasonable standard of road surface.

Destinations visited in different chapters might be quite close together. The aim of this book is to provide progressive trips in some cases, and round trips in others. For example, when you reach the vicinity of Hobart, you have the choice of exploring that city, or of taking three alternative drives from the same starting point.

Each destination is dealt with in detail only once, although you might pass close to one particular feature during several of the drives. For example; several routes include signposted turn-offs to Cradle Mountain. These will be noted, and in most cases, there will be a cue directing you to the appropriate chapter in which the destination is covered in detail.

Historic buildings. Public buildings such as churches and hotels are usually open for inspection, although some churches may be locked against vandalism. Some historic houses offer colonial accommodation, teas or conducted tours, others are private homes.
As the circumstances of many houses are subject to change, you need to rely on signs. Generally, houses which welcome inspection will advertise the fact.

Entry fees and hours of entry are subject to changes and seasonal fluctuations.

Museums, displays, tea-gardens and special-interest shops may sometimes close or relocate. Most of those included in *Tasmania—a Guide* are well established. Others which are not mentioned are usually clearly signposted, so you can discover those for yourselves.

National Parks are usually easily accessible. A range of passes is available, including (at the time of writing) the Tassie Holiday Pass which allows your car and its passengers access to any park within the state for a period of two months. In May

1997 the price of this is set to rise to $30.00. Daily and annual passes are also available.

Poppy crops look pretty, but don't enter the paddocks for a better look! Those *Keep Out* signs on the fences aren't for decoration.

Suggested walks in the country. Most of these are short and fairly easy.

Suggested walks in towns. Where walks are suggested within a city or town, it's usually because the buildings and other features are too close together to enjoy while driving. It's both inconvenient and dangerous to keep stopping and starting every ten metres or so.

The weather is usually temperate, but it can change very quickly in mountainous areas and the Central Highlands.

Highways. Bypasses are currently under construction near some of our towns. In some cases, it's difficult to know, in the early stages, just where these begin and end. If you encounter a bypass not listed in this book, simply stay on the highway to bypass the town, or turn off at the appropriate sign to visit.

Tasmania is a place of contrasts. Despite its small size, there are many different landscapes. The west coast is rocky and forbidding, with fog-shrouded mountains and roads which wind to and fro among the hills. It is in the west, that the mining town of Rosebery cowers in unlikely pockets beneath Mount Murchison wrapped around in bush which contains the strange plants known as horizontal scrub.
The east coast is dry and balmy, with delightful fishing villages like Scamander and Bicheno, and unspoiled white beaches, some of which boast impressive sand dunes.
The north-west contains some of the most

fertile grazing land in Australia, while the north-east has a temperate rainforest—and the first commercial lavender farm in the Southern Hemisphere.

The rugged south-west is uninhabited and largely unexplored, the Midlands flat and bare, and the Central Highlands mountainous. There are strange rock formations: limestone caves at Gunns Plains and Mole Creek, the Blow Hole and Rocking Rock at Bicheno, The Nut at Stanley and Table Cape which juts out into the ocean near Wynyard, the eerie Devils Kitchen and the Blow Hole at Eaglehawk Neck.

There is a variety of wildlife, including kangaroos, wallabies, bandicoots, ring-tailed and brush-tailed possums, platypus, echidna and the well-known Tasmanian devil. Colourful rosella parrots swoop through the trees, black and white cockatoos and kookaburras squawk and laugh. White cattle egrets can be seen around the pastures in winter, and in the east the black swans, which so astonished our early explorers, flourish.

There are a number of wildlife parks and forest and coastal reserves.

The climate is generally cool to mild, lacking the extremes of much of the mainland. Generally, the hottest weather comes in January and February, the coldest in June and July. May and September are particularly beautiful times of the year, for Tasmania has deciduous trees, and spring bulbs, like snowdrops and daffodils, grow wild in many places.

Due to frost and ice, some roads may become treacherous in winter, but these stretches are well marked with warning signs. The highway speed limit is 100 km/h, except on Route Al, where it is sometimes 110. The town limit is 60 km/h, with 70 or 80 in some places.

The visitor who concentrates on the cities will miss much of the charm and the strange contrasts of the countryside. You can't hope to see Tasmania in a weekend—or in a week—but take the time to enjoy your holiday. Remember, you can always come back.

ORGANISATION

The island of Tasmania is the smallest Australian State.Lying about 200 km south of Victoria, separated from the mainland by Bass Strait, Tasmania was discovered in 1642 by Abel Tasman (1602(?)–1659), who named it Van Diemen's Land in honour of his patron. However, as early maps of New Holland (as Australia was once known) show, Tasman thought it to be attached to the mainland.

In 1798 the explorers George Bass (born 1763, disappeared after leaving Sydney in 1803) and Matthew Flinders (1774–1814) circumnavigated Tasmania in a boat called the *Norfolk*, thus proving it to be an island. In 1803, Lieutenant John Bowen led a party to Risdon Cove, and the first settlement was made. Settlements in the north followed.

Transportation of convicts to Van Diemen's Land ended in 1852, and in 1856 the island's name was officially changed to 'Tasmania'. Tasmania has a number of industries, including farming, mining, fishing, forestry, and orcharding. The Hydro Electric Commission (H.E.C.) has made dams on many major rivers: these are of interest and one at least (Devils Gate at Barrington), is a scenic attraction.

Although Tasmanian roads are generally good, the State's relatively small size, (6 883 000 hectares) makes distances deceptive. Tasmania is roughly the size of Ireland, and, although it has six cities, much of the population is scattered throughout the smaller towns and country areas, Anyone driving straight from Launceston to Hobart will miss a great deal. The best way to travel is by car (either your own or a hired one). Tasmania's small population (around 447 000 people) means that the bus services are limited, although coach tours are available. There is no regular long-distance passenger train service.

This book assumes that you have arrived at the port of Devonport in the central north, and will be travelling first to the east. Words printed in **bold print** denote general headings or special points of interest. Many of the buildings and properties referred to are privately owned and not all are open to the public. The author disclaims any responsibility for trespass by tourists.

Escorted tours are available to most destinations in Tasmania. These include trail riding, cruises, bushwalking, and four-wheel drive and coach tours. Up-to-date information on these is available from any branch of the Tasmanian Travel and Information Centre. Branches are located at 5 Best Street, Devonport; Civic Square Precinct, off Little Alexander St, Burnie; corner, St John and Paterson Streets, Launceston; and corner Davey and Elizabeth Streets, Hobart.

1. Devonport and Latrobe

Features of this drive

If you have arrived in Tasmania by sea, this will probably be the first drive you take from this book.

Like most of the trips that follow, it offers a wide range of interest. You'll visit the city of Devonport, the historic town of Latrobe, and several smaller towns out in the country. Some features along the way include a good selection of Georgian and early Victorian buildings, wide, white-sand beaches, secluded bays, rural pasture land, Aboriginal rock carvings, an historic railway museum, a history walk detailing Australia's experiences during World Wars I and II, an art gallery, and a ruin once inhabited by a scholar who labelled jam jars in Latin! The roads are good, and the distances not at all taxing.

The ferry

The *Spirit of Tasmania* roll on/roll off ferry sails from Station Pier in Melbourne at 6 p.m. Monday, Wednesday and Friday, arriving at the T/T Line terminal at East Devonport at 8.30 a.m. on the day following. Built in Germany in 1985 and commissioned the following year, the ship was first known as the *Peter Pan*, a name which has since been changed to the present *Spirit of Tasmania*. The ship took over from its predecessor, the *Abel Tasman*, in November 1993.

About Devonport

Devonport, known locally as 'the gateway to Tasmania', is an ideal place to begin your tour of Tasmania. Situated at the mouth of the Mersey River, Devonport is the fourth of

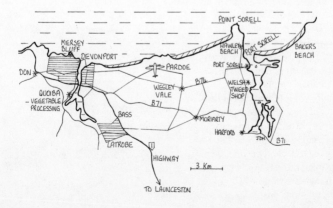

Tasmania's six cities, and was first settled in the 1840s. Originally, it comprised two main towns, Formby (on the western bank of the Mersey) and Torquay (on the east), as well as the properties known as Appledore and Wenvoe. Appledore (a property owned by Bartholomew William Thomas, and named for a village in Devon) was settled in 1852, Wenvoe, (belonging to Charles Thomas and named for a village in Wales)in 1854, Formby in 1853, and Torquay in 1851. In 1890 the villages merged. Torquay is now officially known as East Devonport, while the west bank is called simply Devonport. The two centres are linked by Victoria Bridge.

The *Spirit of Tasmania* docks on the eastern bank of the river.

The Mersey River was first mentioned in a book published in 1820; it was then known as the Second Western River and was re-named the Mersey in 1826 by Edward Curr, the manager of the Van Diemen's Land Company. The Mersey rises in the Central Highlands and runs through Kimberley and Latrobe to Devonport at its mouth.

Tour of East Devonport
On leaving the ferry terminal, turn left onto the Esplanade. In front of you at the first intersection is Number 13 Thomas St (c. 1861). Here Miss Catherine Dean ran a small school. In 1875 the postmistress, Miss Annie Cocker, had an office here. Just across Church St, as you turn right into Thomas St, are St Paul's Pioneer Park and St Paul's Church of England. St Paul's is a simple building, with arched windows and a steeply pitched roof and graceful spire. Its foundation stone was laid on 13 December 1896, and the first rector was the Reverend G.F. Archer, B.A., who had founded the Formby Grammar School the previous year.

St Paul's Church of England and Pioneer Park, East Devonport

In the park are monuments to early settlers in the region. These were moved some years ago when the old graveyard fell into disrepair, and date from the 1880s to the early 20th century. Among them is the headstone of Marion Winspear (nee Stewart), wife of William Dean Winspear. Some of their descendants still live in these parts. Many

of the stones are in good condition, and are standing upright. Others, cracked or broken, have been set flat in the gravel pathway. A plaque nearby reads thus: 'St Paul's Pioneer Park. This wall is erected in memory of the East Devonport pioneers. The names of all interred here will be found in St Paul's church.'

Turn left off Thomas St into Wright St, the Abel Tasman caravan park at East Devonport beach. There is a pleasant picnic area. Return along Wright St, and to your left you will see the pleasant building known as The Old Rectory. For many years a parsonage, it currently caters for banquets and other functions.

Turn left into Stephen St. At the intersection of Stephen and David Streets on the hill, in large grounds surrounded by trees, is historic homestead Mt Pleasant, built in the 1860s. In the grounds is a brick-lined circular well, more than 20 m deep.Return along Stephen St and turn left into Tarleton St.

on which you will see numerous small boats. An interesting feature, at 57 Formby Road, is Taswegia, identified by its striking Tasmanian tiger motif. It is a combined printing museum, craft studio and gift shop. Taswegia opened 4 December, 1985, and, as well as calendars, cards and posters etc., produces the *Devon County Times*. Taswegia is open daily, 10 a.m.–5 p.m. The printing presses, some of which are 100 years old, have been beautifully restored and are in full working order.

78 Formby Road is The Alex, the Alexander Hotel, which was built around 1904.

The first street after the traffic lights is Best St, and at Number 5, on the left, just at the entrance of the car park, is the Devonport Showcase, which houses Impressions Gallery, displaying high quality Tasmanian-made craftwork, and the Old Devonport Town Coffee Shop. Tourist information, including free brochures, is available as well. If you continue on the Esplanade (Formby Rd), you come to Oldaker St, named after

Touring Devonport

Follow Tarleton St until it branches off. Follow the right-hand branch, which runs right under Victoria Bridge. Take the next left-hand turn which sweeps you right around and over the bridge towards Devonport City.

Victoria Bridge. The original bridge was opened in 1902, and the present structure in 1971. In March 1993, work was begun on a second Mersey River Bridge, which is now complete. This expansion was deemed necessary when traffic volume on the existing bridge reached 26 000 vehicles per day.

Follow the route to the town centre, driving along Formby Road. This road hugs the west bank of the river,

Solaqueous Fountain, Victoria Parade, Devonport

Charles Oldaker, an early settler. A few hundred metres from the corner is the Devonport Library (1985), which has a good display of old and rare books dealing with Tasmania. In the foyer are some large glass cases, where displays are held. The library (housed in the Lyons Library building) is open five days a week excluding public holidays. Continue to the end of Formby Road and turn right into Victoria Parade. This street was originally known as The Esplanade, but was renamed in 1897 during Queen Victoria's Jubilee celebrations. Victoria Parade once more hugs the foreshore. On the right are colourful gardens and, just past Nicholls St, the city cenotaph.

An interesting feature nearby is a fountain clock, set in a surround of raised crazy paving garden beds and with a natural rock centrepiece. This is the Solaqueous Fountain, which uses sun and water to give eastern standard time. It was designed by K.C. Davison, and donated by the Soroptimists Club of Devonport, in 1974. Just opposite Point Frederick, in Gloucester Avenue, is the Tasmanian Maritime and Folk Museum, open in the afternoons from Tuesday to Sunday. Admission fees are very reasonable. First housed at East Devonport, the collection outgrew its accommodation and is now in the old Harbour Master's residence and Pilot station.

This was built in 1920, for the sum of £1,434/10/6, and its several rooms are crammed with items, all donated. A large brass bell hanging in the foyer is a bit of a mystery: it is stamped with the letters H.M.C.S. One room is devoted to the ferries which have plied the Bass Strait route: there are scale models of the ferries *Abel Tasman*, *Empress of Australia* and *Princess of Tasmania,* all predecessors of the current *Spirit of Tasmania*. There are also a number of photographs of these ships while they were in commission. Here is the *Oona*, built in 1888, and the *Nairana*, which ran aground in Port Phillip Bay in 1951. Another room is devoted to Devonport itself. There is an old diving suit, complete with lead-weighted boots and an air compressor which predates scuba tanks. There are whaling tools, ships' logs, paintings, ships in bottles, and photographs. Everywhere are scale models, many meticulously made by Mr W. Parker of Somerset.

The four-masted barque *Lawhill* used to bring cocoa beans from South America to Cadbury's factory in Hobart. The guide tells a story of a lad who ran away from home in 1936, fell in love with the *Lawhill* and signed on as cabin boy. He sailed to the Falkland Islands, collected the cocoa beans, and returned to Hobart—only to be locked up by his outraged parents. He promptly ran away again and joined the navy. There are even models of the *Titanic*—as she was when she was launched and as photographic evidence has shown she is now.

Devonport from Mersey Bluff

Victoria Parade leads on to the headland known as Mersey Bluff. On the right is an adventure playground for children, a bike track and skate bowl. Turn right into William St, and ahead lies Mersey Bluff Reserve. Here is a caravan park and a winding road (closed at night) which leads to the top of the Bluff. At the top of the headland is the Mersey Lighthouse (1889).

The 25 000 candle power light, (electric since 1955) is visible up to 27 kilometres out to sea. From the light, a short walking track leads down to steps and a concrete viewing platform, where you may look out over the sea and rocks at the foot of the bluff. Here also is the start of a walking track which leads back to the cenotaph.

Tiagarra

Behind and to the left of the Mersey Light is **Tiagarra**, the Tasmanian Aboriginal Culture and Art Centre. Tiagarra, ('Keeping Place') opened in 1976, and is a popular tourist centre. The main building, with many meticulously prepared displays depicting Aboriginal life, is open daily. Apart from this centre, many well-preserved Aboriginal carvings may be seen scattered around the rocks of the bluff. A detailed plan of the walking track taking in these carvings is available from the craft and gift shop at the centre.

The **Tasmanian Aborigines** are known to have occupied the island over 20 000 years ago. They were a small race of nomadic hunters and gatherers with their own culture which developed quite apart from that of the mainland tribes.

With the coming of European settlement, Governor George Arthur (1784–1854) attempted to resettle the Aborigines onto reserves, including Tasman Peninsula and Oyster Cove. This venture failed, and the race tragically declined. The last full-blooded Tasmanian Aboriginal man, William Lanne, died in 1869, the last woman, Trugannini of the Bruny Island tribe, in 1876.

There are plenty of historic buildings in Devonport, but there isn't room to cover them all in this chapter. If you have time, ask at The Showcase for directions.

Coles Beach Road. Coming down from Mersey Bluff, turn right into Coles Beach Road and take a pleasant drive round the foreshore to Coles Beach and Don Heads. Coles Beach is an ideal place to get out of the car and stretch your legs. It is a lovely unspoilt beach, and favourite haunt of children who delight in scrambling over the rocks and collecting shells. Take a picnic lunch. The local seagulls will appreciate any spare bread you happen to have!

Return to William St, turn right and drive right along to Middle Road. On top of the hill to the left at 77 Middle Road, is 'Home Hill',

'Home Hill', Middle Road, Devonport, home of Joseph and Dame Enid Lyons

the gracious home of the late Sir Joseph and Dame Enid Lyons. Beautifully restored and furnished, 'Home Hill' is open to the public daily from Tuesday to Sunday, 2 p.m.–4 p.m. **Dame Enid Lyons** was born Enid Muriel Burnell in Leesville, near Smithton, in 1897. At the age of 18 she married Joseph Lyons (1879–1939), a fellow Tasmanian who was Premier of Tasmania from 1923 to 1928 and became Prime Minister of Australia in 1931. They had eleven children, and many of their descendants still live in Tasmania. In 1949 Dame Enid became the first woman to hold Federal Cabinet rank. She retired in 1951 and died in 1981. Her story is told in her autobiography *Among the Carrion Crows*. 'Home Hill'—always her favourite haven—is just as Dame Enid left it.

The Don

At the end of Middle Road, turn right into Stoney Rise Road. About 2 km along this road, is the tiny Anglican Church of St Olave's (1880) on your right. Next, you arrive at the Don River Railway Museum. The Don River Railway was established in 1973 and the trains have been running since 1976. The result of voluntary work from members of the Van Diemen Light Railway Society Inc, the museum and train rides are popular attractions with residents and visitors to Tasmania. Engines and carriages dating from 1869 are being lovingly restored, and personnel are enthusiastic and very willing to show visitors around and answer questions. Vintage trains run every day except Good Friday and Christmas Day and steam trains run most Sundays and holidays. Sometimes, special trains run farther afield. Ask at the railway for up-to-date news. The museum has Tasmania's largest collection of steam locomotives and carriages.

At the time of writing, the Don River Railway Museum is expanding. It now has a large collection of ephemera and other railway memorabilia, which covers not only the history of local rail travel but also a good deal of social history.

Don was first settled in 1840, when Thomas Drew began a small timber business. By the early 1950s there was a sawmill but along with many other townships in the district, it declined when the railway was extended to Formby (West Devonport) in 1885.

The Road to Latrobe

To reach the town of Latrobe from Don, return down Stoney Rise Road (Route B19). Bypass the turn-off into Middle Road, and continue, crossing Horsehead Creek. Drive through the town of Spreyton and the hamlet of Tarleton, bypass the right-hand turn-off into Route B13 and continue towards Latrobe.

Latrobe's history

Latrobe is a town of 3000 inhabitants. It was named for Charles Joseph La Trobe. La Trobe assumed temporary administration of Van Diemen's Land in 1846 and later, in 1851, became the first Governor of Victoria. The region, first known as 'the La Trobe reserve', was marked out in early 1851, and the town settled in 1858.

Before the growth of Devonport, Latrobe was the largest town on the north-west coast, with coal and shale mining, (now abandoned), farming and the wharf at Bells Parade. There are several places of historical interest in and around the town, which is now classed as an Historic Village.

Places to see in Latrobe

The large brick house on your left is 'Frogmore', built in the 1880s by George Atkinson Jr, who had purchased the property originally granted to Captain Moriarty in the 1830s. 'Frogmore' has a little square tower at the top. Cross the bridge, and turn off to the left to visit Bells Parade.

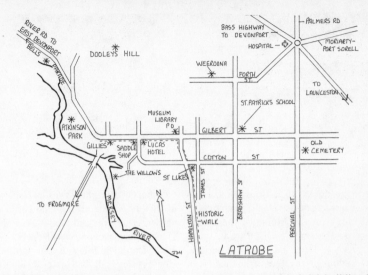

Towards Bells Parade. On your left, as you drive along beside the river, you'll pass Atkinson Park, where there is a monument to George Atkinson, who was often known as 'the Father of Latrobe'.

George Atkinson was born in London in 1833 and arrived in Tasmania in 1852. George was the son of George Atkinson Senior (1804–1872) and his wife Ann (1804–1856). The Atkinsons moved north to Ballahoo, where together with one Zephaniah Williams and others, they began mining for coal. In 1864, George married Rhoda Williams. George Atkinson Sr bought land in Tarleton and Latrobe where he built the first general store and helped decide on the site for the original Latrobe Bridge. He built the first hotel (The Royal Charter Inn, later The Latrobe Inn), in 1858, and was postmaster sometime during the 1860s.

In 1864, George Jr took over the hotel. Twelve years later the inn, now leased, burnt down and was replaced by the stone building on the corner of Gilbert and Victor Streets, now known as Lucas Hotel. By 1873 Atkinson had opened his saleyards and three years later he erected a brick building for a mart, and became an auctioneer. He followed this occupation until retiring in 1916. In the 1880s, George bought the Frogmore property, which had been granted to Captain Moriarty in the 1830s, Here, he built the gracious brick residence which still stands today. When he retired at 83 he was given a handsome illuminated testimonial, signed by men of Latrobe and the surrounding districts, which is still hanging in Frogmore house. Descendants of these signatories still live in the district, but the Atkinson family line died with George's daughter Joan in 1965. When George died in 1920, he was buried in the Anglican cemetery at St Paul's, East Devonport, joining wife Rhoda, parents-in-law Zephaniah and Joan Williams, and Edmund Llewellyn, another family member. His second wife Sophia was buried at Latrobe. In 1987 Latrobe Council gained permission to move to Atkinson Park the white marble monument to George Atkinson and his wife's family.

Bells Parade. Just past Atkinson Park, Bells Parade is seen on the right. Here,

Mersey River near Bells Parade, Latrobe

where the docks once flourished, is a pleasant picnic spot, the setting each summer of 'Henley on the Mersey', the local riverside festival. Bells Parade was extensively restored and beautified during 1986–87 through the efforts of the combined service clubs and the C.E.P. Scheme.

At the Settlers Wharf is a bronze sculpture, by Stephen Walker of Campania, depicting scenes from local history. There is a bridge across the river to Pig Island: an attractive spot which belies its name. A feature of Bells Parade is restored Sherwood Hall.

Sherwood Hall was built by Thomas Johnson and his wife Dolly Dalrymple in the 1850s, and later owned by the French family, of whom one, Daniel French, was Sally's own great-great-grandfather. Members of the French family lived there until 1970 when a severe flood caused the original site to be condemned. During the 1990s, it was moved to this present site and restored. Sherwood Hall is open to the public.On the hill to your left, visible from Settlers Wharf, is an old white house, built in 1887 by Henry Murray M.H.A. the later residence of his daughter Hannah Murray, the town's school mistress. Bells Parade is named for Mr Robert Bell who, with his half-brother Henry Bentinck, made a wharf and store on the site in 1855.

Gilbert Street. Return towards town and drive down Gilbert St, the main street of Latrobe. On the right is Tynsley Hall, built in 1879 by Stephen Kelcey, and used as a residence and tailor and habit-making shop. The building is recorded with the National Trust. The old building on your right, soon after Tynsley Hall, is Samuel Ready's old shop, built in 1866, and just across Victor St stands Lucas Hotel, built in 1872.

If you turn right into Victor St and continue to a Y-fork in the road, you will see to your right the entrance to the property known as The Willows. Here the old wooden homestead was built by William Bonney in the mid-1850s. Originally, The Willows was part of a large property which encompassed land far as Cherry Hills at the opposite end of Latrobe, but William's son, also William, sold off a great deal of the land. William Sr's father, James, donated the land where St Luke's Church of England was built in what is now Hamilton St. William's grand daughter Miss Elsie Bonney (1899–1997), lived in the old homestead until 1962. Owing to its peculiar structure (the foundations were rock on the outside only, with the inner part consisting of great rounds cut from tree trunks); the house is now in a poor state of repair.

Number 84 Gilbert St was a drapers shop known as Kenworthys. It was first operated as a book arcade in the early 1890s by Jabez White, but was taken over by J.P. Kenworthy. Mr Kenworthy, known as 'Pa', was lame, owing to a boyhood accident, and his habit of rubbing his hands and saying 'Come along this way', was mimicked by local boys. His daughter, Mercia Kenworthy, born in 1900, managed the shop until the early 1980s. It is now an antique shop.

On your left, not far from Kenworthys, you will see the Teddy Sheean Memorial. The bronze statue of this local hero marks the beginning of a short walk bounded by native trees and plaques detailing Australia's involvement in war time.

At Numbers 108–114 Gilbert St is William Wells and Sons, a family business which has operated for over eighty years. The store was first opened by a Mr Oppenheim in the 1870s, then taken over by Samuel Sternberg in 1880. William Levitt Wells bought the business in 1893, and his great-grandson Garth Wells runs it today. In 1988 a new grocery department was added to the store, carefully designed so as to be in keeping with the original building. More expansion was under way in 1996. Station Square, site of the old railway station, has the novel Hands of Fame, handprints and information from country singers who have visited the Square. Opposite Wells are the post office, library and Old Courthouse Museum, which has an impressive collection of local items. It is open on Sunday and Friday afternoons. Next in Gilbert St comes the Baptist Tabernacle, built in 1892. Also in Gilbert St is the Information Centre, featuring crafts, book and local tourist news.

Hamilton Street. Turn right into Hamilton St. On your right are old cottages and on your left the Uniting Church, bult in 1879, replacing a small wooden one.

On the corner of Hamilton and Cotton Streets on the left is Number 19 Hamilton St, called Sternbergs, and traditionally the schoolmaster's residence. This lovely house was built as a gentleman's residence for Samuel Sternberg during the 1890s. On the other side of Cotton St is St Luke's Church of England. Inside the church is a memorial to Reverend William Hogg, a much-loved rector who was well known for his favoured method of transport: he rode a tricycle!

St Luke's Church of England, Hamilton St, Latrobe.

Pass Thomas St to your left, and you will see an unusual Italianate-style house with a cupola on top. This is Hamilton House, built for Alfred Ellis, from Bothwell, in 1872. Mr Ellis, who married a Miss Hedditch and had twelve children, ran a general store in Latrobe until being forced out by problems with flooding. He then moved to Ulverstone. Internally, the house is built round an octagonal vestibule. It is now listed with the National Trust. Also in Hamilton St, No. 78, is Vermont, another early Victorian house, built c. 1863 by J.H. Bellion. Vermont may have been one of the first 'spec' homes in the area: it is thought that the design and much of the outer timber were imported from Scotland. At one time Vermont traded as McKenzie's Cash Store, and was the last cash store to the east before Deloraine.

Hamilton St continues into Shale Road, then branches into a Y-fork. The right fork leads on to the Mersey River at a place known as the Great Bend. The left fork is the old Deloraine Road.

Shale Road bounds the hills where the abandoned shale works may be seen. The whole hill is honeycombed with tunnels: one especially impressive one being known as the Ballroom! Even in the hottest weather a cold draught can be felt at the mouth. The hill is now a grazing property. The road from here on is very rough, but at the end is a very pleasant picnic area and a bush walk.

More places in Latrobe. Return to Gilbert St and turn right to visit the old Latrobe graveyard, where many early settlers are buried, including Sophia Louise Hogg, the second wife of George Atkinson. Nearby is St Patrick's Church, built in the early 1870s mainly through the efforts of Kilkenny-born priest Father James Noone known locally as 'James the builder'. A small street nearby was named Noone St in his honour and when he died in Hobart in 1901 he was buried in the churchyard here.

Dooleys Hill. Before leaving Latrobe, you may like the drive over Dooleys Hill (named for James Dooley M.H.A. who owned a great deal of the hill and died in 1891). Heading back past Bells Parade, you will see a steep road leading off at a sharp angle to your right. Drive up, taking a sharp right-hand bend, and continue over the hill. For the first part of the drive you can see down over the Parade. From the top are views over river flats. Follow the road to the right. This brings you to the top of Forth St. From here you can see most of Latrobe. As you descend into Bradshaw St, you will see on the left a big brick house set in large grounds. 'Weeroona' (1891) was built for Dr William Stewart and was later a Girls' Home. It is now Lucinda Colonial Accommodation. Drive to the end of Forth St.

Palmers Road. Another short drive takes you up Palmers Road. Turn left out of Forth St into Moriarty Road. Continue to the roundabout. Here, the Mersey Community Hospital (first hospital on the north-west

coast) is on your left. Take the part of the roundabout which points the way to Moriarty, and turn left up Palmers Road. Palmers Road climbs steeply and there is a sharp bend to the right at the top of Stagg Hill.

Soon after, the bush on your right opens into paddocks and here, smothered in ivy, can still be seen the remains of Palmer's Cottage, an old clay and stone cottage hand-built by Old Palmer, a classics scholar who reputedly labelled his wife's renowned home-made jam in Latin. Please note—this cottage is on private property.

At the top end of Palmer's Road, turn right onto Frankford Road, right again at the first turn-off into Wesley Vale Road and return to the Bass Highway (Route A1) via Moriarty Road.

The country district

From Devonport. North of Latrobe and east of Devonport lies the district known locally as 'Out the Country'. It can be reached from Devonport if you leave the city on the Bass Highway and travel east over Victoria Bridge. Turn left into Route B74, and take the Pardoe road.

From Latrobe. To reach the country district from Latrobe, turn left out of Moriarty Road into Route A1 (the Bass Highway) and turn right into Route B74.

Things to see

The original Pardoe was a 250-acre property taken up by William Francis Wright, a Shropshire man, in 1841, and given his mother's maiden name. Pardoe Road leads you to Pardoe Airport on the left. If you continue on this road, you pass the Associated Pulp and Paper Mills on your right.

Left is the short, rough Moorland Beach road. Sometimes fairy penguins may be seen on the beach in the evenings.

Wesley Vale

Take the roundabout onto Port Sorell Road, Route B74, leaving behind you the hamlet of Wesley Vale, probably named for the Wesleyan Methodist Church erected there. On your left is the property of Northdown, once Van Diemen's Land Company land but occupied in the 1820s by the Thomas family. A descendant owns it today. The history of Northdown and surrounding properties is detailed in the excellent book *Sam Thomas and His Neighbours*, by Harold Thomas. If you turn to your right, into Wrights Lane (named for the Wright family that settled Pardoe), you will be driving through the gently rolling hills of cropping and sheep-farming land. The soil here is rich and red. Along the Port Sorell road to your right you see the signs to Gallerie Chantilly, which is open from 10 a.m. until 5 p.m. every day except Saturday. Gallerie Chantilly is run by local artist Cheyne Purdue, and houses a display of local artwork and crafts.

Hawley Beach and Port Sorell

Farther along the Port Sorell road is a left turn which takes you to Hawley Beach, a series of lovely sheltered beaches and coves and a popular holiday area. Also along this road is Shearwater, which has a country club, with a swimming pool and golf course. Take this turn-off and drive along the straight, taking a sharp right-angled turn at the end. This takes you into Dumbleton St, which leads right down along the foreshore. There are fine-needled she-oak trees between the beach and the road, and down on the sand itself are yellow-flowered boobiallas. The rocks on the beach are distinctively coloured by orange lichens. Away to your right, over the Port Sorell inlet, you will see Bakers Beach and the Asbestos Range National Park. At the far end of Dumbleton St is a scenic walking track to Point Sorell (return trip 3 hours). On your left, off the road, is Hawley House, the first home built in the area (late 1870s), by Major Arthur Dumbleton and named for his mother's old home. Hawley House is now a guesthouse and vineyard. The wine labels are works of art, and the house itself has a bath on top!

Back at the main Port Sorell road, drive straight on to Port Sorell, at the mouth of the Rubicon River. The port is a sheltered inlet, with a charming little fishing village, once called Burgess after the Chief Police Magistrate of the island, and settled in 1844. Now, town and beach alike are known as 'Port Sorell'. Drive to the end Of Wilmot St. This turns sharply to the left, and the first sealed right-hand turn brings you to the jetty, a favourite spot for fishing.

Opposite the Hawley turn-off is Parkers Ford Road, Route C708. Along this road a roundabout takes you to Squeaking Point, rather quaintly named after the long-ago escape of a piglet! Squeaking Point is a rather muddy beach, so wear old shoes.

Port Sorell jetty; in the distance is Bakers Beach

Moriarty

Continuing along Route C708 you may turn right to return through Thirlstane and Moriarty to Devonport. Moriarty is a farming district named after Captain Moriarty, an early settler.

Drive along the Moriarty Road towards Latrobe. On your left near Wescombes Road, is the land originally owned by Donald Wescombe. From the old homestead near the top of the road, Sarah Wescombe used to walk into Latrobe every week to do her shopping.

Asbestos Ranges National Park

If you prefer, you may stay on Parkers Ford Road. Take the next sealed turn to the left, cross the muddy Rubicon and Franklin Rivers, and turn left onto the unsealed road (Route C740) to the Asbestos Ranges National Park.

The Asbestos Range was once a gold-mining area and the Park runs right up to Badger Head. Follow the road right through; you come to Bakers Beach, a quiet white-sand beach with impressive sand dunes. A right-hand turn about 1 km from the beginning of Asbestos Range Road will bring you in a long loop through the Dalgarth Park Forest Reserve, and Route C741 runs right through the Dazzler Range to Beaconsfield, which you will be visiting in Chapter 5.

BIBLIOGRAPHY

Books
COCKER, Kathleen, *Early Houses of the North West Coast of Tasmania*, G.H. Stancombe, 1973.
RAMSAY, Charles, *With the Pioneers*, 1957, revised edition 1979, Latrobe Group of the National Trust, Australia.
THOMAS, Bertram, *Prints from the Past*, 1981, Latrobe Group of the National Trust, Australia,
THOMAS, Harold, *Sam Thomas and his Neighbours*, Harold Thomas, 1975.

Pamphlets
'Let's Talk about Tiagarra', Tasmanian Visitor Corporation, Ltd. Gallerie Chantilly.

Maps
Tasmania 1:100 000 Topographic Maps, Land Tenure Index Series, Edition 2, published by Lands Department: 'Forth', 'Tamar'
UBD Street Directory, Universal Press.
Tasmania Visitor Atlas.

Information
Thanks to Elsie Bonney, Kath Devereaux, G. and P. Farrell, Tony Hendricks, the T/T Line, staff at Gallerie Chantilly, Don River Railway, the Maritime Museum, Sherwood Hall; and to the citizens of Devonport and Latrobe.

2. Kentish: The Cradle and Roland

Features of this drive

The Kentish area, less than an hour's drive from Devonport, is proud possessor of two of Tasmania's better-known mountains: Cradle Mountain and Mt Roland. You'll have a chance to see these and many other delights, ranging from the impressive heights of Devils Gate Dam to an enormous maze, the village of Lower Crackpot, the lovely murals at Sheffield and the charm of Paradise, Roland and Promised Land. At least two days should be set aside for exploring Kentish, as the Cradle Mountain drive alone is usually regarded as a day trip.

Cradle Mountain

Cradle Mountain, popular with naturalists, botanists, bushwalkers, climbers, fishermen, skiers, tourists, artists, photographers and children is situated in the Cradle Mountain/Lake St Clair National Park, and proudly claims World Heritage listing.

History of Kentish Plains

Kentish Plains was named after a Government Surveyor appointed to the area in 1841. His name was Nathaniel Lipscombe Kentish. In 1842 Kentish and his assistant, with a party of assigned convicts, were given the job of surveying a road from Deloraine to the north-west coast. Their route led through grassy plains, referred to by Kentish as 'August Plains' after the month of their discovery. However, the area became officially known by the name of Kentish.

At one time gold and silver lead were mined in the region, but it was more generally used for grazing. By 1862 the beginnings of a town had sprung up. This was named Sheffield, probably by Edward Curr of the Van Diemen's Land Company. A man named James Powlett built the first building, the Kentish Inn.

The road to Cradle Mountain

To get to Cradle Mountain, take the Roland Highway. Pass the turn-off to the left towards Tarleton and turn right into Route

C146 towards Eugenana (pronounced 'you-zjen-arn-a'). Drive through Aberdene.

Pass on your left the turn-off to Lower Barrington, and the Kelcey Tier Road on your right. This is orcharding and sheep country, and very hilly. Like many other names on the Tasmanian map, Eugenana is a district rather than a town. Lakeside Road, leading to the caravan park, is to your right as you enter Eugenana. At the caravan park is Melrose Quarry, a favourite local swimming hole.

Arboretum. Just out of Eugenana, you might like to turn right into Old Tramway Road to visit the Arboretum, which covers 45 hectares, and features a lake nature walk and a Tasmanian section.

Once through Eugenana you will come to a T-junction. The right fork leads toward Forth, and the left, C145, to Melrose and Lower Barrington. The left one is the one to take. On your right, just through Melrose, is a right turn to Paloona and Wilmot. Pass Route C145 to Lower Barrington on your left traverse some winding road through blackwoods and there is a turn-off to the left (C144) to Paloona Dam. This sign faces away from you. Go straight ahead, over a single lane bridge on Route C144 over the Forth River. Just past the bridge is another T-junction.

Turn left, on C132, towards Wilmot and Cradle Mountain.

Three km along this road is the Alma Reserve. After crossing the river again the road begins to climb quite steeply between massive hills.

Along the highway towards Wilmot you travel through thick bush with wattle and blackwoods (*Acacia melanoxylon*). Do this trip in spring, when these trees are in bloom—unless wattle pollen gives you hay fever! The road rises quite steeply in the hill known locally as Gentle Annie. Above Annie is Chinaman's Hill.

Soon you will pass a turn-off into Upper Castra Road. This is also known as the back road to Leven Canyon. (For a trip to Leven Canyon, see Chapter 18.)

Just beyond this turn-off you should see a good view of Mt Roland. On the left hand side, 3 km away, is Lake Barrington, reached by taking Route C135. As you come to the top of the rise a bit farther on, you look down on Lake Barrington with Mt Roland directly above it. The view is almost too perfect. Beside the road is a stout wooden viewing platform, and a colourful signboard depicts the view and indicates the several mountains visible from this point. These include Mt Claude and Cradle Mountain.

Lake Barrington, created by the Mersey-Forth Power Development Scheme, is the

Mount Roland

venue of Australia's International Rowing Course. You'll get a closer look at Lake Barrington later in this chapter.

Next, you come into Wilmot, a farming area. Wilmot is the site of the first of the Coles shops. Erriba (pronounced 'err-ribba'), comes after Wilmot, and is a very small village with a handful of houses. Another excellent view of the local mountains can be seen to your left.

The Naming of Mt Roland. Mt Roland was once known as Rolland's Repulse, after Captain Rolland of the 3rd regiment who took an exploring trip there in 1823. Owing to illness, he had to retreat from the foot of Mt Roland. Somehow the name was corrupted to its present form. Mt Roland is a great favourite with artists and photographers, as it displays great variety of colours according to light and season. Like Cradle Mountain, it has an inconvenient habit of retreating into the clouds when menaced by a camera. Soon after leaving Erriba, you will reach 3 km of winding road. On a sunny day, there are more very impressive views to be had to the left. At Moina, you will come to what might be called the gateway into Cradle Mountain. There is a turn-off onto Route C136 to Cethana and Sheffield. Straight ahead, on Route C132, is Cradle Mountain, and to the right is the road to Wilmot Dam. At this crossroads there are tea rooms, some pleasant accommodation venues and craft shops.

Wilmot Dam. This road is a private H.E.C. Road, and visitors use it at their own risk. Wilmot Dam is situated on Lake Gairdner. When we visited it the water level was extremely low. The rocks about here have a reddish lichen growing on them, which gives the dam and its surroundings rather a surreal appearance. There is a narrow metal ladder leading up the cliff to a viewing platform from which you can see both sides of the dam. Wattles on the hillside opposite add to the colourful surroundings in early spring. Part of the large Mersey-Forth Power Development, begun in 1963 and completed in the early 1970s, the dam is rock-filled, with a concrete face, and is roughly 35 m in height and 138 m in length.

Back on the main road, drive on for 2 km and turn left. Continue for 8 km to Lemonthyme Lodge (accommodation and meals). The lodge is said to incorporate the largest log cabin in the Southern Hemisphere!

Return to the main road, follow the signs to Cradle Valley, and begin the 30 km drive to your destination.

Middlesex Plains. At first you drive through pleasant bushland, but when you pass the old tree known as the Post Office Tree, (once used for this by timber workers and prospectors), and reach the area known as Middlesex Plains, the surroundings change. Much of the land around here is privately owned, and during the 1930s some was partially cleared for grazing. Most of the eucalypts were ringbarked, but the ground proved unsuitable. Woodchippers have cleared away much of the dead wood and some areas have been fenced off for re-afforestation projects. Cattle graze in many parts and there are cattle grids in the road. The future of the area is still uncertain. The road forks, with one branch leading directly to Cradle Mountain Lake St Clair National Park and the other to the west coast to intercept the Murchison Highway near Que River.

Cradle Mountain Lodge. As the road winds on towards the mountain, you will be passing through buttongrass plains and crossing bridges over beautifully clear creeks and tiny rivers. Iris Rivulet and Black Bog Creek are only two of many. A short distance before you reach Cradle Mountain Lodge, you will see to your right the official camping area. Next comes the lodge itself, and the cluster of timber cabins with individual names such as Emmet, Fagus, Anne, Cradle and Blackwood. Inside the lodge is a lounge with a featured stone fireplace in the middle. Meals are available to passers-by as well as to residents.

Small wallabies hop unconcernedly around the cabins and black currawongs with white-rimmed tails and wings swoop about with the huge confidence of those in possession of the biggest beaks in the region.

Several walks begin from the Pencil Pine Creek area, ranging from the half-hour Enchanted Walk, which is ideally suited to families with young children, to more demanding half-day trips.

The Enchanted Walk is a narrow path which hugs the pretty little Pencil Pine Creek and weaves through mossy dells and glades. It crosses the river via a small bridge, then doubles back on the other side of the river, passing Pencil Pine Falls and the Waterfall Pool. As with most of these mountain creeks, the water is very cold and clear.

At night, a spotlight is turned on outside the lodge and many of the native animals come from the park and surrounding areas to feed. We saw Bennett's wallabies and pademelons and brush-tailed possums, but apparently native cats and Tasmanian devils

Cradle Mountain and Lake Dove

also roll up on occasion. Many of the animals are very tame, but beware of the possums: they can inflict a nasty bite! Just behind the lodge, you can enter the Cradle Mountain National Park, and drive the 7 km to the start of the track to the mountain itself.

Cradle Mountain Lake St Clair National Park

The National Park comprises 168 000 hectares of wilderness country, listed by the World Heritage Committee in 1982. There is a permanent rangers' station where those intending to go on walks within the park must register their intentions. The wild beauty of the park has a perilous quality: the weather can blow up to snow, rain or sleet in a matter of minutes during any season, so walkers must be sensibly equipped to deal with any conditions. At the station there is a warning that children under the age of eight years are not advised to attempt the walks in the park. The road leading through the park towards Lake Dove is narrow, winding and gravel-surfaced.

Cradle Mountain was named by Joseph Fossey (who also named Middlesex Plains) in 1827 for its resemblance to a miner's (or possibly a baby's) cradle.

From the car park near the lake radiate a series of walking tracks, including walks to Mt Campbell (3 hours), to Hansons Peak (3 hours; named for a young boy who died in the area), to Twisted Lakes (3.5 hours) and Lake Rodway (5 hours). There are also routes to Lake Lilla (1 hour), Marions Lookout and the Ballroom Forest (each 3 hours).

The walk through the National Park to Lake St Clair to the south takes about six days and is best only attempted by very experienced bushwalkers. The less experienced now have the option of commercially guided tours, where heavy packs are no longer necessary.

Gustav Weindorfer. The best known character in relation to Cradle Mountain is Gustav Weindorfer, the man who first explored and opened up the area. Weindorfer was a scientist and a recognised authority on Tasmanian flora. The youngest child of Johann Weindorfer, the then Austrian Bezirkshauptmann, (or Lieutenant of a country), and his wife, Gustav was born in Spittal, Carinthia, in 1874.

From an early age he was interested in botany, and so was sent to an agricultural high school near Vienna. He did military service with the Austrian Hungarian army, but was discharged in 1894 as being medically unfit. His chosen career was that of an estate manager, but although he obtained excellent references after his first position, he was unable to find another one. Later he became an accountant, and then a commercial traveller. Apparently feeling that he was getting nowhere, he decided in 1900 to emigrate to Australia. As he could afford to travel only third class steerage, young Gustav acquired the job of kitchen boy to augment his meals. From that unpromising beginning he became assistant purser.

For a time Weindorfer worked in Melbourne, where he joined the Victorian Field Naturalists' Club and began writing papers on botany.

In 1906 he married a Tasmanian, fellow naturalist Kate Julia Cowle, and the couple moved to Tasmania. After a honeymoon spent collecting plants on Mt Roland, they took up farming. In 1908 Gustav's parents arrived for a long visit, and during this time, the older Weindorfers took charge of the farm, allowing Gustav to fulfil a long-time ambition to visit Cradle Mountain.

In 1831 the explorer Henry Hellyer had been the first person known to have climbed Cradle Mountain, but since that time it had been rarely climbed. In 1909 the only 'road' was a packhorse track. With one of his friends from his Melbourne days Gustav visited the mountain that year, and he so loved the area that he and Kate made a return with a local friend, Major Smith, a descendant of James 'Philosopher' Smith. The Weindorfers travelled by horse and cart, and Smith on a bicycle.

In 1910, Gustav first formulated his plan to open up the Cradle Valley for tourists, and after much thought he and his wife and friend bought some land there. In 1911 Gustav explored more and named many of the features including Dove, Crater and Hansons Lakes and Mt Kate.

Lake Dove

During 1912, while Kate managed the farm, Gustav worked to establish Waldheim Chalet, which was opened as a tourist resort at Christmas that year. During 1916, Gustav's parents, brother and wife all died; also, despite the fact that he was a naturalised Australian, he met with some distrust as World War I progressed.

The next year he sold the farm and from then on spent most of his time at Waldheim until his untimely death from a heart attack in 1932.

Lake Cethana

On the return trip from Cradle Mountain you may wish to visit Lake Cethana. To do this, turn off to the right at the tea room corner into Route C136 towards Sheffield. There are 10 km of winding road, and on your way down the mountain you will see a right-hand turn into a private H.E.C. road to Cethana Lake and Lookout and the Wilmot Power Station.

Lake Cethana is one of the more beautiful of the hydro dams, and just round the corner from it is Wilmot Power Station. Looking across to the mountainside we saw a vast pipe plunging straight down and, a hundred or so metres across the hill, a narrow waterfall which followed the same course. The Cethana Dam is 215 m long and 120 m high. Like Wilmot Dam it is rock-filled with a concrete face. When it was built, in 1970, Cethana was one of the largest rock-filled dams in Australia.

The name 'Cethana' (pronounced 'se-tharna') is Aboriginal for 'hair'.

Near Lake Cethana

Farther down the mountain again you cross the Forth River over a large concrete one lane bridge. On your right, immediately past the bridge, is another H.E.C. road to Cethana Dam and Cethana Power Station. This road leads in a spiral around the side of the mountain. An interesting feature is the number of small trickles and tiny waterfalls seeping out of the rocky cliffs. These are attended by miniature forests of ferns and mosses.

Farther down the mountain take Route C136 to Gowrie Park and Sheffield. There is a turn-off to the left to Lake Barrington. Four km from Gowrie Park you pass a road to the right, C138 to Mole Creek on B12, 41 km. It is now 18 km into Sheffield. Straight ahead at this point is Mt Roland.

Gowrie Park was a flourishing hydro village during the late 1960s while the seven Mersey-Forth dams were under construction. At its peak, its population included 1800 H.E.C. employees and their families. Now there is little of it left, and what remains is virtually a service centre. During 1970, when the town was in decline, many of the prefab houses were moved to Latrobe to replace buildings condemned after the devastating floods of August/September of that year.

Driving or walking through the remains of Gowrie Park is a rather eerie experience. The paved streets are all there—named after local mountains—but there are very few buildings left. The bush seems to be quietly taking over again. There is, however, a reasonably priced backpacker lodge, and also Weindorfer's Restaurant. Look at the noticeboard at the entrance to the town for opening days and times.

Return to Devonport via Sheffield.

The Railton Road

A pleasant day trip through parts of the Latrobe and Kentish regions is as follows:

Leave Devonport via Spreyton and Tarleton. Take Route B13 towards Railton. Pass Coal Hill Road on your right: this name echoes the early coal-mining history of the Latrobe/Tarleton area. On your left is a long row of basket willows, screening the Mersey River. Shortly after this on your left, you will see the Dolly Dalrymple monument. This is also the original site of Sherwood Hall, which is visited in Chapter 1. To see the monument turn off the road to the left, into the lay-by, and walk back along the road.

Dolly Dalrymple (c.1808–1864) was the wife of Thomas Johnson (1806–1867) and was part Tasmanian Aboriginal. Her maiden name was Dalrymple Mountgarret Briggs—the 'Dalrymple' being derived from the Dalrymple tribe and the 'Mountgarrett' from a Doctor Mountgarrett at Georgetown who brought her up and educated her. A friend of Dolly's often lent her books, and reported that she most enjoyed reading about travel, history and poetry. Many descendants of Thomas and Dolly Johnson still live around Latrobe.

Dolly Dalrymple is remembered for her bravery in defending her home and children against attack when she was only 23 years of age. A sculpture of her, made by Peter Taylor, is in the library in Devonport. In the carving Dolly holds a bird in one hand. The other hand is jointed at the wrist, and at the level of her head is an unusual set of moveable doors depicting Bass Strait. These may be closed over her face.

Shortly after leaving the monument, cross over Caroline Creek, which is named after a daughter of Thomas and Dolly and was once a favourite lobster-catching spot with the locals.

On the left, not far past the creek, is the Henry Somerset Conservation Area where there is a forestry programme. There is a nature walk here through the eucalypts.

If you happen to drive this way in late spring, you will see a great many of the so-called snake lilies (actually *Diplarrhena moraea*, or white iris) by the roadside. When we were children it was a popular myth that these lilies contained baby snakes, and if you picked one, the parent snakes would come and get you!

On your right is Dawsons Siding Road, and soon after, the site of the former brickworks at Dulverton. Early attempts at brick-making in the area involved primitive pits, the clay from which was made into bricks, replaced in the pits, piled with wood and fired. Certainly some useable bricks resulted from these rough and ready methods, but the waste must have been tremendous. By the 1890s fire bricks were being commercially made nearby, and in 1914 a timber merchant-cum-builder from Devonport brought modern brick-making equipment to the site. The brickworks was in use during the 1980s, but has since closed down.

Tasmanian Heath. If you are travelling the Railton Road in the winter or spring, keep your eye out for the lovely pink, red and white flowers of heath *Epacris impressa*. (This name is Greek, and its elements are *epi*, which means 'upon', *aknos*, which means 'the top' and *impressa*, which means 'dented'.)

So much for the scientific side of things! Heath is a small and very prickly plant, growing to a maximum height of about one metre. It is very widely distributed in Tasmania, thriving at sea level and up to one thousand metres, and extends up into south-eastern mainland Australia. The flowers are bell-shaped and very pretty, but the sharp, pointed leaves put most people off making any attempt to smell them! Apparently some species of heath are grown as hothouse plants in the UK. The red and white flowers are rather less common than the pink but all make a cheering display in the colder months.

Much of the roadway between Latrobe and Railton is bounded by pine to the right and eucalypt to the left.

Railton

As you enter Railton, which was surveyed in 1853 by J.M. Dooley, there is a sign off to the right pointing to the Goliath Portland Cement Works, 2 km from the road. The cement works was established in 1930, and may be visited by appointment, 10 a.m.–3 p.m. daily. Railton area relies heavily on the cement works, agriculture and the timber industry for employment. Railton Lime is on your left, beside the quarry. On your right is the H.E.C. building, 1942, and Railton Railway Station is on your right, where you will probably see piles of logs awaiting transport. Farther along to your left, just before King St, is the King's Hall, built in 1926. Railton township is remarkable for its very wide central street: it is one of the few Tasmanian towns with angle parking. On your left, Route B13 leads to Elizabeth Town, on the Launceston Road.

Just past the Railton Primary School, is Newbed Road. It is a pleasant drive around this road, which crosses ferny hills, and pasture land and emerges back behind the cement works.

Near the school is a large mural—a foretaste of things to come—and on your left is the route to Sunnyside.

Sheffield

It is about 11 km from Railton to the larger town of Sheffield. On the winding road between Railton and Sheffield, look out for masses of wild flowers in the late spring. The orange pea-like flowers on short prickly shrubs are known as 'prickly beauty' and there are also white-flowering daisy bushes and many varieties of fern. Shortly you will come to the turn-off into Route C156 towards Kimberley on B13, and B14 on your right goes to Sheffield, 4 km away. Sheffield is known locally as the 'Town of Murals', and as you enter the town you are bound to see why!

Mural sign board at Kentish

The Murals were instigated by the Kentish Association for Tourism Incorporated, in 1986. Since then, a great many murals have been painted, originally by John Lendis, (born in England, moved to Sydney, holidayed in Tasmania and stayed on), Birgitte Hansen, (Danish-born, living in Newcastle), Bruce Lamrock, (born in Sydney, living near Scottsdale), David Hopkins, Cheyne Purdue and Wayne Strickland, (all Tasmanians). Since 1988, when we first investigated the murals, their number has increased enormously. The artists' styles differ greatly, and pamphlets and a book giving up-do-date details of artists and murals is available from local shops and centres.

Route C136 on your left leads to Gowrie Park and nearby are the two Kentish Museums. Just off High St, in Pioneer Crescent, is an information centre which currently incorporates an art gallery and shop. Books featuring the area are available inside, and outside is a set of miniature signposts pointing to some of the more intriguingly named destinations within easy reach of Sheffield.

To see all the murals (which depict sometimes colourful and exciting and sometimes homely scenes from Tasmania's past), you will need to cover Sheffield pretty thoroughly. Check out Main St, High St, Henry St, Hope St and others. Even the toilet block has been pressed into service to act as a canvas!

Another interesting sight in High St is Slaters Country Store, established in 1899.

For those interested in pottery, crafts etc., Sheffield is a wonderful mine of local talent. It's well worth parking your car and walking around the town to avoid missing some of the smaller shops. The No Where Else Pottery and the Blacksmith Gallery are interesting places to visit, and you may also buy locally produced honey or take a steam train ride.

West Kentish

From Sheffield, Route B14 leads through to Spreyton 23 km and Devonport, 29 km away. Turn left into Route C141 to West Kentish (7 km) and Lake Barrington, (14 km). Directly ahead as you turn you will see Mt Roland and one of its fellow guardians. Walking tracks to the top of the mountain begin at Gowrie Park and Claude Road.

Throughout the Sheffield district you will see many hawthorn hedges, particularly lovely in October/November, when they are covered in white and sometimes pink blossom, and then again in autumn and winter with their red berries.

Soon you will come to a Y-fork. The left-hand side leads off to Gowrie Park and the right to West Kentish, Lake Barrington and Roland. Take this right turn. At the top of the hill you come into little West Kentish, and the right-hand turn-off into C143 to Barrington. Continue on C141 to Lake Barrington, 7 km away. West Kentish is a small and rather sleepy township in the middle of a farming district, raising sheep and cattle. As you leave West Kentish you will see huge electricity pylons across to the front and right and to your left, Mt Roland. At the top of the hill C140 leads to Cethana, C141 ahead to Kentish Park. Follow C140

to the left to see the rowing course at Lake Barrington. Drive through the tiny township of Roland, and look out for wildlife. Just as we left the township we saw an echidna waddling along.

Tasmazia

Drive through Promised Land to see Tasmazia, the world's largest maze complex. Apart from seven different mazes, Tasmazia offers lavender products, a Three Bears Cottage and the model town of Lower Crackpot. Check locally for opening times.

Lake Barrington. Just after Tasmazia, a turn-off to the right leads into 3.5 km of very steep and winding road down into the recreational area and Lake Barrington, provided and managed by the Lands Department and closed 8 p.m.–8a.m. On your right about 800 m down the hill, is the start of the Billet Creek Nature Way, which

Billet Creek Nature Way

Lake Barrington

is a a 90-minute walk down to the lakeside. The track is gravel and very attractive.

If you decide to continue by car, shortly after the beginning of the walk you can look down to your right for a glimpse of Lake Barrington, created by the Mersey/Forth Power Development Scheme. To the left is Murfets Creek, just before you enter the Recreation Area and reach the other end of the Billet Creek Nature Way, at Murfets Bay. At the lake are toilets, kiosk, parking areas and boat shed, but no camping is allowed. The Lands Department Office is there for enquiries.

The Lake Barrington International Rowing Course was funded by the Tasmanian and Commonwealth Governments under the International Standard Sports Facility Programme. It was officially opened in 1984. The world rowing championships were held here in 1990.

Retrace your path up the hill. There is a choice of ways: right to Staverton and Cethana, or left towards Barrington. Turn left onto the road, return through Roland and, to visit Kentish Park, turn left into Route C141. As you head down towards Kentish Park you pass another turn-off left to Roland. Unless you want to drive around in circles, don't take it! Kentish Park is also on Lake Barrington, but has camping facilities and a playground.

No Where Else. Return to West Kentish, then take the turn-off to the left into Route C143 to Barrington, 9 km away. Along the Barrington Road, you pass one of the most photographed sights in Tasmania: the signpost pinpointing No Where Else. The story goes that, before the road was a through road, the owner of the property here, Mr Charles Ivory, used to inform travellers that the road led to his farm and 'nowhere else'. When the road was continued, the name became official. A large roadside sign used to tell this story. It has now been replaced by the current small version.

Devils Gate Dam. Just before you reach Barrington, turn left into the Devils Gate Road. Caution! The sign is quite easy to miss, so keep an eye out for it. On your right, halfway along the road, is a picnic area with barbecues and toilets. Follow the road right down the hill to the pumping station and the river.

Although Devils Gate isn't a particularly big dam, (height 79.25 m, crest length 117.35 m, power station commissioned 1969), it is one of the most picturesque and interesting. Children love to stand near the pumping station and yell and listen to the echoes that reverberate from the impressive cliffs and the dam itself, and the dark and slightly sinister river (no throwing stones; hydro personnel or other visitors might be underneath!). The flora around the dam is interesting, including yellow bottlebrushes and many other plants we hadn't seen before.

Back towards Latrobe or Devonport

Return up Devils Gate Road and turn left towards Barrington. It was in a paddock somewhere around here that an old man addicted to chewing tobacco was bitten by a snake while stooking hay. His workmates took him in a horse-drawn cart to Sheffield, where the doctor declared him to be quite unaffected and suggested that he check up on the snake. The snake was found, quite dead—poisoned by the concentration of tobacco in the old bloke's blood—or so the story goes!

When you come to another turn-off where Spreyton and Devonport are to your left on Route B14 and Sheffield is to your right, turn left. On your left just after the turn-off is a property called Glencoe which offers bed and breakfast. Come into lower Barrington and on your left on C144 is Paloona Dam, 6 km away. There is also a turn-off to Melrose. Coming down to the foot of the hill, cross over the tiny Don River, passing the turn-off to the farming district of Nook on C150. Pass James Road on your right and cross Coal Creek. On your left are the Forest Glen Tea Gardens. Continue towards Tarleton on C156, passing Clovelly Orchards and the Castle Node Riding School on your right. Pass Coal Mine Road. The road ends at a T-junction, with Spreyton and Devonport on Route B19 to the left and Latrobe to the right.

BIBLIOGRAPHY

Books
BERGMAN, Dr G.F.J., *Gustav Weindorfer of Cradle Mountain*, 1959.
COCKER, Kathleen, *Early Houses of the North West Coast of Tasmania,* 1973.

Pamphlets
'Welcome to Sheffield, Town of Murals.'
'Let's Talk about the Kentish District.', Tas. Visitor Corporation.
'Power in Tasmania' The Hydro Electric Commission.

Maps
Tasmap 1:100 000 Land Tenure Index Series 'Forth', 'Mersey', 'Sophia'

Information
Thanks to Ted and Stella Best, Bess Pagel, the people of Sheffield, and others.

3. Elizabeth Town to Chudleigh, Caveside and Mole Creek

Features of this drive

One of the most attractive and varied drives in Tasmania is the trip through Mole Creek and Caveside. Not only does it have charming scenery and an enviable selection of interesting mountains around the horizon, it also features creeks, caves, temperate rainforest, rocky outcrops of limestone (and the local limeworks), peaceful rural scenes, varied wildflowers, birds and a wildlife park. And then, perhaps you'd like to buy some honey? The district offers a wide range of country accommodation. This drive is neither long nor taxing, so you'll have time to enjoy it at leisure.

The Mole Creek district

The bush is more attractive around Mole Creek than farther to the east: blackwood trees are almost as common as eucalypts. There is plenty of birdlife around; in a couple of hours we saw a white goshawk, some kookaburras, blue cranes and magpies. On other occasions we have seen rosella parrots and a sulphur-crested cockatoo. The roads twist about, but there isn't much traffic and there is always plenty to look at. You'll see wild scenery, cliffs and mountains, but there is also the cosy aspect of small storybook farms. We saw cattle, sheep, goats, horses, chooks, donkeys, earthworms (farmed) and bees... you name it, they rear it, around Mole Creek. Oddly, (despite the name of the place), the one thing they don't have is moles. It seems that the town was named after the creek which rises in the Great Western Tiers, and the creek was named after its own odd habit of flowing placidly and then abruptly disappearing underground before emerging once again some metres farther along. In other words, it burrows.

Lakes. The Great Western Tiers are covered with lakes, including Lakes Explorer, Douglas, Mackenzie, Johnny, Chambers, Nameless, Pitt, Lucy Long, Furmage, Field, Meander and Halkyard. It is thought that there are over three thousand of them, many unnamed! During 1895 a party of local men and boys carried a load of fish fry up the mountains and stocked the lakes with trout. A local remembers catching fifteen-pound trout in the lakes during the late 1930s. The land between the Meander and Mersey rivers was explored by Captain John Rolland in 1823. Cattlemen looking for grazing moved in the following year. There are several different routes to Mole Creek, but we took one recommended by a friend. Drive east from Devonport to Elizabeth Town (see Chapter 4 for details) and, just after the Elizabeth Town Museum and antique shop, (a long stone building on the right side of the road), turn right into Route C163 to Red Hills. Pass the right-hand turn-off to Dunorlan, the old property once owned by Captain Moriarty. Mt Roland is visible to your right. For some reason Mt Roland is always changing colour, from grey to blue to purple or white; no wonder it's a favourite subject with painters and photographers. Mt Roland dominates the area around Sheffield, but here at Mole Creek its dominance gives way to the local peaks and ridges.

Drive through rolling farmland between hawthorn hedges. In late October to late November, these hedges are covered with white and pink blossom, and in the autumn, with red berries. Even in winter they bear a crop of deserted birds' nests. During the early summer, the roadsides are covered with groves of large white daisies.

Turn to the right onto Route B12, the Mole Creek Road, passing Route C168 to Dairy Plains on your left. Continue past a property named Askrigg. Ahead and to your right you can see a mountain range with an unusual folded appearance: this is the Gog Range. Look out on your right for a narrow track leading to Lobster Falls.

Pass the property Oakden on your right, and continue between more hawthorn hedges into Chudleigh. Bentley is on your left just before you enter the township.

The Gog Range runs from the east of Mt Roland towards Deloraine, and is separated by a creek from another ridge called, inevitably, Magog. The original Gog and Magog, apparently, were legendary giants or monsters. Until burnt in the Fire of London, large statues of the pair stood in that city. Gog and Magog are referred to in the Bible (Rev. 20: 7, 8), and in the book of Ezekiel.

Bentley Estate was first occupied by a European in 1827, when Thomas Cookson Simpson grazed cattle there. Simpson had an occupation lease, which allowed him to run stock on the crown land for a fee of 7 shillings and 6 pence, (75c) a year. He built a hut and stockyard. In 1829, John Badcock Gardiner was granted 800 acres. In 1832 he applied for more land. Gardiner's daughter was the first white child born in the district in that year. Nearby Gardiners Ridge is named after the family. The original Bentley was a village in Devonshire. Gardiner sold Bentley to Edward Bryant, who sold to Philip Oakden, of Launceston. In 1870 Donald Cameron bought it. The single-storey brick homestead at Bentley was built in 1879 for Cameron's son Norman.

The Cameron family had Angus cattle, merino sheep and a linseed oil mill, established in 1888. Another source states that Bentley was part of the property owned by Lt Vaughan in the 1830s, and occupied at that time by his nephew, Godfrey Bentley.

Chudleigh

Chudleigh, named after a village in Devonshire, England, is small but very pretty. Its history is greatly bound up with that of one well-known character, Sir Henry Reed, who had a large property there in 1837.

Henry Reed was born in Yorkshire in 1806, the son of postmaster, Samuel Reed. At 13 years old he was apprenticed to a Hull merchant. At 21, Henry sailed for Van Diemen's Land as a steerage passenger on the *Tiger. He* arrived at Hobart, and walked to Launceston. In late 1827 he was granted land at Nile, and named the property Rockliff Vale after his mother. He cleared much of the property, and when it was a profitable concern, let it.

By the time he was 24, Reed had built his store in Launceston (see Chapter 6), and later went into shipping and whaling, sailing for England in 1831. While in England, he married his cousin Suzanna Maria Grubb. In 1837, the now very successful Henry

Reed bought the property called Native Hut Corner at Chudleigh from Lt Travers Hartley Vaughan, who had had the grant since 1830. Reed renamed it Wesley Dale, in honour of the founder of Methodism. It is not known whether Vaughan or Reed built the farmhouse, once open to the public and known as Old Wesley Dale, but Henry Reed is certainly responsible for the building during the 1860s of Mountain Villa, and a church also at the Wesley Dale property. Henry Reed was a great builder: one source says that he had Mount Pleasant in Launceston built, another that he merely improved it. Whichever it was, for some years he lived there for nine months of the year and returned to enjoy the summer at Wesley Dale.

He was a Justice of the Peace in 1838, and became known as the 'Convicts' Friend', sometimes spending the night with the men in the Condemned Cells at the gaol. Reed was a great evangelist, and an oak tree has been planted on the site of a wattle under which he used to preach. Although he

Chudleigh

became very well-to-do, he was well loved by the locals and his employees: it was said that in his whole life he never had a servant punished, which must have been considered remarkable in those days of indentured labour.

In 1847 the Reeds left for England, where they stayed for the next 26 years. During this time the Reed family had increased: eleven children were born—Henry John, Maria, Charlotte, Elizabeth, Mary Hannah, Hannah, Georgina, William, Edward, Frederick and Arthur. Only five of these children survived past their twenty-fifth birthdays. In 1860 Suzanna died, aged 46. Three years later Henry married his second wife, Margaret Sayres Elizabeth Frith. More children, Walter, Annie, Margaret, Mary and Henry, were born during the next six years. In 1873 the Reeds returned to Tasmania, where Henry died in 1880. Margaret died in 1924.

Other Early Settlers. During the 1830s, Henry Reed brought free settlers from England to take up some of his land. Notable among these settlers were James How (b. 1796) and his wife Sarah Reed (b. 1794) who arrived in 1836. James was the son of Richard How and his wife Sarah Simmonds. The Hows had so many descendants that present-day Hows are still trying to work out exactly how they are related—particularly since some spell their name with a final 'e' and some without it. Fourteen-year-old Leslie How was one of the group who stocked the mountain lakes with trout. Another early settler in the district was John Francis Parsons from Devon, (b. 1823), who jumped ship in Launceston and settled at Chudleigh. He helped build Mountain Villa and married Susan Ryder, with whom he had twelve children.

As you go through Chudleigh look out for a large brick building which is the old surveyors' building, built around 1840.

Opposite is a building which was once a two-storey hotel, begun in the 1850s by ticket-of-leave man Dan Picket and his wife Mary (daughter of James and Sarah) How. It is now only one storey. Dan Picket is locally famed for having lived to the age of 105! He was well respected in the district and it was well known that even the bushrangers would always leave him unharmed.

Chudleigh

Mole Creek Road

Drive on through Chudleigh and turn right (still on Route B12) towards Mole Creek and King Solomon's Cave. About 200 metres from the turn-off is an old cemetery in a paddock on your right, guarded by an ancient oak tree. Look out for the grave of James and Annie Cubit and their daughters. The Cubits are a well-known local family, and their number includes Simon Cubit, who has written a number of books concerning the high country around the Tiers.

Others buried in the cemetery include Sylvie Howe, who died in May 1900, at the age of four, Barry Picket, who died in 1866, and the Warren family, dating from the 1860s and 1880s, and George and Jane Bellchambers. Some of the gravestones are broken, and some are indecipherable. This graveyard was established in 1861, and is accessible via two gates. In a typically Mole Creek District touch, sheep graze around the fenced-in graves.

On your right as you continue past the graveyard is the turn-off to the Mole Creek Holiday Village. There is also a turn-off to the Alum Cliffs.

To visit the **Alum Cliffs**, you can take this turn-off or drive on to the right of the wildlife park. Just past a grey brick house on the roadside is another route to the cliffs. The Alum Cliffs are not made up of alum but of decomposing limestone. This sounds unattractive, but the view is well worth the short walk.

Follow the road up to a small lay-by and climb the stile. It takes around 15 minutes to walk uphill and downhill, to the Alum Cliffs. The track is not muddy even in winter, but is rather rough and stony. If you are quiet and lucky, you may see kangaroos, wombats or Tasmanian devils and possums in the evening. On your right. you can hear and sometimes see the Mersey River at the foot of the hill. At the top of the hill is a magnificent view of the Alum Cliffs, pale grey and white and covered with lichen. Small trees grow in pockets on the cliffs.

The path continues down very steeply to your left, marked by red arrows. Mt Roland is on your far left and Gog Range over to the right. Vegetation includes Tasmanian heath, bottlebrushes, gums, tea-tree and wild cherry. If you climb down any of the faint tracks made by the local wildlife, it will take you about an hour to reach the banks of the Mersey River.

Wildlife Park

Close by is the Mole Creek Wildlife Park and Koala Village, opened in 1979. The owners have a long-term plan to breed endangered native animals and, with the co-operation of the National Parks and Wildlife Service, to re-establish them in the bush. The park is one of the few places in Tasmania where one can see koalas since these do not live here in the wild. As well as koalas, you can see (and feed from specially provided feed bags) kangaroos and wallabies. There are wombats, echidnas, snakes, possums and a nocturnal house containing a number of species in a controlled environment. See the Tasmanian devils, too: fierce little black creatures, rather like dogs, with an impressive mouthful of teeth and a custom-made jaw which locks shut. A Tasmanian devil will be quite comfortable hanging by his teeth from a broom handle, and could bite through your finger as easily as you would deal with a baby carrot. Luckily, the ones that live in the park are domesticated and quite tame—and separated from the public by a stout barrier!

The Tasmanian Devil, (*Sarcophilus harrisii*). Apart from the impressive dental equipment mentioned earlier, the devil has a backward opening pouch in which the young

Illustration from The Tasmanian Devil *(P. Reilly and W. Rolland, Kangaroo Press, 1988)*

spend the period immediately after their birth. On your right just past the Wildlife Park is Old Wesley Dale, which was open to the public for some years but is now run solely as a farm.

Mole Creek

Return to the Route B12 and turn right. When you reach the sign for Mole Creek, drive straight ahead. The chief industries around Mole Creek are logging, honey, dairying and beef. It is a close-knit community, and the locals we met were happy to give directions or just to pass the time of day. On your left as you pass through the town is the honey factory. and in front once again you can see Mt Roland.

Along Den Road is **The Limeworks**, which opened in 1972 as a small crusher up on the hill and, as our informant laconically commented, 'a fair bit of the hill's gone missing since then'. The company has existed since last century, and it hopes that current stocks of limestone will last another fifty years. New sites will have to be chosen with care, as the limestone hereabouts is riddled with caves and underground creeks. The hill being mined at present is unusual in that it was a single blob of solid limestone without other rock or unwanted waterways. Not all the lime produced is used for agricultural purposes. Unprocessed limestone (or calcium carbonate) is crushed into all sizes from head-sized chunks to fine dust. The dust is used for glass manufacture and fertiliser. Processed lime is that which has been burnt and turned into calcium oxide, or quicklime, which goes to the west coast mines such as Copper Mines of Tasmania and Renison Bell and used as a pollution control treating the run-off from the mines, by balancing the pH. The quicklime can also be processed again with water to produce calcium hydroxide, or limil, which goes to

the building industry and also into the water supply. Gravel and limestone are used for road-building.

The limeworks and surroundings are not a picturesque sight, but rehabilitation is already under way. As each part of the quarry is mined, the overburden (or unwanted rock) is scraped off and topsoil spread over it. Very quickly the bush begins to regenerate, with the quick-growing wattle seedlings appearing first, and other species following. There are no organised tours of the works, but any interested person may ask to be shown around.

Note for Would-be Industrial Spies, who are not welcome at the limeworks. Apparently spies from rival quarries can accurately determine costing and production, and use the information to undercut local tenders. Would-be spies are warned that their camera films will be confiscated. One such spy was apprehended at the local fish and chip shop some years ago. So, if you go wandering uninvited into the quarry with a telephoto lens camera slung round your neck, your coat collar turned up, a false beard, a notebook in hand and a clipboard under your arm, be prepared for a hostile reception.

Towards the Caves

As you come out of Den Road, turn right and drive on to a Y-junction. Route B12 continues to the King Solomon's and Marakoopa Caves, while Route C137 leads off over the hills to Paradise and the road to Sheffield (see Chapter 2). Look for signs to a deer farm along this road. Also along the way is Union Bridge.

Union Bridge crosses the Mersey River. It's a long narrow wooden bridge covered with tarmac and supported on giant telegraph pole-type legs. Apparently locals dive from the bridge in summer, but this is definitely not recommended for the casual visitor: should you miss the only hole deep enough for safety it might be the last dive you ever make. From Union Bridge you may see platypus at dusk and dawn. Down to the left is an easy access through a small gate to the river, an ideal place for fishing or picnicking.

Limestone caves are formed by the seeping of water through the limestone rock. This dissolves the calcium carbonate in the rock, which in turn forms the stalagmites (the 'mites go up') and stalactites (the 'tites go down').

There are 180 known caves in the Mole Creek area, but **Marakoopa** and **King Solomon's** are the only two open to the public. Quite a few others are accessible to experienced cavers, but the forest rangers have locked some of the larger ones to prevent unauthorised entry, lost or injured cavers, and possible damage to formations. Members of speleological clubs may get a permit to explore these. **Marakoopa Cave** is very large with two streams running through it. It was formed thousands of years ago by two rivers which ran through it after the ice age. It features reflections and quite a good display of glow-worms. It is also inhabited by a species of mountain shrimp, by cave crickets around the entrances, and by cave spiders—fearsomely leggy creatures with a span of 15 to 17 cm, which eat the crickets. **King Solomon's** has more formations in striking shades of apricot, orange and brown.

Marakoopa Cave was discovered by the local Byard family in 1910 while they were searching for cattle. They opened it in 1912. 'Marakoopa' is an Aboriginal name meaning 'handsome'. Marakoopa extends some 6 kilometres, but guided tours cover only 600–700 metres, which take about an hour.

King Solomon's Cave is a dry cave now, but was formed by a creek. It was discovered by hunters when a wallaby which they were chasing fell down one of the two entrances and the dogs barked around it. King Solomon's is named for one of its formations, a rock profile of the biblical king. Around the cave are a number of sparkling calcite crystals. King Solomon's is less than 200 metres long. The caves (which maintain a constant year round temperature of 9°C), are said to be equal to any in Australia, and it is quite possible that more will still be discovered in the thick bush. Cavers come from all over Australia to explore. Near Marakoopa Cave is a nature walk following the creek which runs from the cave. It takes about 20 minutes.

To visit King Solomon's Cave, return to the Y-fork and take the indicated route.

West Moreland Falls. To visit West Moreland Falls, go back to Mole Creek. By the Mole Creek Guest House you'll see a large illustrated map of the area. Drive on through the town and turn right at the Hall. The sign indicates South Mole Creek, Presbyterian Church and the school and service station on Route C169.

Follow this road on out of town until you reach a T-junction. To the left is Route C169 to Chudleigh and Caveside, (once known as Watery Plains), and to the right is the way to West Moreland Falls, the Wet Cave, and Honeycomb Caves.

Turn off towards the Wet Cave. If you stop at this point to have a look at the mountains, you will see three easily recognisable features.

The rounded one to the left, shaped like an inverted mixing bowl, is Quamby Bluff, the sharp peak in the middle is Mother Cummings Peak, and the cleft to the right is Lobster Gorge, through which Lobster Rivulet (known locally as Lobster Creek) flows. Not far from the cleft is a huge lump of sandstone, in which many generations of climbers have carved their names.

Mother Cummings Peak is named after Miss Cummings, a school mistress at Western Creek. Some youngsters bet her that she couldn't walk to the top of the peak, so she did!

The road is a bit rough, but it isn't far to the beginning of the Falls track.

It is a 10-minute walk through the rainforest to a picnic area (merely a primitive fireplace and log seats) and a 2-hour return walk to the falls. Look out for native clematis twining around the trees, and for giant tree ferns, easily three times the height of a man. Other trees include dogwood and musk, and sometimes in rotten logs you may find rather disgusting-looking worms the same size as an earthworm but butter yellow in colour. Other creatures include a tiny semi-transparent pale green spider. It is fairly easy walking, downhill at first and then climbing, and crossing the creek at several different points by small wooden bridges.

At one point, about half an hour from the road, you will see a long stone trough through which the creek flows. This is part of a man-made system known as The Nine Foot, used for many years to bring water out of the bush and into the farm lands. The creek has a habit of disappearing down deep holes in the hill, to reappear kilometres away in an unexpected direction. The trough persuades it to continue on a straight course over these holes. The Nine Foot continues out across the paddocks as a channel, originally nine feet wide, twisting through Caveside as far as Chudleigh. Originally twelve inch fluming was used to cross the holes, but in 1966 this rusted through and the present trough was installed. The cost was shared by many local farmers on a pro rata basis, and came to 88 pounds. The Nine Foot was convict built, and it is said that one of the overseers of the work had a splendid white stallion. It was his proud boast that the animal was the finest jumper in the country. He took up a bet that the horse could jump the Nine Foot and during the subsequent attempt the unfortunate animal broke its back. No mention is made of what happened to the overseer.

Local farmers walk into the forest regularly to maintain the beginning of the Nine Foot, because without due care it easily becomes choked with leaves and branches. The final few metres of the walk to the falls is inclined to be slippery, so be careful.

The Wet Caves Reserve. On the left as you return from the West Moreland Falls track is a cyclone gate leading into the Wet Cave State Reserve. About 100 metres from the gate, on your right, is the first cave, known as The Honeycomb Cave. Anyone intending to visit these caves needs torches, hard hats, and appropriate clothing, perhaps including fishermen's waders! The Honeycomb Cave has water through it most of the time but does occasionally dry up. Another entrance to the Honeycomb Cave is a few hundred metres farther along. These caves are very popular with cavers and often during long weekends and holidays a tent city will spring up on the short green grass among the trees. Inside, out of sight of the open mouth, is a maze of small entrances giving a beeswax appearance which has given these caves their name.

The Wet Cave is so called because it is wet all the year round. Depending on the rainfall for that season, you may wade through water up to your ankles or up to your thighs. To see the Wet Cave follow the creek upstream several hundred metres from the Honeycomb Cave. The pebbly 'beach' at the entrance may be under water if it has been raining recently.

To return to Devonport, you may drive back through Chudleigh. If you stay on this road, you'll end up in Deloraine. Turn left to return to Devonport. Alternatively, take the Paradise Road over Union Bridge to Sheffield, Railton and Latrobe.

BIBLIOGRAPHY

Books
FYSH, Hudson, *Henry Reed, Van Diemen's Land Pioneer*, Cat and Fiddle Press, 1973.
EMMET, E.T., *Tasmania by Road and Track*, Oxford University Press, 1953.

Pamphlets
'Bentley Estate, Chudleigh, Tasmania.' Undated paper.

Maps
Tasmap Topographic 1: 100 000, 'Mersey' and 'Forth'.

Information
Thanks to Margaret and Kelvin Howe, Keith How, Rodney How, Natalie Harrison, Kaye Mathews, George Shaw, the staff of the Limeworks and the Wildlife Park at Mole Creek and other local residents.

4. Devonport to Launceston

Features of this drive

The route from the city of Devonport to Launceston takes in several towns of historic interest. Most of them have been bypassed by the highway system, but they are well signposted and it takes only a few minutes to reach them. Along the way you'll see a small castle, a large orchard, waterfalls, some interesting displays of gemstones and trains, historic houses and estates, and calm, rural scenery.

To reach the city of Launceston, roughly 110 km from Devonport, take the Bass Highway (Highway 1) out of Devonport eastward over the Victoria Bridge. Shortly before the hospital at Latrobe, you will see on your right a house called 'Wyndarra Lodge'. An attractive white building, 'Wyndarra' was originally a private residence, but has since been used for functions and a child-care centre. The large grounds contain some 180 different species of trees. Inside, there are some particularly interesting ceilings, featuring cupids and birds. The earliest record of the land on which 'Wyndarra' was built is in a conveyance dated 1893. In this document the block is described as being 30 acres, part of a lot of 320 acres. The parties concerned in the conveyance were Peter John Douglas, Edward Bartlett and William Lee Bartlett and Richard Mitchell.

A Latrobe resident, the late Mr Perce Hicks, remembered helping his grandfather to lay pipeline which brought water to 'Wyndarra' from a spring at the top of the hill. Every year, the pipes had to be cleaned out!

'Wyndarra Lodge'

'Wyndarra' was built in about 1920 for a Spanish gentleman named Joseph Theodore D'Oliveyra on land which belonged to his wife Winifred Stewart, (a daughter of Dr Stewart of Weeroona, Latrobe). A wealthy man in his own right, who had been a planter in the Solomon Islands, Mr D'Oliveyra owned a sawmill and furniture factory in Gilbert St, Latrobe, near where the TAB building is now. He used to arrange trips to Cradle Mountain in his special caterpillar-tracked vehicle, long before there was a decent road or even a track there.

The most direct route to Launceston

The most direct route to Launceston is the Bass Highway, Highway 1. This route bypasses the towns of Deloraine, Carrick and Exton, but passes through Hagley and Westbury. For anyone hoping to make the most of the historic buildings of the district, it's better to diverge from the highway into Deloraine. This allows you to pass through Exton and Carrick before rejoining Highway 1.

The road to Deloraine

The road to Deloraine was first planned and built in the 1830s. To reach Deloraine, bypass Latrobe at the roundabout, and proceed south-east. On your left, you'll pass the Speedway. On your left, at Route C704, is Oppenheims Road, and on your right, Oppenheim Hill.

Benjamin L. Oppenheim was a German Jew who left Germany to go to San Francisco where he opened a music emporium. Later, having moved to Tasmania, Mr Oppenheim owned a number of different businesses in Latrobe during the 1870s, and took up farming near Sassafras in 1880.

He carved his 600 acre property Forest Hill out of virgin bush, and very successfully raised sheep. Benjamin married Jane Robinson from Westbury, and they had nine children. A new house was built at Forest Hill in 1881.

Shortly after passing Oppenheim Hill, you will come to the East Sassafras Road, Route C706, on your left. This road leads you through the country area to join the Exeter Highway (see Chapter 5).

On your way through Sassafras, look on the right-hand side for a small white castle known as 'Liberty Castle'. Built in the late 1980s, 'Liberty Castle' is a private home.

Sassafras

The district of Sassafras covers approximately 40 km of rich farming land. It was settled in 1857, and was probably named after the sassafras trees found in the district at that time. As in the Penguin area, it was the very thickness of the bushland which discouraged settlers. Among the early pioneers were George, Henry, John, Francis and Hannah Rockliff from Yorkshire.

The Rockliff Family in Tasmania. George Rockliff was born in 1831, and arrived in Tasmania in 1852 on the *Lady Bute*. He settled in Sassafras in 1837 and married Ann Levick (1829–1925) in 1860. The couple had five sons and a daughter. George died in 1909. Henry Rockliff was born in 1815, and arrived in Tasmania on the *Essex* in 1841 and became overseer at Wesley Dale (see Chapter 3). He married Hannah Spurr (1818–1891) in 1842 and they settled on their Skelbrook property in Sassafras two years later. They had eight sons and three daughters. Henry died in 1889.

John Rockliff was born in 1835, and married Alice Scholey (1840–1897) in 1858. They arrived in Tasmania on the *Donald McKay* that same year and established Westfield in Sassafras in 1 859. They had six sons and four daughters. John died in 1905.

Francis Rockliff (1829–1893) and his sister Hannah (1824–1906) arrived in Melbourne on the *Merchant Prince* in 1859. Francis established his property Robin Hood's Well and returned to England to marry Elizabeth Wass in 1867. Hannah married Jonathan Graham (1833–1905) in 1866 and they established Rock Field. Neither couple had any children, however a nephew from England, John Rockliff, took over Robin Hood's Well and married Henry and Hannah's daughter, Harriet. This marriage produced six children. Many descendants of the Rockliffs and of other pioneering families still live locally.

Just past Sassafras is the picturesque **Parramatta Creek** Roadside Park. This spot offers a rest stop for motorists, and a pleasant picnic area supplied with a barbecue and toilets. The Conservatory Tea House building can be seen in The Conservatory Road just beyond the park. Nearby is one

Old Conservatory, Sassafras

of the largest orchards in Australia, run by Clements and Marshall.The orchard contains about eight varieties of apples, and the first plantings began in 1989.

Elizabeth Town is the next settlement along the highway. Elizabeth Town (see also Chapter 3) is tiny, with a school, an hotel, a garage and two churches, and a few houses clustered together on the road. Be aware that the town speed limit still applies! Route B13 to Railton and Latrobe leads off to the right at Elizabeth Town. The large hill to your left is Christmas Hill. On your right is the Elizabeth Town Hotel (1903), with an old bluestone building next to it. On your left is Holy Cross Anglican Church, and on your right the Church of Our Lady Help of Christians, built in 1938. There is a right-hand turn-off to Cradle Mountain, which is 94 km away. For a trip to The Cradle see Chapter 2.

The next turn-off to the right leads to a fork: the left hand road Route C163 taking you 8 km to Lemana, and the right hand (Route C161), 3 km to Dunorlan.

History of 'Dunorlan'. 'Dunorlan' was originally owned by an Irishman, Captain William Moriarty R.N., after whom Moriarty near Latrobe was named. Captain Moriarty, a friend of Sir John Franklin, was a retired naval officer from Dunorlan, County Cork, and in 1829 he was granted a large block of land, which he made up to 4000 acres. He named his property after his native place in Ireland. He became the Port Officer at George Town, and later, the Police Magistrate at Westbury.

While he was thus occupied, his sister, the redoubtable Miss Lucinda Moriarty, looked after the estate with the help of her 15-year-old nephew, Roddan Douglas. Miss Moriarty later took up a grant of her own at Latrobe, where the house called 'Frogmore' now stands.

In 1838 Moriarty advertised 'Dunorlan' for sale. It was later, in about 1846, bought by Henry Reed, who subdivided the property into thirteen farms, and leased these to tenants who included Joseph Cox, James Bonney and John Hicks.

Deloraine

The main highway bypasses Deloraine, but we do recommend a visit—not only to the town itself but to the pleasant countryside around it.

If you enjoyed the drive through the Mole Creek district in Chapter 3, you'll enjoy this too, for the routes lie close together and link up through the Montana Road. Since Deloraine is a larger town than any of the settlements visited in Chapter 3, there are more buildings to be seen.

To visit Deloraine, turn-off to the left of the bypass and follow the signs through to the town. Deloraine straddles the Meander River, and is, in our opinion, one of the prettiest of the northern towns. The river and its park make a good place for a picnic, and the town has a large number of well-preserved and well-documented colonial buildings. Deloraine hosts a big annual craft fair.

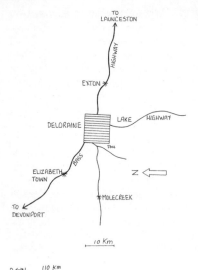

TO
LAUNCESTON

HIGHWAY

EXTON

DELORAINE   LAKE   HIGHWAY

BASS

34

ELIZABETH
TOWN

N ⇐

MOLECREEK

TO
DEVONPORT

| 10 Km |

D ↔ L   110 Km

Some historical facts about Deloraine

The first bridge over the Meander, (which
was once called 'The First Western River'),
was built by convict labour, and destroyed
by flood in 1844, the second was pulled down
in 1877.

The first property settled was 'Alverston'
estate, and the township was laid out in the
1830s. Daniel Griffin, writing for *The Daily
Telegraph* in 1893, thought the name of the
town, being of Scottish origin, had probably
been suggested by James or Thomas Scott,
the surveyor (see Chapter 9).

Historic buildings in Deloraine

If you drive into the town there are a number
of interesting buildings within easy walking
distance of the bridge over the Meander.
On the west bank of the river is a park with
a train and picnic area, and a board offering
a map of the town with interesting buildings
highlighted. From this point you can look
across the river to see the weir and the site
of the first power station. If you walk west
along West Parade, you can see the
Deloraine Tabernacle, built in 1880 on your

right. Close by, at No. 17 West Parade, is
Bonneys Inn, established in 1831 by John
Bonney. The Inn now provides light lunches
and Tasmanian crafts. Built of convict-made
bricks, it was Deloraine's first brick building
and first hotel.

Next to it is the Deloraine Hotel, also built
by John Bonney and established in 1848.

Turn right into West Barrack St. At the
corner of Beafeater and Blake Streets,
directly ahead, is a red brick building, one of
the old shops. Turn left into Beafeater St.
On your left is an old brick building known
as Claytons Mill. Turn left into Church St
and left into Tower Hill St. On your right is
a stone building called 'Eldersyde' which
used to belong to the Misses Edith and
Marion Pitt: Sally's father, who lived in
Deloraine as a boy in the 1930s, remembers
the Misses Pitt well. They were very elderly,
and they collected stamps. They rode
bicycles through the town until they were in
their nineties, riding down the hill and pushing
the bikes back up with a load of shopping.
Their sister was Mrs Bishop Blackwood.
Turn left back into Church St. On your left,
next to Roberts Ltd, is the cream and red
brick visitors' centre. It was once a grain
store, built by James Bennett, who lived at
that time on the 'Roberts' site. He had a
merchant shop and an office. Later, during
the 1930s, it was a clothing factory: one of

Bonney's Inn, Deloraine

Deloraine Hotel

Sally's aunts worked there. A lot of machinists were brought from Victoria to make mattress covers, mens' clothing etc. Later the building was used as a general meeting hall for Guides and, (under the name 'Annie's Room'), as a rehearsal venue by the Deloraine Dramatic Society. In 1982 it became the Old Sewing Box Museum, and then an antique shop. It is now a visitors' centre, stocked with pamphlets and information—and very friendly staff. Directly ahead at this point, you can see a view of Quamby Bluff. On your right is Simpson's Butchery, in another old building which once housed Spurrs Drapery. The top floor was then a gymnasium.

On your right, straight ahead, is Ye Old British Inn, built as a shop by a Mr McCormack. Turn right into Parsonage St before you reach the hotel. On your left is a pink building that used to be known as Folly's Teahouse. If you look through the trees you can see the big house at 'Calstock'.

Cross over Church St and immediately on your left is the old Deloraine Christian School, once a convent, more recently a private residence. On your right is the Catholic Church of the Holy Redeemer, a very handsome bluestone building. It was blessed and dedicated by Rev. Daniel Murphy, Bishop of Hobart, in 1886. Above the door is a plaque in memory of Rev. Edward Francis Walsh, pastor of the church for 22 years. He died in 1902. Inside, the

church is very beautiful, with a particularly lovely window above the altar. The Stations of the Cross are framed with wood, each dedicated to a past member the congregation. The church cost £4000 to build, this being raised by a Father Walsh. Turn right into West Goderich St, and on your left is the Convent School, (1924) and on your right the Presbytery.

St Andrews Theatre, once the Presbyterian Church, was built in 1883. The old Manse is next door. Walk (or drive, if you're doing this bit on wheels) into Emu Bay Road. On your left is number 118, which is well over a hundred and twenty years old (dating from before 1871) and which was once the W. Harris Store building. You can see a thriving W. Harris's at Latrobe. During the 1970s and '80s, the building housed a business called Berry's Antiques. Mr Berry Sr was the owner of the property called 'Bowerbanks' behind Bowerbank Mill. On the site of Beaurepairs there used to be a Chinese shop that bought and sold everything!

Go along Emu Bay Road and on your left at No. 95 is an old brick house called 'The Gables' and next to it the Oddfellows Hall and Masonic Hall, built in 1889.

Drive down to West Parade along the river; going east. On your left look for an old, tall, grey building with gables, St Mark's Rectory. Crossing the river, you can see St Mark's

St Mark's, 1851, Deloraine

Anglican Church (1859) up on the hill directly ahead of you. If you turn up East Barrack St from East Parade, you can see Deloraine Police and Citizens Youth Club: this was once a school. The big building next to it is Grenoch Home for the Aged, and next on the right is 'Arcoona', once Dr Frank Coles' old private hospital. Cross the street and on the left opposite the High School is the old house of James Scott. Turn right past the High School, turn right again into East Barrack St Number 5, an old cream-coloured house, was the surgery of Dr Rock. If you turn right into East Parade, 'Booroongia', at No. 24, was the original home of Dr J.R. Robertson, a well-known medical practitioner of the early 20th century. Continue along East Parade and turn right onto the Bass Highway. Cross Westbury Place to see the old Alveston Cottages, Nos. 16–20–22, or turn up Westbury Place to visit St Mark's and the interesting old graveyard. Near the Alveston Cottages is another building erected at the same time, and past them, over Railway St on your right is the Old Plough Inn built by Frederick Rudge in 1841. Next to that is Aubreyville, the home of the late Miss Ruby Harris.

In Emu Bay Road, opposite the Fire Station, is the Folk Museum.

Also at Deloraine is a turn-off to the right, Route B12, the Mole Creek Road (see Chapter 3). Close to this road is 'Red Hills House'.

'Red Hills House' was probably built by William Mason, but bought by James Bennett, who ran it as the Jolly Farmer Inn. Bennett had arrived in Australia in 1837 and by 1893 was well known as one of the richest and most successful men in the district. He died in Deloraine in 1898. In around 1882 James' son George and his wife Kate and family moved to 'Red Hills House'. By 1950 the house was in bad repair, but it has since been restored.

The Lake Highway

The Lake Highway (see also Chapter 17) is Route A5 out of Deloraine. Drive over the bridge and turn right into Route A5. On your right as you enter the highway is the Meander River, rather marshy just here, with a number of willow trees growing around. Willows are not indigenous to Tasmania, but the climate and soil make them common around the northern rivers, despite the control efforts of many centres. Pass a large sawmill and then the Deloraine Showgrounds. On the left you can see Calstock again.

'Calstock' property was 3500 acres granted in 1832 by Governor George Arthur to a Lt Pearson Foote, R.N. He apparently built a strange, ship-shaped brick house which he ran in true ship-shape manner, nautical and Bristol-fashion, naming it after his family's estate in Devon.

In 1845 he sold the property to Archdeacon Marriott, Rector of St Mathew's Church, New Norfolk. He in turn sold it in 1853, to John Field, whose family already owned a large amount of land around Westbury. John Field's father, William Field, arrived from Hertfordshire, England, in around 1816. He named his home at Carrick, 'Enfield', after his hometown, and bought up more land, including 'Westfield', which you'll see near Westbury. John Field, who married Mary-Ann Lindsay, largely rebuilt the house into the gracious building you see now. He and his brother Thomas bred horses, two of which won fame by winning the Melbourne Cup: Malua in 1884 and Sheet Anchor in 1885. John Field died in 1900, leaving the property to his son John Thomas. After his death, 'Calstock' was bought by the Bowman family, and later owned by a syndicate.

Continuing on the Lake Highway. On your right, look out for the triangular peak of Beafeater Hill, and on your left is the entrance to Barra Farm, owned in the 1940s by John and Jean MacNeill (nee Bowman). We always used to look out for the distinctive white wrought iron gates of this property, but at the time of writing the have been removed—temporarily, we hope! On the left, immediately after the gateway is Barra Road. Pass Pumice Stone Ridge to your left. During the 1920s the school children of Deloraine were taken on class walks to The Pumice! Pass Beaufield, on the right, and come around a bend. The rounded hill is Cubits Sugarloaf. Six kilometres from Deloraine, you will come to Route C166. Pass that, and turn off to the right at Route C167, Meander Road. Pass Cubits Sugarloaf to your left. Meander is now 9 km away.

Meander

On your left, soon after the turn-off, is 'Stockers Plains'. Another property on the left is 'Mulvhill'. On the right is 'Pleasant Park'. On the right is a turn-off to Western Creek, Caveside, and Mole Creek (see Chapter 3). Past this turn-off is Nuttings Road. Pass on your left a turn-off to Jackeys Marsh and East Meander, and continue towards the Meander Forest Reserve. Just after the turn-off, you will reach the quiet township of Meander, surrounded by storybook farms with a mixture of animals: cattle, goats, sheep and chooks. Watch out for roosters crossing! The Meander River is crossed by a one-lane bridge, so be prepared to give way if necessary. Down to the right of the bridge is a gauge for measuring flood level. At this point, the river is lined with native trees, blackwood, wattle and gum. Perhaps because the river comes down from bush-mantled mountains, the water is very clear.

Pass Sandy Lane on the right and there is a school sign ahead. Pass Reiffers Road, and the recreation ground. On the left is the

The Meander River

Meander Primary School and St Saviour's Anglican church, weatherboard buildings that match in style. Just beyond is the little graveyard. People buried there include John George Reiffer, from Ceres, who died in 1926, George and Harriet Proverbs, and Margaret Elizabeth Proverbs, Joseph Whitely, 1891 and Joseph Nutting, 1895. Pass Barbers Road on the right and continue past a little gully with man ferns, *Dicksonia antarctica* (called 'tree ferns' on the Australian mainland), and then climb a hill. The road becomes gravel at this point. Continue on the Meander Falls Road into the Meander Forest Reserve.

Meander Forest Reserve offers various walking tracks, and information about the routes to take. In the reserve there are shelters, toilets and barbecue facilities. It is a beautiful place, with moss and lichen everywhere, ferns, pink mountain berries, (*Cyathodes parvifalia*) and red, white and pink Tasmanian heath.

Meander Forest Reserve

Near the take-off point for the Meander Falls Walk is the Huntsmans Hideaway, a cabin erected by the Apex Club. Inside is a fuel stove and wooden bunks.

To continue your tour—return to Meander and turn left into Sandy Lane. Drive on until you come to a junction; on your left you will see 'Cheshunt', a large imposing white house with a number of outbuildings gathered around it.
pic 185

'Cheshunt' estate was granted to **Thomas Archer** of 'Woolmers' in Longford, (see Chapter 7) sometime in the late 1820s. He kept the estate in trust for his son William Archer. The grant, some 6000 acres, took up most of the left side of the Meander Valley, south of the estate of 'Woodlands', belonging to William Gunn. Thomas Archer and William Field battled over the ownership of 2000 acres on the other side of the river (Stockers Plains). After this, Thomas Archer never returned to 'Cheshunt', but after his death his son William came to the estate.

William was born in Launceston in 1820. He is known as the first Tasmanian-born, and possibly the first Australian-born, architect. In 1846 he married his cousin Anna Hortle. He designed the house at 'Cheshunt' and began building in 1851. He moved in 1852. 'Cheshunt' is unusual for its time, as it is a Victorian-style house: most others in Tasmania of comparable age are Georgian. In 1863, William Archer became the first Warden of Deloraine, but resigned after a

'Cheshunt', near Deloraine

year, the distance being too great to travel regularly. He and Anna had thirteen children. In 1873 **William Bowman** of 'Cross Marsh', Melton Mowbray, bought the estate, and his descendants are still in residence. The outbuildings were workmens' cottages: now all but one are used for storing machinery.

Montana Falls. The road to the left is Cheshunt Road, Route C166, leading to Caveside, some 18 km away. Turn right and drive about 1 km to a left-hand turn into Route Cl64, the Montana Road. From the turn-off Montana is 4 km, and Red Hills 11 km, to the left. If you drove straight ahead, you would reach the A5 highway and return to Deloraine. Follow the Montana Road towards a one-lane bridge.

To see Montana Falls, turn right into Leonards Road, just before the bridge. The sign may be difficult to see, but there is another sign indicating Montana Falls a little way farther on. A few metres up Leonards Road, a walking track leads off to the left. The first stage of the falls is about five minutes' brisk walk away. You can climb right down to an odd little sandy beach in the middle of the falls.

Back to Deloraine. Back on the Montana Road, drive over the bridge. The road comes out onto the Mole Creek Road, Route B12. Turn right to return to Deloraine. On your

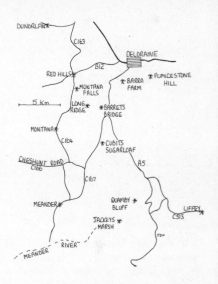

Montana Falls

way, you will pass 'Woodlands' which was granted to William Gunn. Leave Deloraine by heading eastward, bearing left. (If you went right, you'd end up back on the Lake Highway!)

On your right as you leave the town is **Bowerbank Mill**. The Bowerbank area originally consisted of around 1 000 acres. It was first granted to Alexander Rose in 1831. He leased the property to William Field, and later sold it to Lt Alfred Horne in 1841. Horne named his new property 'Bowerbank'. He died the next year and his widow Mary-Anne and her five children moved onto the property. Mary-Anne had Bowerbank Mill built in 1853. It was designed by William Archer. Mary-Anne died in 186l, and left the property to three sons, Leslie, Robert and James. Part of the property was purchased by Lionel Berry in 1832. Bowerbank Mill is now an art and craft gallery and also offers colonial accommodation.

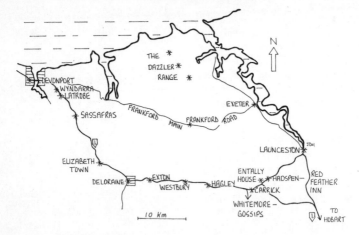

Exton. Route B54 leads into Exton, a small town offering such delights as tea rooms, antiques, farm cheese and even a connection with television personality Dr Harry Cooper!

'Exton' estate was once the property of the Rev. Samuel Martin who arrived in Van Diemen's Land in 1833. Rev. Martin's wife's maiden name had been 'Exton', so this was the name they gave to their new home. Later, the land was managed by his son, John Martin.

During the 1850s, the present house was built, replacing the original homestead. In the mid-1880s, the house, 'Exton', was sold to William Hart, a businessman from Launceston, a wealthy man who owned a generous slice of the Tasmania Gold Mine at Beaconsfield. In 1924 'Exton' was sold once again, and has since had a number of different owners. After leaving Exton, you will be able to rejoin Highway 1 at the junction. Turn right and continue towards Westbury.

Liffey Falls State Reserve. To reach the Liffey Falls State Reserve follow the signs from near Westbury.

Touring Westbury

About 3 km west of Westbury is the property 'Westfield' which, like 'Calstock' was once part of the Field family holdings. 'Westfield' homestead was completed in 1835, and was made of handmade bricks with blackwood doors. It remained in the Field family until 1946. Westbury is an attractive town which was settled in 1823 by the Field family. It has a number of historic buildings, many beautifully restored, and also features three unusual and interesting attractions of a more recent date.

When you enter Westbury, cross Quamby Bridge and turn right into Lonsdale Promenade. On your right is the village green—the only one in northern Tasmania, and once the place where the Irish garrison went to parade. The Green features a maypole base, the maypole itself having been donated by the people of Westbury, Wiltshire, England, when its Tasmanian namesake town had its one hundred and fiftieth anniversary. By the War Memorial on the Green is a 25-pounder gun and a drinking fountain and playground.

On your left is St Andrew's Anglican church. Inside this church are carvings done by local artist Mrs C.A. (Nellie) Payen. Farther along on your right, on the corner of King St, is the 'White House'. This was built in 1846 on land granted to Thomas White in 1842. Thomas White borrowed 600 pounds to build the house, which was originally known as Thomas White's Token Store. Later it became White's Hotel. The 'White House' is open to the public, and inside you can see a splendid collection of period pieces, all meticulously catalogued and described in a booklet available at the house. Most of the outbuildings are also open for inspection, including the reconstructed bakery and the stone coachhouse and stables. In the coach-house and garage are old vehicles, ranging from a penny-farthing, (dating from about 1888) through to a ladies park phaeton to a locomobile steam car made at the turn of the century.

The bakery is now working again, having re-opened in 1995. Inside, you can buy bread, cakes and biscuits baked in a traditional wood-fired oven. Directly opposite the bakery is a Georgian cottage that was built by James Earles in the late 1830s. It has been restored.

Turn up King St and on the corner of King and William Streets is the Old Rectory and the Old Bakehouse, and along the same street you'll see plenty of other interesting buildings.

Part of Westbury is known as Pensioners' Bush. This name dates from the period when Irish soldiers retired from the garrison and were granted five acre blocks in the town. Back on the main road, you'll see the Catholic Church on your left. Opposite this is the Westbury Hotel, originally one of seven hotels in the town! Another of them was Fitzpatrick's Inn, built in 1833.

Before you leave Westbury look to your left for the extensive Pearn Steam World Museum and the Westbury Gemstone and Mineral Display, and to your right for Westbury Maze.

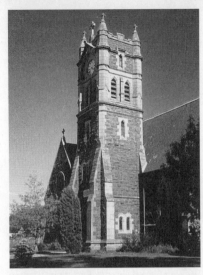

Westbury Roman Catholic Church

Pearn Steam World Museum houses a joint project of the State and Local Governments, Rotary and Apex. The collection was made by the Pearn brothers, Jake, Verdun and Zenith, during the 1940s.

Westbury Gemstone and Mineral Display. Many of the stones in this extensive (the largest in Australia) collection of gemstones and mineral samples were owned by Terry Green of Gladstone, in North East Tasmania, He sold them to Frank Bardenhagen (see Chapter 9), who has set up an impressive display area decorated with murals by artist Dallas Sutherland.

Hagley

The next town after Westbury is Hagley: a small town featuring the Hagley Farm School and Environment Centre and St Mary's Church, built in the early 1860s. Sir Richard Dry, Tasmania's first Knight and a one-time Premier, who laid the foundation stone, was later buried in a vault there. His wife, Lady

Dry, gave the lovely East Window to the church. Hagley Farm School was one of the first two area schools in Tasmania. It was begun in 1931, then housed in a building erected in 1865. The old school house is still used by students visiting the environment centre, and the school itself is now a primary school only.

Carrick

To visit Carrick, you will need to turn-off the highway at the roundabout just after Hagley and take Route B54 for 8 km. We think Carrick is one of the most interesting townships on this route, perhaps because it is so small and perfectly preserved. Just before you reach the township, you pass Route C508 which leads off to the right to Whitemore and Gossips Restaurant, built in the early 1840s and run as the Glenore Hotel. For some years it was the only hotel in the district. Since then, it has been, variously, a general store and post office, and a store room for hay. By 1977 the building was almost derelict, but the predecessors of the present owner restored it and it re-opened as 'Gossips'.

This area is the venue for the annual Agfest agricultural festival.

Cross the Liffey River, and on the right is a bluestone building covered with ivy, the old Mill House. It replaces an original wooden building erected by a man named William, (or Edward), Bryan in 1828. Bryan had been granted 3000 acres of ground around the river in 1820. He called his property 'Cluan'. The river was at that time known as Penny Royal Creek. The embryo village was originally known as Lyttleton, but this was later changed to the present Carrick.

The Old Mill House was bought in 1867 by Thomas Wilkes Mends, later of Mends and Affleck), who became very successful. The Old Mill was for some time run as a restaurant.

Next on your right, visible up the hill and entered via Route C513, is Hawthorne Villa, built by Mr Mends in 1875 for his wife and eight children, and now operated as a tearoom offering country accommo-dation. Beyond it in C513 is the burnt remains of a brick building known as Archers Folly, begun (though never finished), in 1860 by John Kinder Archer. Near it is Malik Copper Art Gallery. Back on Carrick road, look to your left to see the old Prince of Wales Hotel, built in 1840 and now a private home, the stables of which have been renovated as a restaurant. On your right is the old Plough Inn, dating from 1841. It was built by John Rudge. Next on your left is the Carrick Inn, built in 1833 and still trading as a hotel. Almost opposite is the Old Watchhouse, built for this purpose by convicts from Westbury in 1837. The Old Watchhouse is a rather attractive Georgian building, with the two holding cells intact. One is now a bathroom and the other a toilet!

Old Watchhouse, Carrick

Just up Liffey St to the right are some old cottages, built originally as part of the Entally Estate. (See later in this chapter for information about 'Entally'.) Next to the right is 'Balmoral', built in 1851, and on the left the red brick building housing Christies'

'Entally House', Carrick

Antiques, built in 1844. Farther away to your left is pretty St Andrew's Church, built in 1848. Carrick Hall is on your right.

Illawarra Road. Just out of Carrick pass the turn-off to your right into the Illawarra Road, which takes you to Perth and the Heritage Highway (see Chapters 7 and 8). If you turn up this road, you will see Illawarra Christ Church, an attractive building erected by Captain Edward Dumaresq as a school house in the early 1840s, and used as a church from c. 1846 onwards. In 1858 Captain Dumaresq gave the church and 9 acres of land to the Church of England. His son Henry married Miss Watson, daughter of Rev. Thomas Watson. The church was expanded and consecrated in the 1880s, but continued to serve as a school until 1899. Edward Dumaresq is buried in the graveyard. Return to the Carrick Road to continue on your way to Hadspen.

'Entally'. Past the Illawarra Road turn-off, you'll see the property (once part of the 'Entally' estate), named The Moat. A few hundred metres farther on is the left turn to Westwood. About 3 kilometres from Carrick is the left turn which leads back and around to Entally House.

'Entally House' was built c. 1819, by Thomas Haydock Reibey, the son of Thomas and Mary Reibey. Mary Reibey herself was an interesting character. She was born Mary Haydock to surveyor James Haydock and his wife in Lancashire in 1777. At the age of fourteen, by now an orphan, Mary 'borrowed' a neighbour's horse, was convicted of stealing, and sentenced to transportation to New South Wales for seven years. In 1792 Mary sailed on the *Royal Admiral*. Also on the ship was young Captain Thomas Reibey. He befriended Mary, found her employment as a nursemaid with some friends, and finally married her in 1794. Mary was pardoned, and they built a warehouse and house combined, known as 'Entally'. Their first son Thomas Haydock Reibey was born in 1796. Other children, James Haydock, George, Celia, Eliza, Penelope Jane and Eliza Ann, followed. In 1811 Captain Thomas Reibey died. Mary took up his business and the family throve. Thomas Haydock Reibey was given a land grant in Van Diemen's Land, near where

Carrick now stands. This he named after his parents' home, which in turn had been named after a place in Calcutta. He married Richardia Allen, and they had three children, Thomas, James and Mary. Mary Reibey died in 1855. Her grandson Thomas Reibey married Catherine Kyle, and became the first clergyman to be ordained in Tasmania. He became an Archdeacon in 1858, and was Premier of Tasmania in 1874. He and his wife had no children and he died in 1912. A nephew inherited the property, but he too died childless.

'Entally House' was opened to the public in 1950. It is well worth visiting, not only for the lovely house itself, but for the numerous outbuildings, (also open to the public) and the spacious grounds. Even the flowers in the borders are kept in period! When we visited, 'Entally' was open every day except Christmas Day and Good Friday, from 10 a.m. to 12.30 and from 1 p.m. to 5 p.m. Check locally for up-to-date information.

When you enter the house, you visit the dining room, with a fine grandfather clock made in the 1740s by John Vise of Wisbech. Next are the drawing room and main bedroom, and a gift shop. The stairs are particularly steep, leading to two small bedrooms, with skylights instead of windows, and a playroom. Beyond the staircase are the music room and library, and the kitchen, appointed in N.S.W. cedar.

Another early estate in this area was 'Sillwood', granted to Colonel William Page Ashburner in 1827. 'Sillwood' was broken up in 1836.

Hadspen

Just before you reach Launceston, you'll come to the turn-off to Hadspen. Turn into the town and drive past Foote, Browne and Reibey Streets. Turn right into Main St to visit some very old cottages, a bluestone church, and the Red Feather Inn.

The Red Feather Inn is a sandstone building, one of the first coaching inns in Tasmania. It was built in 1844 by John Sprunt, who also built other coaching inns and the Paterson Barracks. The Red Feather is a licensed restaurant, and includes a craft shop.

From Hadspen, continue towards Launceston. You may now choose to turn

Red Feather Inn, Hadspen

left and go through Prospect on the old route into the city, passing the turn-offs to the Velodrome and the Casino, or else go straight ahead on the new route.

BIBLIOGRAPHY

Books and Booklets
EMMETT, E.T. *Tasmania by Road and Track*, Melbourne University Press, 1952.
MEREDITH, Louisa and GRIFFIN, Daniel, *Early Deloraine: the Writings of Louisa Meredith and Daniel Griffin*.
NATIONAL TRUST, *Early Pioneer Estates of Deloraine*.
NEWITT, Lyn *Convicts and Carriageways*, Dept of Main Roads, 1988.
WHISHAW, Mary Kinloch, *Tasmanian Village, A Story of Carrick*, 1963.
Sassafras, A History of its Settlement and people, 1988. White House Village Green Westbury, Tasmania.

Pamphlets
'Guide to Historical Deloraine'
'Come Visit Tasmanian National Trust Properties'
'Pearns Steam World and The Westbury Gemstone and Mineral Display'

Maps
Tasmap 1: 100 000 Land Tenure Index Series:
'Forth', 'Meander', 'South Esk'

Information
Thanks to Pat Bell, George Farrell, Rev. Tony Hendricks, the late Perce Hicks, proprietors of 'Wyndarra', 'Red Feather Inn', 'The White House' and 'Gossips' and the people of Deloraine, Westbury and Carrick, especially Jan Atkins and Denis and Robyn Whishaw.

5. The Exeter Highway, and round the Tamar

Features of this drive

One of the most pleasant drives in northern Tasmania is the trip which takes you along the Exeter Highway and through the valley of the Tamar River. The Exeter Highway is also an alternative Route to Launceston from the North West Coast. This is a good trip to take if you don't mind winding roads, and also if you are interested in historic buildings, penguins at Low Head, gold mines, maritime history, and breathtaking views of the river and ocean. You'll also visit the oldest town in Australia, a Swiss lakeside village and a town that isn't there.

The Tamar River begins with the merging of the North and South Esks near Launceston. The name Tamar dates back nearly 4000 years to the wife of Judah, grandson of Abraham. Her name was given to a river between Cornwall and Devon in England, and came to Tasmania with English settlers.

To reach the Exeter Highway from Devonport leave Devonport eastward on Highway 1 (the Bass Highway), turn left at the roundabout near Latrobe and head for Moriarty on Route C702. Just past the Moriarty Hall, you turn right onto the Exeter Highway, Route B71, and head for Exeter, 53 km away.

Poppies. Driving through the Moriarty district in the summer, you will sometimes see opium poppies growing. These form a very pretty crop, with large pink flowers interspersed with a scattering of darker ones. Tasmania is the only place in the Southern Hemisphere where opium poppies may legally be grown. They are processed at Glaxo Australia Latrobe, for use in pharmaceuticals. Please note; it is against the law to enter the paddocks where the poppies are being grown. Most crops are protected by warning signs and/or formidable fences.

Pass Route C709 to Squeaking Point, which is visited in Chapter 1.

Thirlstane. Not far from Moriarty, you reach Thirlstane. On the right is a signpost indicating Thirlstane House. The Thirlstane property was owned by the Sams family in the 1840s. George Sams built a small unlined cottage there which became the temporary home of Charles and Louisa Meredith (see Chapter 11), when they moved north from Swansea. Louisa jokingly named the cottage 'Lath Hall', a name which stuck to it for many years. The property was divided by Robert Stewart in the late 1890s into a number of farms. He had plans for the building of a new township there. He sold it to the Parsons family, who had recently arrived from the south, in the late 1890s. The house, (which cannot be seen from the road) was extensively rebuilt in 1910. It is a private residence.

A little farther on is a T-junction. Turn right.

Towards Exeter. Soon the road veers left. Follow it round, and as you top the rise, you will see the Rubicon River. According to the time of day, the Rubicon may resemble a small lake, or a large expanse of mudflats. After crossing the muddy Rubicon (in which a foolhardy person who tried to wade across at low tide is said to have sunk from sight), cross the Franklin River. Some confusion exists about this name, because there are in fact *two* Franklin Rivers in Tasmania. This one in the north is muddy like the Rubicon, the one down south is a true wilderness river, which you'll be visiting in Chapter 15. A turn-off to the left, Route C740, goes to Baker's Beach (14 km), a wide beach with sand and impressive dunes.

Continue along Route B71 to Exeter. On your left are plantations of radiata pine, extensively grown for use in building and paper making.

Cross Saxons Creek, and just before Frankford, you will see a tiny church perched on a hillside to the left—St Saviour's Church of England.

Frankford

Frankford is on the Exeter Highway, just after the turn-off to Holwell Road. It is a small country town, scattered along the side of the Exeter Highway. At the end of last century, the only way to Frankford was by river. You would then be put on a horse which found its way to the small clearing where several people had taken up selections.

From Frankford, you have a choice of routes. You can:

(a) continue on the Exeter Highway to Exeter, and then head left to Beaconsfield and George Town or right towards Launceston.

(b) drive about 7 km farther on then take Route B72 to Westbury and join the Bass Highway (Highway 1).

(c) turn left into Route C715, the Holwell Road, and go straight to Beaconsfield.

Frankford to Exeter. If you choose option (a), you'll continue through Frankford towards Exeter. The next town after Frankford is Glengarry. On the left is Glengarry Presbyterian Church. Cross Tunks Bridge, probably named for a Mr Tunks who once leased the Huntly property of Joseph Robertson.

'Huntly' (since renamed) belonged to Joseph Robertson (1824–1905), a Scot from Perthshire, in the 1870s. Joseph and his wife Christine Pringle arrived in Tasmania in 1861 and first settled in Ross in the Midlands. After a number of moves, the family settled at Huntly where Joseph became the first successful hop-grower in northern Tasmania. The house once included a post office, run by Joseph's daughter Mary, and a later post office may still be seen in Glengarry. 'Huntly' has lately been restored. Joseph and Christina are buried in Winkleigh Cemetery.

Route C731 is a right-hand turn from this road leading 7 km to **Notely Gorge** in the Notely Gorge Reserve. Notely Gorge is a lovely place to visit, with walking tracks through ferns, a picnic area and toilets.

As you come into Exeter, you'll cross Stony Creek. To the east of Exeter, on the West Tamar Highway, is Bradey's Lookout, a favourite place with photographers. Beyond Exeter to the east it is 25 km to Riverside, one of the outer suburbs of Launceston.

If you choose to drive along this route, you may visit Legana, and, on the right, the Swiss lakeside village of **Grindelwald**, the inspiration of Roelf Vos. Grindelwald is well worth a visit, and is particularly pretty on a sunny day. It has plenty of accommodation and tourist facilities.

To reach the East Tamar Highway, which takes you to Launceston by a different route, turn left at Exeter and follow the signs to the Batman Bridge.

Frankford to Westbury. If you choose option B, you should probably turn back to

Grindelwald, West Tamar Highway

Chapter 4, where the trip from Westbury to Launceston is covered in some detail.

Holwell Road. If you choose option (c), you'll take the Holwell Road to Beaconsfield. You still get to Exeter later on!

It is 9 km from Holwell Road turn-off to Holwell, along a rather narrow winding road, some of which is gravel.

In 1839, when Surveyor George Frankland made a map of the Tamar area, a whole large tract of land west of the Tamar, including Holwell, Badger Head, York Town and Beaconsfield was known by the all-inclusive name of 'Ilfracombe'.

Holwell is a tiny town, but you might like to stop there to enjoy the fine view of Bass Strait, or follow the signs to the Holwell Gorge State Reserve. It's about another 11 km to Beaconsfield.

As you approach Beaconsfield, you come to a choice of ways. Follow the right-hand road into the town.

Beaconsfield—some history

Settlers had arrived on the site of Beaconsfield by 1805, but the town's history really began in the 1820s, when its first industry—limestone quarrying—was established to assist with the building of nearby George Town. This venture continued, first under governmental control and later as a privately leased company, until the 1870s. Iron was also discovered in the area, and this was officially confirmed in 1866 by Charles Gould, the geologist for whom the little wooden town of Goulds Country, near St Helens, was named. (See Chapter 10.) Strangely, he seems not to have noticed the gold.

Unfortunately, although several iron-based companies began mining and smelting the iron ore, it was later found to be unacceptably contaminated with chrome, and by the end of 1877, the mines had closed.

In that same year, gold was found in respectable quantities (there had been smaller finds earlier), by William and David Daily, on Cabbage Tree Hill, west of present-day Beaconsfield. William, David and their three brothers became major shareholders in the later mine, known as Tasmania Gold Mine, which at one stage produced nearly 48% of Tasmania's gold.

The area between Cabbage Tree Hill and Middle Arm became known as the 'Brandy Creek Field', and in 1877 was recognised as a town and granted a post office. The Daily brothers appointed a Wesleyan preacher, Joseph Davies (fresh from the Ballarat goldfields), as their manager and the next year a Wesleyan Chapel and an Anglican Church were built. A Roman Catholic Church (Weld St) followed in 1890. Holy Trinity church was designed by Alexander North, who also designed St Matthew's in Bothwell and Holy Trinity in Launceston. In 1879, the town was given the more dignified name of 'Beaconsfield', after the then Earl of Beaconsfield, Benjamin Disraeli. Five years later came a major town upheaval: the bank was robbed! During the '80s and '90s, the town grew rapidly. More miners arrived, some like John Peart (1824–1894) and his family coming in from mainland goldfields. By 1900, Beaconsfield was the third largest town in Tasmania, but water seeping into the mine shafts caused so many problems that, despite the fact that the possibilities of the gold seam had by no means been exhausted, the mines were closed down some fifty years after they opened. The Tasmania Mine itself shut down in 1914.

The Tasmania Mine Today. During the late 1980s interest re-awakened in the Tasmania Mine. Gold has been recovered from the Golconda tailings factory at Middle Arm, and it is expected that the mine will be re-opened on a commercial basis by the end of the 1990s. New techniques, such as the sealing of tunnels with quick-setting concrete, promise to control the water seepage problem which bedevilled the mines last time around. Dewatering of the shafts is already well under way.

Touring Beaconsfield

The main street of Beaconsfield is Weld St, named for Governor Weld. Turn out of Weld St into West St, opposite the Post Office, to visit the Grubb Shaft Goldmine Museum. The Grubb Shaft was named for Launceston businessman W.T. Grubb who, with W. Hart, brought the main reef claim in the Tasmanian Goldmine from the Daily brothers in 1877. The Grubb Shaft building was erected in 1905. It is an old boiler house, which housed twelve coal-fired boilers that supplied steam to the engines in the Hart and Grubb Shaft Buildings. The museum is open every day of the year except Christmas and Good Friday, and features a waterwheel-driven ore-crushing stamp battery (the only one in Australia) and pump rods (made of pitch pine) used to connect the pumps down the shaft with the steam engines on the surface.

John Robertson was a son of Joseph and Christina Robertson of 'Huntly', Glengarry. He was born in England in 1860 and arrived in Tasmania at the age of 10 months. John built a house called 'Rookery Nook', which can still be seen at Winkleigh. He was married twice: once to Mary Gottfried (with whom he had six children) and later to Hannah Peart, (with whom he had a daughter). He was a member of the Salvation Army from 1884, John Robertson died at the gold mine at Beaconsfield (where he was head pitman), in 1911.

Next to the site is the ruined Hart Shaft Engine House (1904), which contained a pump engine, the Hart Shaft Mine winding

Hart Shaft, Beaconsfield

engine and air compressors. Enquiries about the present mines may be made at the museum.

Farther up the road on the right of the Hart and Grubb Shaft buildings is the Beaconsfield Council Chambers and on the other side is a children's playground. Inside the Council Chambers are old photos including pictures of members of the successive municipal councils, beginning in 1912. A range of pamphlets and books is available for sale. There are also books at the museum.

Just outside (to the right) is a copper beech tree presented to the people of Beaconsfield, Tasmania, by the people in Beaconsfield, England, and planted by the Governor of Tasmania, Sir Ronald Cross, in 1957.

Opposite the Grubb Shaft is the Miner's Cottage, a reconstruction of the type of cottage in which the miners used to live. Behind this is the original Flowery Gully School House (1891–1937). Donated by the residents of Flowery Gully as a museum piece, the little timber building was re-erected and restored, and opened in 1971. Inside, it is furnished with desks, slates, books, a teacher's desk, an old map of Tasmania, and all the other paraphernalia used in the early schools.

From the bank beside the school, you can look across to Alicia Hall, (est. 1899) in Weld St.

Leaving West St, turn left into Weld St, to pass Manions Jubilee Bakery (1887). Next is the Exchange Hotel.

Beauty Point—then and now

To visit Beauty Point, leave Beaconsfield by continuing along Weld St.

Beauty Point, as the name implies, is a charming place. Oddly enough, however, its appearance had nothing to do with the way it got its name.

It seems that in the 1890s a Mr Garret had a prize bullock named Beauty. In those days, possession of an animal such as Beauty was the equivalent of owning a truck today, and when Beauty died, the spot was named after him.

At Beauty Point, apart from some very choice scenery, is the Australian Maritime College and fisheries, as well as the Underwater Training Centre.

A road leads down to the waterside: to the north-east you look over Port Dalrymple, and south-east down to Middle Arm and across to Shag Head.

Drive around the Esplanade past Sandy Beach (right) and Ilfraville (known as Sandy Beach until the early 1970s), (left).

Beauty Point

Beauty Point

If you drive out to Redbill Point there is a good view over West Arm. Beauty Point has plenty of picnic areas, and accommodation is available.

Apples at Ilfraville

Once there were many flourishing orchards in the area between Beaconsfield and Kelso. When the British were leaving India earlier this century, a husband and wife partnership, Sadlier and Knight, went into business developing orchards and selling them to transplanted Anglo-Indians.

They caused between 20 and 50 twenty-acre blocks to be cleared by bullock teams and planted with apple trees around Kelso, but unfortunately the climate was too windy and this combined with bad drainage caused most of the orchards to fail.

One orchard which does remain is at Ilfraville, and has belonged to four generations of the Taylor family, with the fifth generation already on hand.

Joe Taylor was a native of Rochedale, in England, and he and his family arrived in Tasmania in 1913. As a descendant rather ruefully points out: 'Joe thought he was on to a good thing, settling between a flourishing port (Beauty Point) and a growing gold town (Beaconsfield). How wrong can you be?'

Although the current Mr Taylor's is the only orchard remaining around Beauty Point, he is quite confident that the industry is slowly improving. 'It will never be anything spectacular,' he says, 'but we think you can safely say the Taylors and their apples will be around for a good while yet.'

Although Tasmania's apple exports have dropped by two thirds, the state's status of being free of the dreaded fruit fly has wakened Japanese interest in buying local apples. The Red and Golden Delicious are the best known export varieties. Orchardists have experimented with new types such as the yellow-fleshed Fuji apple and the Nashi, a cross between an apple and a pear.

Currently, the local market is important, with Royal Galas, Granny Smiths and Croftons among the most popular.

Growers are trying out a New Zealand variety, but at the time of writing the jury is still out on its success in Australia.

York Town—the town that isn't there

Continue on Route A7, (here known as the West Arm Road) and follow it sharply round at the junction with Route C720. To your right, just before Andersons Creek, is a small lay-by at an historic site, where a brick cairn commemorates the discovery of Andersons Creek by Ensign Robert Anderson in 1804. Andersons Creek was named by Lieutenant Colonel William Paterson, after its discoverer.

In around 1805, there was an effort to establish settlers from Norfolk Island on farms in this area, but poor conditions drove the settlers upriver to the more fertile ground where Launceston now stands. Frankly, if Andersons Creek was as muddy and unprepossessing a stream then as now, you can scarcely blame the Norfolk Islanders for moving on!

Masseys Creek comes next, and then, to the left, is a turn-off to Bowens Road (Route C740), named for an early orchardist. This leads to the Asbestos Range National Park and Bakers Beach, and is unsealed.

Turn into Bowens Road and drive round to the picnic area, where there is a stone monument (1954), which includes a plan of the historic settlement of York Town. The York Town plaque reads (rather oddly, as York Town was by no means permanent), 'Site of the first permanent settlement in Northern Tasmania'. Perhaps the meaning here is that previous explorers of the unknown north had set up camps rather than towns.

The plaque continues:

'I have investigated most parts of the country and being still of the opinion that the head of the western arm is most eligible situation for the permanent residence I have taken the liberty of naming it Yorktown'. Lt Governor William Paterson, December 1804.'

York Town

The town 'Yorktown' was laid out but although there was plenty of water and timber, there were problems with the site. Shipping could not come within six miles of it, and loaded boats could come only at high water. Winter rains reduced the area to a swamp, so in 1806 the settlement was moved to the head of the port, where the North and South Esks fall ito it. The new town was named 'Launceston'.

It is said that Governor Lachlan Macquarie (often called 'Macquarie the Builder'), was not at all impressed with York Town when he saw it in 1811.

During Lt Col. Paterson's early enthusiasm for York Town, he had had buildings erected and trees planted, and when the town was abandoned, a convict named Harry Barrett stayed behind as caretaker. He lived there until 1870, when he died—aged 101! Perhaps the area wasn't so insalubrious after all.

Towns that aren't there. When first researching this book, we discovered that many towns which appear on the map are almost impossible to find. This is not the fault of the maps—in fact, there are many excellent road maps available—but is due to the fact that many farming communities are so spread out that they cannot be termed 'towns' in the ordinary sense. 'Blink and you'll miss it!' is a common description of these places.

To avoid confusing the modern-day explorer of Tasmania. these places will be referred to as 'farming areas' or 'settlements' rather than as 'towns'. York Town, which really isn't there at all, is an exaggerated example.

A7 to Kelso and Greens Beach

Cross the York Town Rivulet, and on your left is Route C721 to Badger Head in the Asbestos Range National Park. On your right, Route C722 takes you 5 km to Clarence Point, up to Arthurs Head and back to the Kelso Road. From Arthurs Head you may look across Port Dalrymple to see York Cove and George Town. The turn-off to Kelso, the next township, is also on the right. You'll see two giant radio transmission masts near the road. Kelso was once the site of a strange disappearance. It seems that during the 1920s, while orchards were being cleared, two brothers named Hinds had a bullock team. One terrible stormy night one told his brother that he was 'going to check on the bullocks'. He went out all right, but never came back, and despite a concentrated search, was never found. One of the more likely theories is that he lost his bearings in the storm and walked into the sea.

If you follow Route A7 you come to the quietly charming beachside resort of Greens Beach. Temptations include a golf club and camping ground and a magnificent view of Bass Strait. If you drive west in Greens Beach and park at the top of the cliff, you can look east to see the lighthouse at Low Head or, (appropriately enough!) west to West Head. To go down to the beach where boats are launched, turn into Greens Beach, and take the right hand road.

It seems a little unfortunate that to reach George Town from Greens Beach there is no real alternative to driving back to York Town on A7, taking the short cut, (Route C720), then continuing (back through Beaconsfield) until the turn-off (Route C725) to the Batman Bridge. This is also a most unusual circumstance: generally, in Tasmania, there are so many attractive alternative routes that the difficulty lies in making a choice! Apart from this example the only real cases of one-way routes we can recall are the roads to Coles Bay (Chapter 11), Southport (Chapter 13), and Strathgordon (Chapter 14).

South of Beaconsfield

Leaving Beaconsfield, and driving south east, proceed along the West Tamar Highway (Route A7), and cross Middle Arm Creek. A turn to the right on C717 would take you to Flowery Gully and Winkleigh and a turn to the left would bring you to Rowella and Sidmouth, where 13 families from the Lowlands of Scotland were settled during the 1840s.

To reach the **Batman Bridge** at Whirlpool Reach and cross the Tamar, turn left onto C725. The Batman Bridge is B73, leading onto Route A8. It is a cable-stayed truss bridge and was built in 1968 and named, not after the Caped Crusader, but after John Batman, an active early settler who later helped to found Melbourne. Soon after crossing the Batman Bridge you come to a turn-off (right), going to Craigbourne and Hillwood.

Towards George Town

Turn left onto Route A8, (the East Tamar Highway) to see Bell Bay 16 km and George Town 18 km away. Launceston is 32 km to the right.

It is rather odd, driving along the modern road toward George Town, to recall that when Governor Lachlan Macquarie travelled this way in 1821, the road was so extraordinarily bad that he and his party gave up and travelled by water instead! They rode horses on the return journey, but left the road to have a look at the Eastern Arm of the Tamar—and, despite (or maybe because of) the presence of a guide, got lost in the bush! Pass the Bridport Road, (Route B82), on the right and the woodchip mill on the left. Bell Bay Power Station is left. Bell Bay is the site of the Comalco aluminium plant.

Bridport Road goes through the small settlement of Pipers River, and bypasses the turn-off to Mount Direction (right). It is a pleasant drive along a straight, well-made road, which passes the huge old property of 'Bowood' to the right and comes out at Bridport. (See Chapter 9 for more about 'Bowood' and Bridport.) Coming in to George Town on Route A8, look out for the right-hand turn-off for Mount George Scenic Lookout, just 4 km from the main road.

History of George Town

George Town is proud of its status as the third settlement in Australia, dating from 1804. Most medium-to-large towns look on with envy when neighbouring settlements achieve cityhood, but George Town probably wouldn't thank you if cityhood were thrust upon it. You see, as things stand, it can claim to be the oldest *town* in Australia!

The site of the town was first visited by Europeans in 1798 when Bass and Flinders, in the *Norfolk*, named Port Dalrymple. Then five years later Colonel William Paterson took possession of the area in the name of King George III. Paterson also named the Tamar River in honour of Governor King's birthplace in Cornwall. Had George Town had a reliable source of fresh water larger than the little York Rivulet, it might have gone on to become the northern capital; as it is, William Paterson moved up-river to Launceston in 1825.

Touring George Town. Because it is so old, George Town is full of historic buildings.

Pier Hotel, George Town

These include the old Watchhouse (1843), George Town Hotel (1846), the cottage called 'Whitestones' 11839), Cable Company House (1870), Pier Hotel (1850), 'Fasifern', Cable Co House (1870), 'The Monument' (1840), 'Ivy Cottage' (1855), 'Laura Villa' (1870), 'The Grove' (1838). BenHyrons' House (1860), 'White Cottage' (1840), and 'Lawton Farmhouse' (1890).

As you come into the town from Route A8, you should see a Visitor Centre and information bay. The centre is open daily. Continue on this road and turn left into Macquarie St. George Town is so full of interest that it is a good idea to park your car and walk around the streets so you can enjoy the charming old buildings at leisure. Remember though—many of them are private homes. Detailed information about tours and history walks is available in the town, but the following is one possibility. You may be interested to note that George Town shares many street names with Launceston. At the corner of Sorell (named for Governor William Sorell) and Macquarie (named for Governor Lachlan Macquarie) Streets, is the Old Watchhouse (l843). This was once a gaol. A few metres farther on, opposite the modern Post Office, is the George Town Hotel. This hotel (c.1880), and known as 'Gray's', is painted in heritage colours and has attractive lacy decorations. Turn left into

'Whitestones', George Town

'The Grove', George Town

Anne St to see the site of St Mary Magdalene Anglican Church (1883), the third church to be built on this site. The church was burned down in 1994. In the churchyard are some interesting headstones, including that of Reverend John Fereday (d. 1871), whose wife, Susan, was a noted artist. There is a memorial to Mary Ann Friend, wife of Mathew Curling Friend, a Port Officer of the district. Mary Ann died in 1838, aged 40. Also buried in the churchyard is William Lashington Goodwin, of 'The Grove'. (d. 1862) or, as his tombstone puts it, in MDCCCLXII!

Go back to Macquarie St and turn left into Elizabeth St to see houses dating from the 1870s; the Pier Hotel, an attractive building established in the 1840s; 'Whitestones' (1839), once licensed as the 'Steam Packet Inn' and the old Bakehouse, owned by the Widdowson family in the 1870s. Turn left into Macquarie St again, with the Bakehouse on your left and No. 27 Macquarie St (1870s) and No. 19 (weatherboard house c. 1848) on your right. Turn left into Wellington St, to see the home of the Widdowson family (1870s), and then turn right onto the Esplanade. Pass Barrack St, and on your right is No. 13 the Esplanade, 'Fasifern', built in the 1870s for William Warren of the Bass Strait Cable Company. 'Fasifern' is restored, and is classified with the National Trust.

Walk on to Windmill Point, to see a monument bearing the date in 1804 when William Paterson of the N.S.W. Corps landed from H.M.S. *Buffalo* and took possession of the northern territory of Van Diemen's Land in the name of George III. Walk up Macquarie St, past Barrack St, and turn left into Wellington St, to see No. 22, built for the Brown family in 1855, and No. 17, built in the 1870s.

Turn right up Cimitiere St, (named for G. Cimitiere, the Commandant at Port Dalrymple c. 1820), to see No. 25, a Georgian building called 'The Grove'. Outside 'The Grove' (1838) is an old-world garden, including lavender hedge, flower borders, and geraniums in pots.

'The Grove' is three storeys high. The top floor contains the attics, where the maids were kept locked in at night. The first floor was given over to bed chambers and the ground floor had the kitchens, parlour and dining room. The parlour is handsomely furnished in gold and red. For a moderate fee, you may explore the house. The main staircase of 18 steps leads up to the bedrooms, furnished in period style with such items as a hip bath and cradle. A rather perilous wooden stair leads up to the attics. There are no windows there, but only skylights, and the doors are much smaller than those serving the lower floors.

The house was once a Port Officer's Residence, occupied by Joseph and Elizabeth Davies. Mr Davies, manager of the Tasmania Gold Mine, bought the house in 1889. He died in 1922 at the age of eighty three. Continue up Cimitiere St, and cross Anne St. On the corner is Ben Hyron's cottage.

Ben Hyrons (1795?–1873), was transported to Van Diemen's Land in 1818 for possessing counterfeit coins.

In Hobart Town, Hyrons worked for a shoemaker until receiving a conditional pardon in 1831. His first wife Amelia, (who had been transported to Sydney), having remarried, Hyrons married three more times, first to Sophia Wood, with whom he moved to Launceston and went into the hotel business. Sophia died in 1832, so he married Mahala Hedditch, moved to Hobart, and then back to Launceston, where he ran the London Tavern and Royal Olympic Theatre on the site of the present Post Office.

Here also, in 1840, he started his Comet coach (built in Hobart Town), on the main Midlands run. Coaches had begun to run a few years earlier, and there was determined competition between the rival coach-owners. Four years later, Ben launched an improved model, again made by Johnson, of Collins St in Hobart Town.

In 1851, Hyrons withdrew his services from the Midlands run, but continued his service from Launceston to Longford and George Town, where he moved in 1855. His wife Mahala died in George Town in 1862. Benjamin then married a woman named Marie Duncan.

Turn off Cimitiere St into Sorell St. On the corner is a brick cottage, the former Post Office (1861), and farther along is the oldest remaining building in George Town, 'Tara Hall', built c. 1830 for William Kneale.

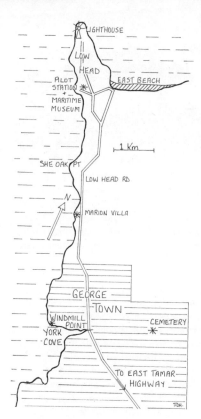

A drive to Low Head

Along the Low Head Road, (reached from Goulburn St or Anne St), you may see 'Marion Villa' clearly signposted on your left. Built in 1834, 'Marion Villa' was the holiday residence of James Cox (see Chapter 7), a prominent citizen whose principal residence was lovely 'Clarendon', near Evandale.

Visitors to 'Marion Villa' may be surprised to see what appears to be a narrow pit (or half a dry moat!) on the side away from the road. This feature, which is shared by 'Clarendon', is an area walk, in which windows were set allowing light into basement rooms. 'Marion Villa' is almost

'Marion Villa', Low Head

as it was in James Cox's day: there has been just one addition, on the east side. A little farther on, on your right, notice leading lights and cottages, built around 1888 by John Gunn, for whom Gunn St in George Town is named. The cottages were occupied by the light keepers. Pass Gunn Parade on your right. Along to the left you can see a stone wall, built in 1890. A cluster of red-roofed white buildings on your left is the Pilot Station Precinct (1835), including the Maritime Museum opened in 1980. This museum is well worth a visit. When we went there we saw a light display, including ships' kerosene navigation lights and a flashing gas light, once used on beacons and islands in the river. There were also examples of scrimshaw, photographs, maps, a diver's suit, models of ships, a teak skylight, a lifeboat mast and rigging and many other interesting items.

Opposite the museum is tiny white Christ Church, built in 1877 and consecrated in 1884. On the wall is a plaque from the National Trust, acknowledging the care given to the building. Just past Christ Church is 'Bermondsdey Cottage' (1850), and the Cable Station Headquarters (1859). Two houses and a castle on your right are 'Braeside' and 'Kuranui', built in 1889. Mr John Gunn built the castle at the rear in 1929. These houses are surrounded by a very interesting garden. At the end of Low Head is the impressive red and white Channel Light (1888), overlooking the Bass Strait and the rocks. On your way back, you may like to visit the pleasant picnic spot at East Beach, or the Low Head fairy penguin colony (tours each evening at Sunset from November to March).

Back to George Town. As you return through George Town, it is interesting to visit the old cemetery. Drive along Cimitiere St, passing Friend St (named for Mathew Curling Friend) Franklin St, Agnes St and Hammond Avenue. Turn right onto Marguerite St and follow it round to the

Maritime Museum, Low Head

Light House, Low Head

cemetery on your left. Straight ahead of you is what is left of the original road to Launceston: the Goulburn St Bridge was not built until the 1850s.

In the cemetery is an impressive crypt for Mary Anne Friend. For some reason her name on the crypt is spelt differently from the way it appears on the memorial we once saw in Mary Magdalene Church. One stone rather intriguingly gives a single name: 'Bertie'.

Deviot and Sidmouth. From George Town, you may go on to Launceston on Route A8, or return towards Devonport via the Exeter Highway, but before you leave the area you might like to visit Deviot and Sidmouth.

You can turn directly into Route C728 as you come off the Batman Bridge, heading back towards Exeter, but it's probably easier if you go straight to Exeter, turn right onto Route A7, and then left into Route C728. This leads into a very pleasant drive along the west bank of the Tamar.

If you wish to visit Rosevears, with its waterbird haven and historic inn, take the second turn to the left instead, onto Route C733. Route C728 takes you first through the little settlement of Blackwall, past Gem Rock and opposite the Crescent Shore Nature Reserve. Pass a jetty on your right and continue to Gravelly Beach. Cross the bridge, and pass the row of palm trees. Next on your right is the Paper Beach Road, leading 2 km to Paper Beach, Lightfoot Bay and Swan Point. Swan Point was named by Matthew Flinders in November 1798, because he saw a large colony of swans there.

Just past the road you reach a sign marking the entrance of the 2.5 km walking track to Paper Beach. In the same area are the ruins of a flour mill, c.1888. Cross the Supply River and on your right is Robigana. Swan Point once encompassed a much larger area, but in 1913 the name Robigana (Aboriginal for 'swan') was selected, to avoid confusion with Swan Port on the east coast. The Peden family chose to call their home Robigana.

Paper Beach was named when an early resident, Mr Law, found a case of lading papers washed ashore from a ship there. The Robigana area was once largely concerned with orcharding, and was the site originally proposed for the town of Exeter in 1866, but gold was discovered in Beaconsfield and the changing point for the horses which drew gold coaches developed into the town now named Exeter.

Next along the road is Deviot, and on your left is Marions Vineyard, open for wine tasting and sales. Continue along the road until you reach the Batman Bridge. Turn off to the right, just before reaching the bridge, and follow the road underneath the bridge, along the bank of the Tamar, to visit an old Presbyterian Church, the Auld Kirk of

Sidmouth. The Auld Kirk is a pleasing building of orange and blue freestone.

'The Auld Kirk'. In 1840 the pioneers of the Sidmouth area wrote to the Government and requested that a church be built for Sidmouth. This letter was signed by people from a radius of 10 miles around.

The first Presbyterian services held in the area were conducted at 'Richmond Hill', the home of James Reid, with the ministers travelling from Launceston and Evandale. In 1843 the first minister, Rev. Alexander McKenzie arrived. He set up a building fund and work was begun on the kirk. Both convict and free labour were used on the local-stone building, and the church originally had a shingle roof. The kirk opened in 1846, and

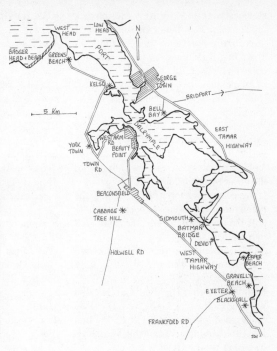

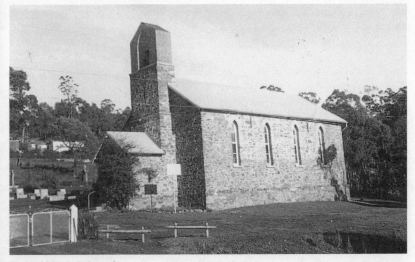

The Auld Kirk, Sidmouth

services were held by Rev. McKenzie's replacement, Rev. James Garrett. Some of the congregation came upriver from York Town and Ilfracombe, and funerals often came up by boat. Rev. Garrett was trained in medicine as well as theology, and was thus a doubly valued member of the community.

When he died in 1874 he was buried in the cemetery at the kirk. In 1900 the building was gutted by fire, and for some years the Auld Kirk was known as 'the church with the tree growing inside'.

It was partially restored in 1913, and as the population of the area was declining along with the Beaconsfield gold, the church fell into disuse.

Services resumed in 1920, the restoration was completed and the kirk formally rededicated in 1933.

Near the church is Highfield Garden, with what looks like a rocket by the fence. Stay on the road following the Tamar. The first turn-off is to the left to Sidmouth, 1 km away. The right-hand turn leads to Rowella and Kayena.

You reach Route B73 at a T-junction. To the right is Beaconsfield, 7 km away, and to the left Exeter is 9 km away.

BIBLIOGRAPHY

Books

ALLEN, Doris and BROWN, Dawn, *Tasmanian Connection· The Peart Family.*

BROWN, Dawn, SHEARWOOD, Glenda and SMELLIE, Grace, *Our Heritage*; *The Robertsons.*

KERRISON, Janet, *Beaconsfield Gold*, Rotary Club.

PHILLIPS, Joan, *Recollections at Robigana*, Boolarong Publications, 1982.

SMITH, Coultman, *Town With A History;* Beaconsfield Museum Committee, 1978.

Pamphlets

'Pilot Station and Museum. Low Head'
'The Tamar Heritage'
'Walk Through George Town'
'George Town—On Top in Tasmania'

Maps

Tasmap Land Tenure Index Series; 'Tamar', 'Forth'

Information

Thanks to Judy Austen, Matthew Williams, Betty Roberts, A.E. Taylor and Don Wright.

6. Launceston

Features of this drive

Launceston is a pleasant city with plenty of well-preserved Georgian and Victorian buildings. It has a pleasant park, and offers museums, churches, curiosity and antique shops as well as modern city amenities. It is the second largest city in Tasmania, but it doesn't take long to drive out into the country again. In Launceston, you may ride a chairlift, take a river cruise, visit an old umbrella shop, a woollen mill, an Automobile Museum, and a country club Casino.

The beginnings of Launceston

Launceston: (NOTE—Pronounced 'LON-sess-ton' locally), is the second city of Tasmania, and the third oldest city in Australia.

Its beginnings coincided with the discovery of the Tamar River in 1798 by Bass and Flinders. They named the area Port Dalrymple in honour of the Admiralty Hydrographer, Alexander Dalrymple. Six years later, in 1804, Colonel William Paterson arrived at Port Dalrymple, having been dispatched there by Governor King. In November of that year, he formally took possession of the north of Van Diemen's Land. During a voyage up the Tamar in the Lady Nelson he named the North and South Esks (Esk is an old English river name which originally meant just 'river'!) and the Tamar, in honour of Governor King of N.S.W., who had been born on the Tamar River, which

forms the border between Cornwall and Devon. The new colony was first called 'Patersonia' in 1806 when Paterson moved his headquarters there from George Town and Beaconsfield, but the name was changed to Launceston a year later in honour of Governor Philip Gidley King's birthplace in Cornwall.

In 1824, Launceston was officially proclaimed a township, replacing George Town as the main settlement in the north. Two years later it was properly surveyed and mapped out by surveyor H.W. Smythe. In 1843 the fight against the transportation of convicts began, becoming successful in the early 1850s. In 1846 military rule came

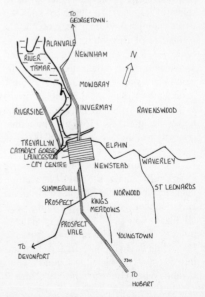

LAUNCESTON
CITY CENTRE

to an end and in 1852 Launceston was proclaimed as a municipality, the first mayor being Mr W.S. Button. The population had grown to over seven thousand people.

The 1850s were a decade of great change. Roads were built and improved, buildings erected, and the population continued to increase steadily. Today Launceston, the 'Garden City', is the unofficial northern capital of Tasmania. It is situated 64 km south of the mouth of the Tamar, just over 100 km south-east of Devonport. The North and South Esk Rivers meet at Launceston, and around the area are mountains, including the well-known skiing mountain, Ben Lomond, in the Eastern Tiers. Ben Lomond (1572 m) is Tasmania's second highest peak, the highest being Mt Ossa (1617 m). The current population of the city is around 67 000.

In and around Launceston. There are several different ways to reach Launceston, but whether you come into the city from the Bass Highway or the Exeter and Tamar Highways you will find plenty of signs to point the route. If you approach from the Bass Highway, you may wish to turn left into Prospect to visit the Country Club Casino. When you reach the city centre, it is a good idea to park your car at the Elizabeth Street Car Park, and walk around the CBD. Here is one route you might like to take. The buildings detailed are just a fraction of the fine old buildings that make up Launceston's city centre, but there isn't room to mention all of them. For information on others, ask locally.

St John's Church of England and George Arthur. As you come out of the entrance onto Elizabeth Street, turn right and walk down to St John Street. On your left, on the corner of Elizabeth and St John Streets, is **St John's Church of England**. The foundation stone of this church was laid by Sir Arthur E. Havelock, who was Governor of Tasmania in 1902. The foundation stone of the original church of this site was laid by the Lieutenant Governor George Arthur on 28 Jan, 1825. Governor Arthur had commissioned the building in 1824, and, on noting that the architect had planned that the church would be as large as the one in Hobart, he decreed that it must be made smaller! The church was built in stuccoed brick and in a Georgian gothic style. The clay was dug from nearby Princes Square. In 1830 the clock tower was finished with one clock face: the present tower was built five years later. Further additions were made, notably by architect Alexander North in 1901.

One of the early rectors, in 1827, was the Reverend James Norman. Inside the church are some interesting carvings, depicting coats of arms, biblical symbols, and plants and animals endemic to Tasmania. These were begun in 1904 by Hugh Cunningham and continued by his apprentice Gordon Cumming. The drawings upon which the carvings were based were provided by architect Alexander North. Unfortunately, the ambitious project of decorating the entire church with carvings was never completed. A particularly endearing set of decorations may be seen on the Tasmanian oak choir stalls, which feature four pairs of possums. **Sir George Arthur** (1784–1854), was born and died in England. During the years 1824–1836 he served as Tasmania's first Lieutenant Governor. He is remembered with mixed feelings: his rule saw bushranging wiped out, the building of Port Arthur Prison—the notorious 'Black Drive' and other equally dubious exploits.

Princes Square. Turn left into St John Street. On your right, on the corner of Frederick Street, is Princes Square, once a brickfield, later a parade ground. It became a park in 1859 and has a graceful fountain with an interesting history. It is one of a kind, designed in Paris and imported to Launceston from the first Great Paris Exhibition.

Chalmers Church, Christ Church and Milton Hall. Cross Frederick Street. The white church directly ahead is Chalmers Church, named for Sir Thomas Chalmers.

Princes Square, Launceston

Originally opened in 1860, the church was built in the gothic revival style, and was extensively restored in 1969. Turn right into Frederick Street. Close to Chalmers Church in Frederick Street is the Baptist Christ Church, featuring an interesting organ and stained glass windows, and near it, Milton Hall, built in 1841 and enlarged in 1858. Originally, this building was known as St Johns Square Independent Chapel, and was used by the noted historian Rev. John West, who preached here for fifteen years. Rev. West was firmly against transportation. He later wrote a two volume history of Tasmania and became editor of *The Sydney Morning Herald*. Milton Hall was built in the Greek Revival style.

Drysdale House and Morton House. Turn right into Charles Street. Directly opposite the turn-off is Drysdale House and on your left, as you head up Charles Street, is Morton House, once St Johns Hospital, built around 1835. This simple Georgian building has the distinction of being the site of the first use of anaesthetic in Australia. The doctor was Dr W.R. Pugh.

Memorial Baptist Church. Turn left into Elizabeth Street. Here you'll see some lovely terrace-style shops. As you turn right into Wellington Street, look across the street to see Trade's Hotel, whose exterior features portraits of famous modern musicians. Cross over York Street and on your left is the Memorial Baptist Church, built in 1885. The site of this church belonged to merchant and philanthropist Henry Reed, who came to Tasmania in the late 1820s. When he died in 1880, his widow paid for this church to be erected as a memorial. The foundation stone was laid in 1883. Behind this building is the original brick church built by Henry Reed.

O'Keefe's Court House. Cross Brisbane Street, and pass Barrow Street. On your right, on the corner of Wellington and Paterson St, is O'Keefe's Court House, established in 1826. The earliest documentation of a building on this site is dated July, 1826, when a Mr George Lyford (Master Builder) had dealings with a Mr Patrick Dalrymple (Gentleman). Patrick Dalrymple died in 1840.

Turn right into Paterson Street. On your right is the *Examiner* and Express Building, established in 1842.

The Examiner, Tasmania's oldest newspaper, was founded in 1842 by a Scotsman named James Aikenhead, who had secretly imported the necessary equipment into Tasmania. At first it was printed weekly, but in 1877 it became a morning daily and since then has never missed an issue. Since 1854 it has occupied the same premises in Paterson Street.

Staffordshire House and Macquarie House. If you turn left into Charles Street, you will see Staffordshire House, built in

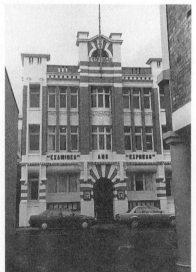

The Examiner Building, Launceston

1833. Turn tight into Cameron Street. This brings you into Civic Square. On your left is Macquarie House, built in 1830. Macquarie House was originally a warehouse, built for Henry Reed. The interior was altered and the building received its present name in 1920, and it was renovated in 1981. Built in the Georgian style, Macquarie House was made from hand-fired bricks and local timbers. It now houses a branch of the Queen Victoria Museum.

Town Hall and Post Office. On your right is the Northern Regional Library, and just past the library, on your left is the Town Hall, built in 1864. The Town Hall is a very fine building, featuring nine Corinthian columns. When it was built it had only four. It is now one of the most impressive buildings in the city. Built in the 1860s, it was designed by Peter Mills. On the other side of St John Street is the Post Office, built in 1886. The Post Office is in red brick, built in the Queen Anne style. The clock was added to the tower much later, in 1909, at the insistence of the citizens of Launceston!

Johnstone and Wilmot Building and the Old Umbrella Shop. As you turn left into St John Street and walk past the frontage of the Town Hall, look over the road to see the Johnstone and Wilmot Building, dating from 1842. Return to Cameron Street and turn right into George Street. On your right, at 60 George Street, is The Old Umbrella Shop. It is manned by volunteers working for the National Trust. The shop was owned by three generations of the Shott family: Robert Shott, his son Robert Martin Shott, and his grandson John W.R. Shott, who left the entire property in his will to the National Trust in 1978. The shop, the last of its kind in Tasmania, was built in the 1860s, and is lined with Tasmanian blackwood. The Shott family not only sold umbrellas, but made them as well. The business began in the

The Old Umbrella Shop

next-door building. In 1891 there was a hairdressing business in the present shop and in 1908 it was a grocery shop. Robert Shott acquired it in 1912, but let it to tenants until 1921 when he moved in with his umbrella and walking-stick business. His son Robert Martin Shott bought it and stayed in business there until 1964. The National Trust has kept the old fittings of the shop and has a display of umbrellas and different artifacts but it also sells gifts and souvenirs. New umbrellas are for sale, and there is a large display of antique ones. Some maps and tourist information books and pamphlets are also available.

Holy Trinity, the Batman Fawkner Inn and Crown Mill.

Walk along Cameron Street towards City Park. On your left is Holy Trinity, built on the site of the second building erected in Launceston, a prisoners' barracks. On your right is the Batman Fawkner Inn. John Batman was born in Parramatta in 1800, and died in 1839. As a young man he was a wheelwright; in 1820 he came to Tasmania as a farmer. He had an eventful life, capturing bushranger Matthew Brady in 1826, and sailing from Launceston to Port Phillip, where he made his famous remark: 'This will be the place for a village'. The Batman Bridge over the Tamar River is named after him. John Pascoe Fawkner was born in London in 1792 and died in 1869. In 1803 his father was transported to Australia, and was able to take his family with him. At the age of 22 John Pascoe Fawkner was deported from Van Diemen's Land to N.S.W. for helping in the escape of some convicts, but he later returned to Launceston to become a respected citizen. In 1819 he was in Hobart Town, which he left to return to Launceston to work in the timber trade. In 1824 he built the Batman Fawkner Inn, which was then known as the Cornwall Hotel. It was then the only two-storey house in Launceston. Later, Fawkner became a market gardener, a baker, butcher, general store proprietor, coach proprietor—and still found time in 1829 to start the *Launceston Advertiser*. Together with John Batman, he had much to do with the settling of Melbourne. He was surely one of the most energetic men of his time!

On your left is Crown Mill, built by John Affleck in 1897. Since he was of Scottish parentage (his father was Thomas Affleck, from Dumfries), it is fitting that he made oatmeal!

Around City Park. As you come out of Cameron St, on your left across Tamar St is Albert Hall, erected in 1891 at the cost of £14 000. Directly in front is City Park, established in the 1820s, and the original Government House Grounds. Outside the park are some imposing iron gates, made by W.H. Knight, Launceston, in 1903. These grounds were originally a Crown Grant to the Launceston Horticultural Society,

Conservatory, City Park, Launceston

transferred to the Launceston City Council in 1863 in perpetual trust for the citizens. Inside the park is the John Hart Conservatory.

Beside City Park is a block of ground which was granted to Charles Price and his wife Catherine in 1836 by Governor Arthur. Here they built an independent chapel and conducted a grammar school for 26 years. For 56 years Rev. Price was pastor of the first independent church in Launceston. He died in 1891 and Catherine in the next year. In 1895 the Price Memorial Hall was erected, and in 1920 the Council bought the building.

The National Automobile Museum of Tasmania. Across from City Park, at 86 Cimitiere St, is the Automobile Museum, featuring many old and interesting vehicles.

St Andrew's Kirk, the Union Bank Building and A.N.Z. Bank. Return up Cameron St to Civic Square. Turn left into St John Street. On your right is St Andrew's Kirk, built in 1849, on the site of the earlier Town Watch-house, the land being granted to the Presbyterians by the Government. Cross Paterson Street. On your right is the old Union Bank Building, built in the 1860s. On the corner of St John and Brisbane Streets is the A.N.Z. bank, built in 1885.

Dicky White's Street. Turn onto Brisbane Street, which was named after Sir Thomas Brisbane, Governor of N.S.W. from 1821–25. It was originally known as Dicky White's Street. On your right is the old Launceston Hotel, possibly the oldest licensed hotel in Australia: built in 1814, and rebuilt in the 1880s. Past the hotel, walk on down Brisbane street until you come to the entrance of the Quadrant Mall on your right. The shop on your left, now known as Centrepoint Arcade, was established in 1870. Just inside the entrance to the Quadrant is the outline of an old well, discovered during the making of the Quadrant Mall in 1978. The well supplied water to Richard (Dicky) White's house and stables in around 1822. Also in the Quadrant Mall is Gourlay's Sweet Shop, established in 1889, and famed for many years for its homemade sweets. Nearby is Dicky White's Lane.

Richard White was one of the early settlers to take up an allotment in Launceston. He shared it with a friend named Whittle (with whom he had come from Norfolk Island, probably around 1810), and the allotment included what is now the Quadrant Mall. White built the Launceston Hotel in 1822, and also an auction mart and his own house with stables and coach house and garden.

The Synagogue. From the Quadrant, turn left into St John Street. Cross York Street. On your right is the Jewish Synagogue, built in 1846. A left turn into Elizabeth Street brings you back to the car park.

To visit **The Queen Victoria Museum**, walk four blocks up Wellington Street from Elizabeth Street. The museum is on your left. Queen Victoria Museum was opened in 1891 on the occasion of Queen Victoria's Golden Jubilee. It is very well worth a visit, with fascinating exhibits ranging from convict relics to engines, to thousand-year-old coins, to the Chinese Joss House from Weldborough (see Chapter 9). A very interesting feature is the collection of stuffed

Customs House, Launceston

birds and animals, including the Tasmanian native hen, the black swan, brush-tailed possums and tawny frogmouths.

Old Customs House and Monds and Affleck Mill. From the museum it is three blocks to Old Customs House and Monds & Affleck Mill, (built 1860), on the Esplanade, on either side of St John's Street.

Cataract Gorge and Penny Royal. To reach Cataract Gorge and the attractions of Penny Royal and Richies Mill, turn right out of the Elizabeth Street car park, past the Colonial Motor Inn and St John's Church. Cross St John Street, and continue down Elizabeth St. Cross Charles, Wellington, and Bathurst Streets. At the end of Elizabeth Street turn right into Margaret Street. On

The Pennyroyal Gunpowder Mills, part of the famous Pennyroyal World

your left is the Church of the Apostles, a grey stone building. Continue up Margaret Street, passing York Street with the Old Bakery Inn on your left. Cross Brisbane Street. Turn left into Paterson Street. It is now 450 m to Cataract Walk. On your left is the Penny Royal Watermill (see section below), a stone building erected in 1825, and part of the famous Penny Royal World, which comprises Watermill, Gunpowder Mill, cannon foundry and fort. Originally these buildings came from a grazing property called Barton, but have been rebuilt in the old quarry here as a major attraction. Richies Mill is close by on your right. The landing stage there is the departure point of the Penny Royal paddle steamer, *Lady Stelfox*, which makes several regular forty-minute cruises up the Gorge each day. For sailing times, check locally.

Cataract Gorge was discovered in 1804 by William Collins in the *Lady Nelson.*
On your left as you approach the gorge is the Zigzag Walk to the first Basin. Cross King's Bridge. Enter Baldhill Road, which brings you into Trevallyn Road. At the top of Bald Hill is the Baldhill Lookout. As you drive on you will come to a fork. The right fork takes you up Bald Hill, the left takes you on the gorge and cliffgrounds. Turn up Fulford Street.
Cataract Gorge and Cliffground Reserve has a carpark at the top, then a fairly steep descent by steps and slopes, or a longer, easier one via the road. As you walk down you will see green lawns left and right, and daffodil beds. Peacocks parade around the lawns. You will now come to the tearooms and the Cataract Walk. There are several pleasant walks around the gorge area, including a half-hour hike to the disused Duck Reach Power Station, which provided the first hydro-electric power in the Southern Hemisphere. The gorge has a chairlift, and is sometimes the venue for open-air concerts.

Lady Stelfox *on Cataract Gorge*

The Lady Nelson. In 1800 the *Lady Nelson* became the first ship to sail through Bass Strait from the west. For the next three years she made a number of voyages around the south-east of Australia, helping with the establishment of the northern Tasmanian settlement at Port Dalrymple. In 1807 she transported Norfolk Islanders to Tasmania, and four years later brought Governor Macquarie to tour the island. She was burnt in 1825, while helping to establish a settlement in northern Australia. The 'new' *Lady Nelson* is a full-sized replica of the original, incorporating modern safety standards. The original was designed in 1798 by Captain Schank, the 'new' edition by Robert Sexton and Brom Knoop in 1985–87.

James Leslie of the Cataract. According to a story passed through the Leslie family of Tasmania, there was once a brewery at Cataract Gorge known, logically enough, as The Cataract Brewery. The story begins in 1830 when a young man named James

Leslie came out from Ireland on the ship *Juno*; he was sent from Dublin, it is said, because he was in 'bad company'. On the ship he met a Dr Cotter, who was coming out to take charge of the workers at the Cascades Brewery. When he arrived at Hobart Town, he went to the brewery with Dr Cotter and there became a malter and distiller. He married an Irish-born girl, and in 1840 the young Leslies, with their baby, ventured north, on foot. The trip to Launceston took around ten days, and they had two brushes with escaped convicts near Oatlands, and met Aborigines at Evandale. Finally, they settled in Launceston, and James went to work at the Cataract Brewery. Later, he went droving. After a fall from a horse he injured his leg, and holed up in a hut for the night. Two escaped convicts approached the hut, but the resourceful James, loudly carrying on a conversation with an imaginary companion, stuck his gun out of a hole in the wall and routed them. Another tale tells how in the 1850s, James

Leslie, now settled around Distillery Creek near the present-day suburb of Ravenswood, decided to run his own still. One day he heard that the troopers were coming, and promptly poured the evidence away into the creek. Unfortunately, some convicts were building a bridge across Distillery Creek near the flour mill downstream (part of which building still remains on the left bank of the creek). The troopers couldn't make out how the convicts managed to get so drunk!

Waverley Woollen Mills

To visit the Waverley Woollen Mills, take Route A3 out towards East Launceston and Newstead. Turn onto Hoblers Bridge Road at Newstead and follow the signs. The Woollen Mills were established in 1874 by a Scotsman named Peter Bulman. From him, they passed to his brother-in-law Robert Hogarth, and remained in the Hogarth family until 1981. Tours of the mill run every day, Monday through to Friday. Ask at the mill for details of times and prices.

Franklin House

To see the National Trust-owned 'Franklin House', head out through the suburbs of Kings Meadows and Youngtown. You will see 'Franklin House' on your left. The house was built in 1838 by Britton Jones, who had

'Franklin House'

arrived in Tasmania in 1820 and settled at Longford. Two years later he married Sophia Kirk, who was one of the first few white girls to be born in the colony.

The bricks for the house were made by convicts on the premises, and it must have been built as a speculation, for as soon as it was finished, Jones advertised it for sale in the *Launceston Advertiser*, the newspaper begun a decade earlier by John Pascoe Fawkner. Jones also had an inn on the other side of the road called the Sir William Wallace Inn. He leased the house for a while, and then in 1842 it was bought by William Keeler Hawkes (1804–1882) who came out from England with his wife and three sisters. He was a schoolmaster, and he ran the house as a boys' boarding school for many years until his death. He built the schoolroom in 1842 to accommodate the boys. The school catered for around twenty boys at a time.

The house had several other owners before the National Trust bought it in 1960. Once named 'The Hollies', the house was re-named in honour of Sir John Franklin. Although dating from early Victorian times, it was built in the popular Georgian style with regular windows and the portico on the front. The house has been very little altered over the years. There was no bathroom, and the kitchen, due to the risk of fire, was built slightly away from the main house. The woodwork inside is New South Wales cedarwood, which was used so much in these early homes that the natural forests from which it came no longer exist.

The furnishings were not originally in the house, but are mainly early Victorian. Some pieces are earlier, because the settlers used to bring out their own furnishings. These include an unusual 1700 bacon cupboard, made of wood (including the lock), and an eighteenth century grandfather clock. Upstairs is a big room, used for parties and as a music room.

St James, Franklin

At the rear of the house are the stables, the cobbles of which are extremely worn, and must have been very hard on the hoofs of the horses.

Opposite 'Franklin House', on the other side of the road, is St James' Church of England, a modest little building opened for services in 1845. To inspect the church, the key may be obtained from 'Franklin House'. In the churchyard are the graves of William Keeler Hawkes, his wife and three sisters. 'Franklin House' is open daily. On the way there you will pass through the suburb of Sandhill.

A pioneer of the Sandhill

The Sandhill has seen many colourful events and characters over the years, not least Mr Thomas Arthur Bailey, who was born there in 1826. Thomas's parents kept the hotel known as 'The Horse and Jockey Inn'. Thomas became a blacksmith, but in his earlier days engaged in bushwork, splitting, sawing and carting. He was a renowned sportsman, horse trainer and pigeon shooter. Later, he had a farm at Dromedary, where he was once mistaken for bushranger Martin Cash, arrested and escorted to Brighton before being correctly identified and released. Over the years Thomas worked at his trade at Green Ponds, Bothwell, Hamilton, Broadmarsh, Bridgewater and New Norfolk. He was married twice, his first wife dying in 1847. Altogether, he had 23 children, 19 of whom were still living in 1920. Also at that time he had 112 grandchildren and over 80 great-grandchildren. Thomas was a tall and vigorous man, and, on the day before his death in 1920, at the grand old age of 94 he was, (as his obituary states admiringly) 'in full possession of his mental faculties and able to take his customary walk'.

Of course, there are many other interesting places to visit in and around Launceston This is only a sample.

BIBLIOGRAPHY
Books
PHILLIPS, Arthur and SMITH, Patsy Adam, *Launceston Sketchbook*, Rigby, 1973.
The Cyclopedia of Tasmania, 1900.
UBD Street Directory, Universal Press.

Pamphlets
'Early Buildings of Launceston'
'Launceston—A Walk Through History' (both available Queen Victoria Museum and Art Gallery)
'Franklin House' (Available Franklin House)
'Lady Nelson Project', the Tasmanian Sail Training Association.
'Let's Talk About The Cataract Gorge and Cliff Grounds Reserve'
'Let's Talk About Launceston'
(both from the Tasmania Visitor Corporation or Tasmanian Travel Centres)

Maps
Tasmap 1: 100 000 Land Tenure Index Series:
'St Patricks'

Information
Thanks to Jenny Gill, Norma Hudson, Betty Sherriff , and staff at Franklin House and Penny Royal.

7. Longford, Evandale and Perth

Features of this drive

Not far from Launceston are three old towns which date from the coaching days: Longford, Evandale and Perth. These three form an almost straight line, and all depend to some extent on the South Esk River. Longford is the largest, with a population of two and a half thousand. Perth is somewhat smaller, and Evandale has fewer than a thousand people.

They can be reached by a number of different routes, and are generally well-signposted. If you enjoy quiet old towns, crafts, stately homes, tea rooms, and peaceful picnics, this is a good drive for you. The distances covered are not great, so you might cover most of the drive in a half-day or choose to take your time and visit quiet rural Cressy and the power station at Poatina as well. Accommodation is varied and plentiful.

Launceston to Evandale

To reach the historic village of Evandale from Launceston, leave the city by the southern outlet. When you reach the roundabout, follow the signs for the airport and Evandale, passing Western Junction Airport on your left, and continuing to Evandale and Nile. Near the airport a good selection of hire car firms can be found, and scenic flights are available close by.

Ben Lomond is visible a little to your left.

Evandale

The Evandale district has been a grazing area since before 1816, when the first land grants were made.

The town of Evandale was established in 1866, the year after the municipality was declared, but there was already a school there ten years earlier. The schoolmistress was a Mrs Chilcot and there were about seven pupils. The town was named after Surveyor General G.W. Evans.

Touring Evandale. On your left in High St as you enter the town is a brick water tower. The reservoir was erected in the late 1800s, and filled by hydraulic turbine from 'Glendessary' on the South Esk River. On your left is the Council Chambers building, erected in 1865, and almost opposite is 'Ingleside'. On the left, just past Barclay St, is the pillared brick Blenheim, built in 1832 by John Williat(t), and run by him as an inn under the name Patriot King William. Williatt also built the white house called 'The Laurels' on the right, in around 1840.

The Two Churches of St Andrew. St Andrew's Church of England on your left was begun in 1871 to replace the earlier 1841 building. The foundation stone was laid by Venerable W.H. Browne, Archdeacon of Launceston. The church is stuccoed.

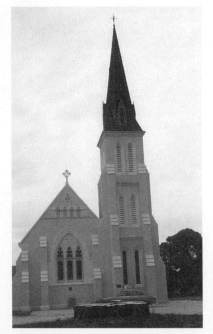

The huge cypress tree in the grounds, now a stump, was planted in 1871 by Rev. Russell. In front of the church is a memorial to George William Evans (d. 1852) and his wife Lucy Parris (d.. 1849), of 'Warwick Lodge', Newtown Bay. This headstone was removed from St John's Burial Ground, Newtown. A plaque commemorates Frank Long, (1842–1908), who discovered silver at Zeehan on the west coast.

He was buried in an unmarked grave in the cemetery. In the foyer is more information and a photograph of Long, as well as a list of all the rectors from 1838 to the present. Also, rather endearingly, is a message to anyone unfortunate enough to find themselves locked in the church: they have only to ring the bell to be released! After St Andrews, on the left, is Church Lane Pioneer Park.

On the right is another St Andrew's, this time the Uniting Church (originally Presbyterian) built in 1839. This is a quite different type of building in the Greek Revival style. The church was erected with the help of a governmental grant of £600 in response to a signed petition from the Scottish community of Evandale who had already raised £400 on their own initiative. In the grounds is a splendid monument in, memory of Rev. Robert Russell (1808–1977), who served the parish from 1838 until 1873. Around the church is a graveyard with many old stones dating from the

St Andrew's Church of England, Evandale   *St Andrew's Uniting Church, Evandale*

early days of the town. Inside the church is another memorial to the Rev. Russell and an intriguing pulpit with such high walls that it must be entered via a staircase and a small door from the rear of the church. An enormous gold candelabrum, personally donated by Rev. Russell, hangs above the lower pews and above is a gallery. Rev. Russell also donated two stained glass windows, and since his day the congregation has continued his devotion. St Andrew's is a delight.

Other historic buildings. Just past the church are the houses 'Eureka', 'Solomon House' (1836), and 'Leighbourne'. 'Solomon House' was built by Joseph Solomon, the father of A.E. Solomon, Premier of Tasmania from 1912 to 1914. Directly ahead is the Prince of Wales Hotel, (built by William Sidebottom c. 1836 and run during the 1850s by coachman Thomas Hannay), and the Village Antiques shop, dating from 1840.

Russell St. Just before the hotel, turn left into Russell St. On your right is 'Ingleside', the Colonial Bakery, Craft and Art Gallery and on your left Russell's Restaurant. 'Ingleside' was built in 1867, and was originally the Municipal Chambers. Inside, is a wood-fired oven, built to the Small and Shattell design, one of the few to be built the twentieth century. Twenty-five

Clarendon Arms, Evandale

thousand bricks were used. The ironwork was cast by the Phoenix Foundry in Launceston. Before coming into use at Ingleside, it was rescued from Beaconsfield paddock. The oven can bake up to three hundred leaves, and is heated early each morning to 500°F (260°C), by a wood fire. The fire is put out, and different products, (including pies and cakes) are baked at varying and appropriate temperatures as the oven cools. 'Ingleside' also stocks up-market gift lines such as pottery, toys, crafts and hand made garments, and paintings.

As you continue down Russell St, you will pass the Colonial Gallery (1840) and, at the corner of Scene and Russell Streets, the Clarendon Arms Hotel (1847), built by Thomas Fall. Farther along, on your right, are several picturesque cottages. On the corner of Russell St and Huxtable Lane is 'Fallgrove' (once known as 'Prosperous House') and built in 1826 by Kennedy Murray. Each February, Evandale stages a village fair which features penny-farthing cycle races down Russell St. Competitors come from many countries. A Sunday market is held at Falls Park, near 'Fallgrove', and 'Evandale' is also the home of artist Greg Waddle.

Clarendon and Strathmore

To visit the historic homes of 'Clarendon' and 'Strathmore', leave Evandale on the

'Ingleside', Evandale

'Clarendon', Nile Road

very straight Nile Road. 'Clarendon' is 10 km straight ahead. Turn off to the right, come to a T-junction and on the left is 'Clarendon'.

'Clarendon'. The three-storey house, which is neo-classic in design, was built between 1830 and 1838 by John Richards for James Cox. At one stage, the foundations sank and the house had to be extensively shored up. It has since been stabilised. The terrace is supported by graceful columns. The bottom floor is a semi-basement, consisting of kitchens and servants' quarters, once lit by an area walk, and on the first floor is a large hallway with fan-shaped windows.

Upstairs are bedrooms and a delightful toy room, with a rocking horse, china dolls and a large dolls' house. The floors are original. Outside is a walled garden and 9 acres of parkland, including a number of out-buildings in the process of restoration. James Cox (1790–1866), was born at Devizes in Wiltshire, England. He was the second son of William Cox. He emigrated to Australia in 1804 and in 1814, two years after his marriage to Mary Connell (1793–1928), he came to Van Diemen's Land. James was granted 700 acres of land in 1817, with a further 600 in 1819. The area was once called Morven, and was the town

which Governor Macquarie proposed to have built about 3.5 km south-east of Evandale. James was County Magistrate in 1817, and was elected to the Legislative Council in 1829. In 1856 he represented Morven in the first elected House of Assembly. Cox helped to establish Merino sheep, with stock from the flock owned by Douglas McArthur. He also imported a ram from Spain, and bred horses.

James and Mary had eight children, with one son and six daughters surviving childhood. Mary died in 1828 and a year later James married Eliza Collins (1809–1869), who was the daughter of Governor Collins, in St John's Church, Launceston. Eleven more children were born, with nine daughters surviving. James Cox died in 1866, after a fall from his horse. His descendants remained at 'Clarendon' until 1917, and in 1962 the then owner gave the homestead to the National Trust.

'Strathmore'. To visit lovely 'Strathmore' continue on the main Nile Road for 50 metres to the next turn-off to the right. A well-signposted road leads to the houses 'Lochmaben' and 'Strathmore', one on either side of Lochmaben Lake. The man-made lake is a wildlife sanctuary, so look out for waterbirds as well as lilies and rushes. Since early 1988, 'Strathmore' has provided very superior colonial accommodation. It is a popular venue for

'Strathmore', Nile Road

weddings. 'Strathmore' is beautiful, set in extensive grounds with many fine old trees and flower beds. The building which once housed the dairy, bakehouse etc have been converted into luxurious motel units and the top floor of the fine brick stable is often hired by wedding parties.

'Strathmore' was built in the early 1820s for Samuel Bryan (1794–1862). Bryan was an Irish gentleman, a B.A. from Trinity College, Dublin. His brother William is thought to have attended the same college. Samuel Bryan arrived in Tasmania in 1822 at the age of 28, and was granted 2200 acres which he named 'Strathmore' soon afterwards. Here he built a mill, taking water by gravitation from the nearby Nile River, (originally known as Cox's Rivulet), to form the 11-acre Lochmaben Lake. Work on the lake began in 1824, and it was used to supply the mill: from 1832. Samuel married a girl named Jane Henty, the daughter of Thomas Henty, but they had no children.

William, who was granted 'Glenore' at Carrick, arrived in 1824 with his son Robert. He also built a mill, on the Liffey (or Penny Royal) River, at Carrick. William's son was later mixed up in some shady transactions involving stolen cattle, activities culminated in Robert's being arrested and sent to Port Arthur, and in

Lake Lochmaben and Lochmaben, Nile Road

Samuel and William having to leave the colony.

'Lochmaben' was built by a member of the Cox family, but the date is uncertain.

One way to Longford. If you wish, you can travel on along the Nile Road for 18 km until the road meets Kingston Road. The drive is rather flat and featureless. Turn right and drive a further 11 km, crossing the South Esk River on a long bridge and passing the lovely old 'Vaucluse' estate on your right.

'Vaucluse' was built by the Bostock family c. 1814. It was then taken over by another family, the Headlams, and has now belonged to the McKinnon family for many years. Since 1987, 'Vaucluse' has been given over to whole-farm planning, demonstration farming and pasture management. The McKinnon family sometimes hosts tours of the pastures and bird reserves on the property.

Continue until you intercept the Heritage Highway, just north of Conara Junction.

If you want a shorter route, you may return through Evandale from 'Strathmore' and follow the signs to Perth and Longford.

If you take the longer route, past 'Vaucluse', turn left off the Midland Highway into Route C521, Woolmers Lane, to visit Longford.

If you take the shorter route, and follow the signs towards Longford, you will turn into the same Route C521, but it will be a right-hand turn instead.

Along Woolmers Lane, watch for the property called 'Rhodes', owned during the 1930s by the Gatenby family.

Longford

The official discovery of the Longford area came in 1807 when Lt Laycock spent the night on the bank of the Lake River during the first journey from the north to the south. Governor Macquarie dubbed the area

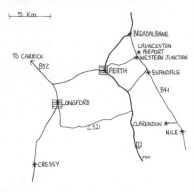

'Norfolk Plains', and in 1812 he directed that the settlers from Norfolk island be given land grants there. Most of these early farms failed, but more settlers came in, many of them from New South Wales. An early estate is 'Woolmers', south-east of the town on the banks of the Macquarie River, just past Point Road on your right. Other old estates include '**Brickendon**', just south of Longford and '**Panshanger**', 8 km farther south. In 1820 the first school was opened, under the name of King's Elementary School, followed by the Rev. R.R. Claiborne's school in 1822. An early church was erected in 1831, and lovely Christ Church was begun eight years later.

Longford was once known as 'Latour'. A road between Launceston and Longford was built in 1813 under the direction of Captain Richie, the Commandant of Port Dalrymple, for the price of one cow in lieu of the £30 originally asked. In 1823 the census showed the Norfolk Plains district to have a population of 553, of whom 204 were free settlers, and 349 were convicts.

'**Woolmers**' was originally owned by Thomas Archer, (1790–1850). He arrived in Van Diemen's Land in 1813 and named his estate after a place in Hertfordshire. The house was begun in 1816, and additions were made in the 1830s. Some of the outbuildings, including the gardener's cottage, 'Woolmers Cottage' (1839); the chapel, summerhouse, Dr Mountgarrett's cottage, and the wool shed (1818–19) still stand. Thomas Archer became Clerk of the Commissariat and a Magistrate. 'Woolmers' is now open to the public.

Cross the Macquarie River on Woolmers Bridge. 'Brickendon' is on your left just as you enter the town.

'**Brickendon**' was built by William Archer, a brother of Thomas Archer of Woolmers.

More historic buildings and a walk through Longford. Along Wellington St watch for 'Northbury', built by another of the Archer brothers, Edward, and his wife Susannah, and for Browns Big Store, established in 1880 by Alfred Brown and, on the right-hand side of the roundabout, the Queens Arms, probably built in the 1830s. On the corner of Wellington St and Archer St is a visitors' information stand displaying a map of the town and a selection of interesting buildings. Since it's almost impossible to drive through a town and look at a great many buildings at the same time, we suggest you park your car and use the map as a guide to find the following (and others) on foot.

The Uniting Church is in High St. The foundation stone of this church was laid by Edward Archer's wife in 1879, and it was built by Thomas Humphrey.

Christ Church, Longford

The Blenheim Inn (1846) is in Malborough St, and, at the corner of William and Marlborough Streets, is 'Jessen Lodge', built in 1827 by Newman Williat, (probably a brother of John Williat of Evandale). The house was made from local bricks and was originally known as the Longford Hotel. It was also a Post Office and later a general store, a savings bank, a library, livery stables, doctor's surgery, nursing home, and finally, 'Jessen Lodge'.

In William St you may see Christ Church, which is set in very extensive grounds. The original church on the site was St Augustine's, built in 1829, but this was found to be structurally unsound and was replaced by the present building ten years later. Christ Church was designed by Robert de Little (1808–1876), who co-designed the Anglican church at Oatlands with John Lee Archer. The west window was designed by William, Archer of 'Cheshunt', (see Chapter 4) and the bell was presented by King George IV. At the rear of the church is the graveyard with a number of early graves including that of Thomas Stephens, who died in 1831, John Pearson, (d.1834) and Solomon Fair (or Farr) who died in 1833. This stone, now broken, was once quite famous for its inscription, which read:

> O silent grave to thee I trust
> The precious pile of worthy dust
> Keep it safe O sacred tombe
> Until a wife shall ask for room.

There is also the family vault of the Archers. Buried here are many family members including Joseph Archer (1823–1914) JP, the third son of Thomas Archer: he lived at 'Panshanger' (pronounced 'pan-sanger'), Edward Archer of 'Northbury' (d. 1862), and his wife Susannah (d. 1890), William Archer of 'Brickendon' (d. 1873), and his parents William (d. 1833) and Caroline (d 1862), and Thomas Archer of 'Woolmers' (d. 1850).

'Kilgour', Archer St, Longford

If you are interested in motor racing, be sure to visit the Country Club Hotel in Wellington St. During the 1950s, and '60s and into the early '70s, Longford was the venue for an annual motor race around the town. This attracted such big names as Jack Brabham. The hotel offers the Racing Car Bistro, and much memorabilia of the racing industry, including a car, a trophy and many photographs and posters. Sally's father remembers this hotel during the 1930s, when it was managed by a man went by the name of Squizzy Taylor! Nearby is Monds and Affleck Mill, and Berriedale, a former inn built in 1842 for Peter Clyne. The Baptist Tabernacle was built in 1880; and was donated to the town by a Mr Gibson who lived at Native Point, during the late 19th century. Mr Gibson was responsible for four of these tabernacles, one each in the towns of Longford, Latrobe and Deloraine, (these three being almost identical), and one, rather more impressive, in his home town of Perth.

Latour St was known in the 1930s as 'Old Maids' Alley' because of the many small cottages there. These cottages are known as 'Noakes Cottages', having been conceived by a Miss Noakes as a haven for elderly single ladies.

Along Archer St opposite the park is 'Kilgour', yet another building to have connections with the Archer family. This house was built by Thomas Archer for his son-in-law and daughter, Dr John Stewart

The Mill Dam, Longford

Kilgour (1815–1902) and Susan Ann (1825–1904).

The Mill Dam. Leave Longford by continuing along Wellington St, past 'Kingsley House'. Turn left into Route B52 towards Burnie to visit a recreation area known as The Mill Dam.

Over to your right watch for the old tannery building, (now a Police Youth and Citizens' Club), at Tannery Corner. To visit the Mill Dam Picnic Area, turn right off Route B52. Follow this road, taking a sharp right angled turn. It is about 1.5 km to the picnic grounds.

Sally's father has mixed feelings about the Mill Dam Road; as a teenaged postal clerk in Longford he used to exercise a neighbour's horse. One day, while cantering along the road, he was horrified when two children and bicycles emerged from the scrub. No time to stop—he was forced to jump both bikes and children, and fortunately no-one was hurt—not even the horse.The reserve has been developed with barbecue facilities and dressing sheds. The weir forms a sheltered pool for unsure swimmers.

When you leave Mill Dam Road, turn left onto Route B52 to visit Perth, about six km away. Just before you reach the town, there's a left-hand turn into Route C531. You might like to turn into this route to visit 'Bowthorpe', and perhaps the Longford Deer Park, but check locally for the opening hours (or days) of each, because they vary according to the time of year.

'Bowthorpe' was built in 1835 by William Mason. It is now classified by the National Trust and Heritage Listed. **Longford Deer Park** is farther along the same road.Just after the turn-off into Route C531 is Perth.

Perth

Perth is an old coaching station town situated near the South Esk River. It was named by Governor Macquarie in 1821, after Perthshire in Scotland. Its original name was 'Punt' because of the Government punt which operated on the river. Until 1835 a ferry crossed the river, but in the year Captain Wood, owner of the 'Hawkridge' property near Powranna, set a letter and petition signed by Perth residents, requesting that a bridge should be built. The first design for Perth Bridge was made by Lt William Kenworthy, in 1835.

William Kenworthy arrived in Van Diemen's Land in 1820 and was appointed Naval Officer and Inspector of Public Works the next year. He held that position until 1835, then returned to England in 1841. His brother, Dr. J.K. Kenworthy, had a property called 'Cambock' in Evandale. John Lee Archer approved the design for the bridge, but altered the piers to his own specifications. The bridge was flood damaged before it was finished, and was redesigned by Captain Alexander Cheyne. This new, improved bridge was finished in 1839, but part of the causeway collapsed in 1841, and three years later a large flood caused further damage. In 1929 a giant flood destroyed the bridge. It was replaced by the present concrete structure.

Alexander Cheyne (1785–1858), arrived in Tasmania in 1835. He was appointed Director-General of Roads and Bridges, and Director of the Department of Public Works, but was dismissed, (apparently through no fault of his own), by Governor Franklin in 1841. He became an alderman in 1858, shortly before he died.

In Perth, look out for the Baptist Tabernacle (mentioned in the Longford section of this chapter).

Cressy and Poatina

While visiting this area, you may also like to pay a visit to the town of Cressy and to Poatina Dam. Cressy can be reached from the Heritage Highway into Route B53 on your way back up from Conara Junction, or by taking Route B51 out of Longford. Cressy has a population of about 650 people, and was established in 1855. It's a favourite destination for anglers. From Cressy, follow the signs to Poatina Dam.

Poatina dates from the mid-1960s, when the power station was commissioned to replace the original Waddamana Power Station which dated from 1916.

Like other H.E.C. projects in Tasmania, Poatina's name was chosen from an Aboriginal word, this time meaning 'a cavern'. It's an appropriate name, as you will discover if you take a tour of the power station.

From Perth you have the choice of going north to Launceston or south, over the bridge, towards Hobart.

BIBLIOGRAPHY

Books.

EMETT, E.T., *Tasmania by Road and Track,* Melbourne University Press, 1952.

SMITH, Roy, *Early Tasmanian Bridges*, 1969.

Pamphlets

DUMARESQ, J.A., Christ Church, Illawarra.

NATIONAL TRUST, The Path of History. Woolmers.

WALKER, Mary, 'The House of Many Changes, A Brief History of St Andrew's Uniting Church, Evandale.'

'Let's Talk About Evandale'

'Let's Talk About Longford' (Tas. Visitors Corporation)

'In and Around Launceston, Tasmania.'

Maps

Tasmap 1: 100 000 Land Tenure Index Series, 'South Esk'.

Information

Thanks to Mrs Cowdery, George Farrell, Jean Phelps, Hawley Stancombe and the manager of 'Vaucluse'.

8. The Heritage Highway

Features of this drive

The shortest route from the north to Hobart is the Heritage Highway which runs through the area known as the Midlands. This drive covers some fine old coaching towns, and passes some of the largest and oldest pastoral properties in Tasmania. If you enjoy convict history, historic bridges, and quiet country towns, this is a good drive. To cover the distance from Launceston to Hobart without stopping would take around two hours, but if you wish to take your time and investigate the towns along the way, you should allow at least six hours. Because the Midlands was an old coaching route, the towns tend to be spaced at fairly short and regular intervals, so you're never very far from food, accommodation and amenities.

Heritage Highway

Drive from Launceston to Perth, and follow the signs. If travelling from the north-west, drive past Hagley and turn at the three-legged roundabout into the lane which says *Launceston*. Take the Route B52 exit to Longford and Hobart, and follow Route B52 through Perth. Now turn into Route 1, which promises Hobart, around 180 km away. Follow this highway in a long curve down through the Midlands to Hobart. The land is dry, but is well suited to wool and beef growing and some cropping. The highway runs straight through Campbell Town but bypasses the old towns of Ross and Oatlands. Many of

the features in the Midlands were named by Governor Lachlan Macquarie.

From Perth, Campbell Town, the first major town, is 48 km away. Cross the South Esk River, over the Perth Bridge. An earlier bridge was washed away during the extensive 1929 floods (see Chapter 7). Pass Eskleigh Nursing Home, once a large pastoral property belonging to the Gibson

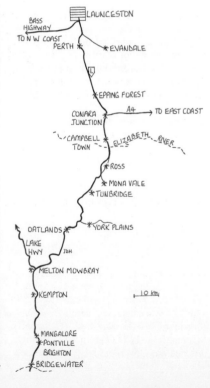

family. The house was then known as 'Scone'. The turn-off to Evandale and 'Clarendon House' on the left is Route B41. You will now be passing through flat countryside right through to Oatlands. This part is called the Epping Straight. The turn-off to Longford is C520.

Symmons Plains car racing course is on the left. The plains were named after two brothers who used to graze their stock in the area early last century.

Powranna Junction was named for the Aboriginal word meaning 'black snake'. Powranna featured in the children's stories of local author Nairda Lyne. The turn-off right into Route B53 would take you towards Poatina (See Chapter 7). Next comes Epping Forest.

St Andrew's Inn, a few km farther along on the right, was once a coaching hotel. Pass the St Mary's turn-off, which leads through Avoca and Fingal to the East Coast. It is 73 km to St Marys, 25 to Avoca and 53 to Fingal. Visits to these towns are covered in Chapter 10.

Blacksmith Creek is just past Conara Junction and 4 km on, on your right, is 'Wanstead House', built by Richard Willis in the 1820s. He came from Cumberland with his family of twelve children, and eventually amassed 8000 acres. He became an influential man in the district, yet sold up and returned England in 1838.

Campbell Town

Campbell Town is an attractive town built on the Elizabeth River. It is in the middle of a pastoral area recognised as one of the best wool-producing districts in the Commonwealth, and is the proud host of Australia's longest running continuous agricultural show, which began in 1838. The town was named after Governor Macquarie's wife, Elizabeth (Campbell) Macquarie in 1821. The journey through this area was Governor Macquarie's second

Campbell Town Show Memorial

trip through Van Diemen's Land, the first having been taken in 1811. The route had been mapped out by Surveyor General Charles Grimes in 1807 under the instructions of Governor Bligh. Mount Grimes at Mona Vale was named after him. In 1821 the road was good enough for use by carriages: in 1823 the first coach service was begun by J.E. Cox, who drove a mailcart from Hobart to Launceston and sometimes took passengers along the way. As you enter the town, look to your left to

St Andrew's, Campbelltown

Gatty Memorial, Campbell Town

see gothic freestone St Andrew's Presbyterian Church, built in 1857, and now classified by the National Trust. The church is charmingly set in trees and, like many of the Midland churches, is floodlit at night. The organ inside originally belonged to Bishop Nixon, Tasmania's first Anglican bishop.

The strange metal globe close by is the Harold Gatty Memorial, commemorating Harold Gatty, an aviator who, with Wylie Post, flew round the world (the first time this had been achieved), in 1931. Gatty was the son of James Gatty, athlete and schoolmaster, and was born in Campbell Town. Beyond the Gatty Memorial is a statue of a sheep, symbolising the town's long-running agricultural show.

The red brick church on the left a block past the memorial park is St Luke's (1837), designed by John Lee Archer. Beyond it is the Sunday School (1845). Both buildings are classified by the National Trust. In the graveyard beside the church are some interesting memorials, including that of William Valentine, surgeon, who died in 1876, his wife Mary Anne (d. 1872), and family members Marian (d. 1910) and William Henry (d. 1831). William Valentine Snr was born at

Martock in Somerset, England and died at Campbell Town at the age of 68.

Hezekiah Harrison, of 'Merton Vale' whose memorial is also in the graveyard, was a magistrate of the district. He died in 1860 on board the steamer *Tasmania* and is buried in Sydney. Other members of the family include his wife Caroline Matilda, and his grandson Charles Hardwicke Harrison and Lt E.W. Harrison who died in 1968 at the age of 94.

Also look for the gravestone of Michael Sharland, who died in 1987 at the age 88. For 60 years he wrote for *The Mercury* newspaper under the pseudonym of 'Peregrine'. Fittingly, his memorial includes the figure of a peregrine falcon. Opposite the Sunday School is Campbell Town Hospital (1855). The big red brick house on your left with all the gables, in the block between William and Queen Streets, is 'The Grange'.

In the Park in front of 'The Grange' is a mammoth tree trunk, easily 2 metres thick, a picnic area—and a notice showing the interesting features of the town.

'The Grange' which now belongs to the National Trust was built during the late 1840s for Dr William Valentine. As well as his medical interests, William Valentine was something of a scientist: he had an observatory built at The Grange and in 1874 he and many other astronomers watched the transit of Venus. Other things he made included an organ and a pair of

'The Grange', Campbell Town

The Foxhunters Return, Campbell Town

telephones! Just past 'The Grange' is a derelict church, and if you turn left into King Street you can visit the Roman Catholic church, St Michael's, a bluestone church erected in 1857 by Bishop Willson. Before you cross the Elizabeth River, you'll pass historic Foxhunters Return, an old inn built during the 1840s. Just over the bridge across the Elizabeth River, is 'Merton Lodge'. The Elizabeth River was named by Governor Macquarie, after his wife, in 1811. It had previously been known as 'Relief Creek'. Route B34, the road to Lake Leake and Bicheno, turns off to the left in the middle of the town.

After Campbell Town, you enter much flatter and rather featureless country, although you'll see Macquarie Tier over to your left. The best time to see the Heritage Highway is during the spring, when the wattle trees are in blossom and the grass is green; in summer it can become very dry. The big properties carry beef cattle and sheep.

Six km from Campbell Town is a cone-shaped hill called Coal Hill, and soon you'll reach Route C305 which leads off to the left into Ross, 2 km off the highway.

Ross

The village of Ross is one of the historic towns, and features buildings made from the Ross sandstone. It was originally conceived as a government stock farm and as a military post, marking the boundary between the northern county of Cornwall and the southern county of Buckingham. As the name suggests, it was named by that lover of Scotland, Governor Lachlan Macquarie in 1821, after the home of his friend H.M. Buchanan who lived near Loch Lomond, Scotland. Argyle Plains was also named by Macquarie.

In 1836 the wonderful Ross Bridge was built, replacing an early wooden structure over the Macquarie River. The bridge was designed by John Lee Archer, who seems to have had a rare eye for graceful proportions in his designs. James Colbeck (burglar) and Daniel Herbert (highwayman) were two of the convict masons employed on the bridge, and Daniel Herbert is credited with the intricate carvings that decorate all six arches. He seems to have had a liking for such work: he also decorated one of the churches at Bothwell. The two men were given their freedom as a result of their work on the bridge. Daniel Herbert is believed to have lived in a cottage in Badajos Street, along near the river.

When you enter the village, along Church Street, look to the left to see St John's Church of England, rebuilt in 1868. The original church was built between 1835 and 1848, with Governor Arthur laying the foundation stone. Robert Quayle Kermode (1812–1870), of Mona Vale, was largely responsible for the rebuilding. He built the 'Calendar House' at Mona Vale in 1862. To the left, along Badajos Street, are a number of interesting stone cottages. The cottage of Irish exile Thomas Meagher is to the right in Bond Street, on your left. In Church Street, past the church, is 'Sherwood Castle', an old inn now known as the Ross Bakery Inn. Attached to this is the Ross Village Bakery, featuring the original wood-fired oven. 'Macquarie House', dating from the 1840s, and an old stone house where Dr McNamara had his surgery are nearby. You may wish to visit the Military Museum.

Cross High Street. On your right is Ross Post Office, built in 1896. Also in this block is the Scotch Thistle Inn, licensed in 1830 and now a restaurant. It is situated in a pleasant walled courtyard. Next to it is the building which used to be a stable belonging to the inn. Across the road is the Man o' Ross Hotel (1835).

Cross Bridge Street to see the Council Chambers and Town Hall, and the Ross Memorial Library. Up on the hill is the Uniting Church, built in 1885 as the Ross Methodist Wesleyan Church. It replaced an earlier chapel situated at the corner of High and Bond Streets.

To see the old graveyard and the Ross Female Factory, walk down the path beyond the church. It's about 200 m to the female factory, (a women's prison) which was established in 1848 in the existing buildings of the chain-gang station. Inside the old building you can read information about the purpose of each part of the prison, as well as potted histories of some of the inmates. Continue along the path to see the old cemetery. The sandstone headstones in the burial ground include two which date from 1817. One of these men, Sir Philip Maher, served as a Quartermaster Sergeant at Waterloo. Many of the stones are illegible, and some have been mended. Down in the 'new' ground, set nearby under tall pine trees, is the Kermode family vault. Here are buried Robert Quayle Kermode, (d. 1870) and his wife Martha Henrietta Elizabeth, their eldest son William Archer Kermode (1816–1901), and many other family members.

From the church it is a short walk to the justly famous and very interesting Ross Bridge. On the side of the bridge is the name of Lt Governor George Arthur, as well as the date MDCCCXXXVI. The name of Captain William Turner, 50th or 'Queen's Own' Regiment Supt is also visible.

Recommendations for walks to see the other sights of Ross are freely available in the town or at Tourist Bureaus.

Ross Bridge

From Ross to Oatlands. The Macquarie River, immediately after the Ross turn-off, is crossed by a long bridge. About 3 km from the crossing is the left-hand turn-off into Mona Vale Road. Towards the end of this road is the Calendar House, the home of R.Q. Kermode. The house is not open to the public, and the road is closed to visitors, so you won't be able to see the house at all. Also in this area are the site of Horton College, which ran from 1855 to 1893, and was demolished in 1919, and 'Somercotes', the home built by Captain Samuel Worton, who arrived from Lincolnshire in 1823. 'Wetmore', the home of the Parramore family since 1823 is also in Mona Vale Road, as is 'Lochiel', built by the same architect who designed the Calendar House.

The next town along the Heritage Highway is Tunbridge, in the Salt Pan Plains. At Tunbridge is an old graveyard with a handsome stone wall. The turn-off is to the left. Route C526, to the right as you pass Tunbridge (named after Tunbridge Wells in England), is to Interlaken, between Lakes Sorell and Crescent.

The Blackman River, which you cross next, is a very small stream that was named in 1824 after an incident in which Aborigines speared two herdsmen who are buried near by. After leaving Tunbridge, you reach hillier country with lots of stones in the paddocks Scattered around the grass are heaps of rocks taken off the pasture; the sheep seem to favour these to stand on. The metal bands around the tree trunks are there to keep possums from climbing up and eating off the leaves.

Antill Ponds is a tiny settlement named after Governor Macquarie's aide-de-camp Major H.C. Antill of the 73rd Regiment and was once a coaching station with an inn named 'White Hart', run by John Presnell in 1830. The name was changed in 1843 to 'Half-Way House', and was a changeover point for horses of the coaches run by Sam Page.

Just after a rest area on the left you will notice examples of roadside topiary, including rams, deer, kangaroo, a giraffe and other animals.

Topiary in the Midlands. The striking topiary figures along the highway between Oatlands and Tunbridge were begun by Jack Cashion of Oatlands, who made his first hawthorn animals in the early 1960s Since his death the remarkable living statues have been maintained by regular trimming.

York Plains Road leads off to the left to York Plains, and Lemont. Not far in from the highway you may see a house set in among pines. This used to belong to the Farrell family, which included Arthur Farrell, who died in the early 1960s at around 90 years of age. Apparently Arthur's father, (the proud father of thirteen children), planted a pine tree for every baby born. The York Plains area is pleasant, with the peaked hills known locally as The Sugarloaves adding character to the land Along this road and the Sorell Springs Road which leads off from it, are such properties as 'Mount Pleasant', 'Sorell Springs' and 'York House', many of which were later cut up for soldier settlers.

St Peters Pass, back on the main highway, is a big old cattle and sheep stud, part of 2560 acres granted to shipping merchant Askin Morrison in 1829. Daniel O'Connor bought part of the land and called it 'St Peters Pass', erecting an inn there known as the 'Kenmore Arms'. O'Connor died on the property in 1856, and the block became re-absorbed into the greater estate. A descendant of Askin Morrison owns it now. 'Pass House' (1829) can be seen on the left. Look out for the statue in the garden!

The turn-off to Oatlands is on the left, after St Peters Pass. The turn-off to Richmond is on B31, via Colebrook, (once named Jerusalem!) and Campania.

Oatlands

Oatlands was another town marked out by Governor Macquarie in June, 1821. He had first passed that way in 1811, naming the area Macquarie Springs. On this second trip he camped on the shore of what he dubbed Great Lagoon. This name was later changed to Lake Frederick and finally to Dulverton, after the birthplace of pioneer Police Magistrate Thomas Anstey. Lake Dulverton has since been stocked with trout and enlarged. The island in the lake was granted to Mary Anstey, wife of Thomas, and is known as Marys Island. On the bank is a cave called Bradys Cave after the bushranger Matthew Brady who was in the area in 1825.

Evidently the countryside around the lake reminded Macquarie of the oat-growing land in his native Scotland, for he chose the name 'Oatlands' for the new town. In 1827 Sergeant Daniel O'Connor helped lay out the town. One of the first settlers was Askin Morrison.

As you enter the town you will see the homestead of 'Weedington', built in 1833

Callington Mill, Oatlands

by the Weeding brothers, John and James. Turn left, and drive alongside the lake to visit the famous 'Callington Mill', which began operations in 1837. It was built by John Vincent, who had arrived in Tasmania in 1823 on the ship Elizabeth with his wife and seven children. In 1840 he conveyed the mill to his son John Jubilee Vincent. The interior of the mill was badly damaged by fire in 1912. It is now owned and restored by the National Parks and Wildlife Service. One viewer of the mill was heard to remark that it looked like a giant Mr Whippy ice-cream—the effect of the new white dome! Around the mill are several of the original stone buildings and the old millstones, and a well.

On your left in the main street, just past the turn-off into William St, is the White Horse Inn. This handsome two-storied building was first built by George Aichison in 1834, He called it the 'Lake Frederick Inn'. Coach owner Sam Page renamed it 'Dulverton Inn' in 1836, and its final name was bestowed in 1853 by Alexander Parker. Opposite is Cantwell's Store, built in around 1857 and owned during the 1920s by Daryl Cantwell.

Turn left into Campbell St to see the Commissariat and guard house, built in 1832. Beyond it near the swimming pool is the site of the old gaol, built that same year. Also nearby are the old school, built in 1886 and the Court House, dating from 1829. Turn into Church Street, and to your left is the Kentish Hotel, once known as the 'Inverary Castle'. The hotel was licensed in 1834 to Joseph McEwan, but has since been largely updated.

The large church at the end of Church Street is St Peter's, designed by John Lee Archer and Robert de Little (see Chapter 7) and built in the mid 1840s. The old rectory is the same age. The graveyard is at the end of the street.

Inside the church are embroidered kneelers and hassocks, by local artists and featuring native flora, biblical symbols, and builders tools, to commemorate the centenary of the construction of the church. A children's corner has cushions decorated with Noah's ark, a rainbow, and barnyard scenes.

Police Magistrate Thomas Anstey, (1777-1851) is buried in the church and also has a memorial in the church. In the square bounded by William, Gay and Dulverton Streets, is St Paul's Catholic Church (c. 1850).

The Uniting Church, the Campbell Memorial Church, originally built in 1856, is farther down High Street, just past Stanley Street. This church was destroyed in 1858 when the 95 foot (30 m) steeple fell during a storm. The present church was built a year later. The founder of the church was Rev. Lachlan Mackinnon Campbell, who served in the district for more than 50 years. He died in 1908. George Wilson Snr of Mount Seymore is also remembered by a plaque in the church: it was due to his efforts that the church was rebuilt.

Just before the church you will see an agricultural museum and historic cottages dating from 1844, and just after is the Manse, built in 1860. The museum may or may not be open, as it was still incomplete when we visited in 1996.

There is a turn-off to the right in the tour which leads to 'Anstey Barton', home of Thomas Anstey and his family.

For a more detailed historical tour of Oatlands, ask locally for leaflets.

Beyond Oatlands

Soon after Oatlands, you come to a track leading off to the right round Lemon Hill to a place known as Lemon Springs. Lemon Springs was named after bushranger Richard Lemon. George Page arrived with the First Fleet and was at Risdon Cove with Lt Bowen in 1803, but was court-martialled by Governor Collins in 1804 for refusing guard duty. He returned to England and then came back in the early 1820s on the ship *Tiger*. In 1832 he built the Lemon Springs Inn at Lemon Springs. He displeased Governor Sorell who re-routed the coach road, so Page built a second inn, the Bath Inn, near the new road. His brother Samuel Page ran coaches. NOTE: one source suggests that the first inn was the one named 'Bath Inn'.

The Stoner Road. A few km from Oatlands, on your left, is Route C314, the Stoner Road. The first homestead along this road is 'Huntworth', on your right. This property was granted to George Meredith (one of the early settlers at Swansea) in 1821. He swapped the grant with Charles Cogle, who had arrived on the *Aguilar* in 1824 and had been granted ground at Swansea. Cogle built a stone house and a tannery, and died in 1857. Stoner was named after the Crown Solicitor of Van Diemen's Land in 1842, Alan Charles Stoner. 'Stoner House' is a large property lying about 2 km from the shores of Lake Tiberias. Neither house nor lake is visible from the road.

Back on the Heritage Highway, you'll come to a right-hand turn to the old Commandant's Cottage.

Jericho and the Lower Marshes Road

Jericho is on the upper reaches of the Jordan, which rises in Lake Tiberias, about 5 km to the south-east. At Jericho, Route C529 leads off to Lower Marshes and meets the Lake Highway at Apsley. If you drive around this route you will pass the following properties: 'Sandhill' (right, 1 km from Jericho), which belonged to James Bryant in 1829, and was later owned by the Bisdee family of 'Lovely Banks'; 'Rose Hill' (3 km farther, right), owned by Benjamin Jones in 1816; and 'Linwood' (or 'Lynwood')—4 km farther on at lower Marshes—which belonged to Robert Jones, son of Benjamin.

To the left at Jericho, Route C529 leads onto Route B3l, the Mud Walls Road, which in turn goes through Mud Walls, the old convict probation station (1844), to Colebrook, Campania and Richmond (see Chapter 17).

One km from the turn-off, on your left, is 'Park Farm', where in 1827 William Pike built a house from which church services were held for many years.

The highest point on the Heritage Highway is the top of Spring Hill, where Governor Macquarie's baggage carts overturned. Sometimes this part of the highway may be covered in snow. A good view down to Mt Wellington can be seen. Halfway down the hill, on the right, is 'Tedworth', once a coaching station named 'London Inn', owned by John Vincent of 'Callington Mill'. Then you come to 'Lovely Banks'.

Melton Mowbray, Kempton and Dysart

Melton Mowbray is the junction of the Midlands and Lake Highways. Here Sam Blackwell, who built the Melton Mowbray Hotel, ran a pack of foxhounds. An old stone drinking trough is a reminder of coaching days.

Kempton was originally known as 'Green Ponds', but was renamed 'Kemp Town' in 1840 for the respected citizen Anthony Fenn Kemp who was granted 'Mount Vernon' in the 1820s. 'Mount Vernon' was named after the home of George Washington. In Kempton on your right is 'Dysart House', built in 1845 for William Henry Ellis. It was once an inn, the 'Commercial', but was more usually known as 'Ellis's Tap'. There were seven inns at Kempton at one time. Also in Kempton is the 'House of Koarlee', built in 1833, St Mary's Anglican Church, 1839, and the Wilmot Arms. These are only a few of the buildings dating from the 1830s and '40s.

Back on the highway, you'll see some trees which form part of the pioneer avenue along the sides of the road. To your right is Dysart, where you may visit St Anne's Anglican Church.

'Chauncy Vale'

Next comes 'Chauncy Vale' on the left, before you enter Bagdad. 'Chauncy Vale' was the home of well-known writer Nan Chauncy, and the house where she lived is still there on the rugged property. It is now a sanctuary, but tours are sometimes taken to Browns Cave, the inspiration for Capra Cave in her book *They Found a Cave*. If you go on one of these tours, be prepared for some steep climbing to the sandstone cave and a breathless scramble down to the creek at the foot of the ravine. The 'Brown' concerned was a bushranger who lived in

Brown's Cave Creek, Chauncy Vale, Bagdad

the vicinity and sometimes found it politic to 'disappear' for a while, hiding out at the cave and terrifying the redcoats by judiciously placed musket shots. The film of the book was made on location here.

Bagdad and Mangalore
Bagdad is situated in the Bagdad Valley, once extensively used for apple and pear orcharding. It is now under pasture. Near Bagdad you may see 'Milford Manor' and historic 'Oakwood'.

Next comes Mangalore. The Mangalore Tier is away to your right. Just south of Mangalore is the Shene Road leading off to your left. 'Shene' was to have been a Georgian homestead designed by Francis Butler for his father Gamelien. However, the father died, and only the opulent stables were built.

Pontville and Brighton

Pontville comes next, a tiny place now recognised as an historic town. On your left, look for the Anglican Church of St Mark. Over the gateway as you enter the church ground is a coloured glass lantern. A number of the Butler family members are buried in the churchyard. Some of the gravestones are quite badly weathered. The older stones are round the back of the church, near the rectory. Also at the back is a vault in memory of some of the Butlers. Buried here are John James Butler and his wife Julia (d. 1876), and Edward Payne Butler (d. 1849).

The pillared sandstone church was built in 1841 and designed by a convict architect. Before entering, turn back towards the gateway to see a magnificent view of Mt Wellington (*the* mountain, as it is known locally) and Brighton Plain. Inside the church (key available at the rectory), is an interesting font, featuring carved angels and a beautifully carved eagle lectern with cherubs on it. John James Butler (1828–1896) and his second wife Diana are

Baptisimal font, St Mark's Church, Pontville

commemorated on one of the windows. On leaving the church, watch for the Crown Inn (1834), and for an old private home, owned by the Butler family.

Climb down the river bank to look under the bridge, supported by four unexpectedly handsome angled sandstone pillars. Notice the water level meter: on dry land when we saw it in early spring. The Barracks (1824), on your left as you cross the bridge, is a large, cream Georgian sandstone building, with two stone lions guarding the entrance. The building was erected as a British Army Barracks, when it was intended that Brighton would be the capital of Van Diemen's Land. St Matthew's, Pontville, is yet another fine old church. While in Brighton, turn into Briggs Road to visit Bonorong Wildlife Centre.

The Jordan River is said to have come by its name in an interesting fashion. It seems that two young men named Jorgen

Jorgensen and Hugh Germain(e) were surveying land, and naming sites alternately as they found them. One had a Bible and the other a copy of *The Arabian Nights*. Thus we have a Jericho and a Jordan River, a Bagdad and a Paradise. Unfortunately (in our opinion), most of the places have since been re-named.

As noted above, Brighton was the original site chosen for Hobart, and Pontville was to have been the centre of the capital. The authorities had the idea of bringing shipping up the Jordan River, which is a very small stream, as far as Pontville, but this proved impractical.

Brighton comes straight after Pontville, with Brighton Army Camp on the right. The Camp was established in 1939 to train A.I.F. units. It is now used by the Antarctic Commission.

To your right as you go through Brighton, look for Mt Dromedary, shaped like a (one-humped) camel. Mt Dromedary was the site of the hideout of bushranger Martin Cash, one of the best known of Tasmanian bushrangers

Martin Cash is one of those folklore figures with an almost Robin Hood reputation. He is known to have killed only one man, although he was always heavily armed. Cash was an Irishman who had been transported to New South Wales for attempted murder. He arrived in Van Diemen's Land in 1837. He was a great escaper, and one of the few to escape from the dreaded Port Arthur by swimming Eaglehawk Bay. He took up bushranging in 1843, and he and his gang became known for their humane methods; they never terrorised women or the poor!

One of his companions, Kavanagh, was wounded and despite Cash's offer to kidnap a doctor to treat him, he insisted on giving himself up, swearing that Cash and Co. were dead. Cash was later betrayed and captured in Hobart, where he shot a Constable Winstanley during the fight. He was sentenced to death, this sentence being commuted to life imprisonment at Norfolk Island.

When the settlement there was abandoned, Cash, now married, returned to Tasmania and settled down to take charge of the gardens of Government House. Later he farmed at Glenorchy, where he died in 1877.

Brighton to Bridgewater. Shortly after Brighton, you pass the turn-off to historic Stonyhurst and Route C322 to Wadaronga Birdlife Park, and then come to the Bridgewater Bridge and Causeway over the Derwent River. This is a very old causeway, constructed during the 1830s by convicts in the chain-gang. Some of the stone was brought from interstate for it. It's a causeway with a lift-span bridge at one end. The bridge was once used extensively, but is now lifted only for yachts and small ferries.

At Bridgewater, there is a choice of ways: Route A10 to New Norfolk, Queenstown and the West Coast (covered in Chapters 14 and 16), or the highway to the left to Hobart City (see Chapter 14).

Watch for swans on the right. On your right, as you turn towards Hobart, is the Convict Museum Old Watch House and Gaol, built in 1838.

BIBLIOGRAPHY

Books

EMMETT, E.T. *Tasmania by Road and Track*, Melbourne University Press, 1952.

NEWITT, Lyn *Convicts and Carriageways*, Dept. Of Main Roads, 1988.

O'BRIEN, G.J., *The Main Road; A Historical Journey from Launceston to Hobart*.

SKEMP, John Rowland, *Shadow over Tasmania*.

SMITH, Roy, *Early Tasmanian Bridges*, 1969.

STANCOMBE, G. Hawley, *Highway in Van Diemen's Land*, 1974.

WEEDING, J.S. *A History of Oatlands*, 1988.

WEEDING, J.S. *A History of the Lower Midlands*, 1976.

Pamphlets
'Let's Talk About Campbell Town'
'Let's Talk About Oatlands'
'Let's Talk About Ross' (Tas. Visitor Corporation)

Tasmania: Hobart to Launceston Travel Tape.

Maps
Tasmap 1: 100 000 Land Tenure Index Series
'Derwent' 'Lake Sorell', 'South Esk'.

Information
Thanks to Mr and Mrs Burberry, Heather Chauncy, George Farrell, Jean Phelps and Betty Roberts.

9. The North-east

Features of this drive

The north-east offers another richly varied drive which takes you from the city of Launceston down to St Helens on the East Coast. The towns you see are a little younger than some others in Tasmania, but all have their own charms. Some of the delights included in this drive are a lavender farm, an unusual forest reserve and a rhododendron garden, wide white surf beaches, temperate myrtle rainforest, two unique pubs, an impressive waterfall, an abandoned mining town, a Chinese cemetery, and a wonderful mining museum. There are plenty of craft and antique shops, food and petrol and accommodation are freely available and the roads, in general, are very good.

Lilydale

History. Around 27 km from Launceston, the Lilydale area was first settled in 1861. During the 1850s, German loggers had begun to clear the area and opened it up for the farmers who followed. Mt Arthur, to the east of Lilydale, is 1187 metres high and is one of the higher mountains in Tasmania.

A gold mine opened nearby in Lisle in 1879 and a track was carved across one slope of Mt Arthur to carry food from Lilydale to the miners. At about the same time a church, school and other public buildings were built at Lilydale, and a railway to Scottsdale opened a decade later.

The area was originally known as Germantown, but during the First World this was altered in the interests of the people who lived there. The name 'Lilydale' was chosen because of its pleasant connotations.

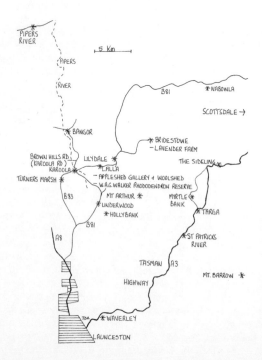

Routes to Lilydale. To visit Lilydale and surrounding areas, enter Launceston city from the Bass Highway and drive through the city on Bathurst Street. Turn right at the Mowbray Junction, then take Route B81 to Lilydale, about 20 km away. Another choice of route would take you on a scenic drive via Pipers River and Turners Marsh to Lalla.

If you take the main route, you'll be driving through bush and pine forest. The Pipers River district is one of the main vine-growing areas in the state. All around the Lilydale area is a complicated maze of roads, so you should take a good road map along. One tiny hamlet called Bangor may be reached by so many different routes that it seems a pity that it isn't bigger when you get there! Seven km before you reach Lilydale on Route B81 you will come to a turn-off to the right leading to the 140 hectare Hollybank Forest Reserve.

Hollybank Forest Reserve. In 1855 a sawmill was established at the site of the present reserve. The manager of this prosperous mill, William Crabtree, planted some of the English trees still to be seen at the reserve today. In 1933 part of the area was bought by Ash Plantation Limited, a company which planned to supply wood suitable for the manufacturing of cricket bats and tennis racquets. Thousands of ash trees and a great many other varieties were planted out, but unfortunately (partly due to the increasing use of artificial materials in sporting goods), the business failed. The Forestry Commission took over the plantation in 1953. There are many kinds of different trees and forests in the Reserve, which is serviced by a network of walking tracks. The Hollybank Forest Centre, located in the Reserve, is open every day Monday–Friday.

Underwood Road. Return to Route B81 and almost opposite the Reserve Road, you'll see Route C823, known as Underwood Road. This road leads you down the hill and across the Pipers River. A feature of the area are the holly bushes; their berries make a cheerful splash in winter and early spring. Turn left into Brown Mountain Road, and take a scenic drive through to Karoola. Turn right out of Karoola into Route C 822, the Lalla Road. On your left along this road, you'll come to the Appleshed Gallery and Teahouse. This is (at the time of writing) open every day except Wednesday and Thursday, but this may be subject to seasonal variation. The Appleshed is housed in an old packing shed which once belonged to Frank Walker, an early settler.

Also along the Lalla Road you can see Pear Walk Cottages and Design Studio and Plover's Ridge Host Farm, and on your right, 1 km from the Apple Shed, is the W.A.G. Walker Rhododendron Reserve, 2 km from the turn-off. This is open at varying times (detailed on the sign).

Rhododendron Reserve. The W.A.G. Walker Rhododendron Reserve is a 12 ha park featuring a number of unusual plants in addition to the rhododendrons that give it its name. The Reserve was established by the son of the Appleshed's Frank Walker who arrived in Tasmania from Kent. He established a nursery, specialising in fruit trees. Later, with his son W.A.G., he added rhododendrons and azaleas to the nursery. As well as looking remarkably opulent during their flowering season (September to mid-December), these rhododendrons have worked hard for their living, becoming the parent plants of many thousands of mainland bushes.

Mt Arthur Road. Along the Lilydale Road is a turn-off to Mt Arthur Road. If you drive to the top of this road, you might like to make the 3-hour return walk to the top of the mountain. As with many walking tracks in Tasmania, this one may be treacherous in bad weather, and locals warn any would-be bushwalkers to make sure they are properly clad and supplied in case of trouble!

In Lilydale township itself, reached on Route B81, you can visit Bardenhagens' General Store: a building classified by the National Trust and operated as a general store since 1888.

The Bardenhagen Family have been in the Lilydale area since the 1880s. As well as opening the General Store, the Bardenhagens ran the first coach service in the district.

Continuing on Route B81, head towards Scottsdale. On the way, you'll see the Lilydale Falls Reserve on your right. The Reserve is a favourite picnic area and the Falls, of which there are two sets, are within easy walking distance.

Lilydale to Scottsdale

It is 42 km from Lilydale to Scottsdale. Follow the winding, hilly road east through thick bush, east towards Scottsdale. Along the way you'll pass through Lebrinna and Golconda. Keep an eye out for signs pointing the way to interesting galleries and craft shops. Also along this road is Heemskirk Vineyards, named after Abel Tasman's ship *Heemskirk*. The Lilydale area is well suited to grape growing, both for the soil and the cool climate. Main varieties grown include Pinot Noir, Chardonnay, Cabernet Sauvignon and Riesling.

Along the way, you'll see signs indicating the way to the famous Bridestowe Lavender Farm. The turn-off from Route B81 is on your left.

Bridestowe Lavender Farm is the oldest commercial lavender farm in Tasmania, and the largest lavender farm in the Southern Hemisphere. It is open to the public, and is probably best seen during the January harvest season. However, it's worth a visit any time.

Bridestowe lavender products are available on site, and throughout the whole state at gift shops, and the lavender is famed for being the purest available. Great care has been taken to prevent cross pollination with other varieties.

Lavender is a popular herb which gets its name from the verb 'to lave' or to wash. It is disinfectant and sweet-smelling, and is used in the forms of sachets and oils as well as in the manufacture of lavender water.

Other ways to Scottsdale

Route B81 is not the only route to Scottsdale from the West. Three others are covered below. Each offers its own charms, but you'd need several weeks to try all routes to all places in Tasmania.

Scottsdale via Bridport. To take this route you turn left at the sign into the Bridport Back Road, drive north to Bridport then south down the Bridport Road to Scottsdale.

Scottsdale via the Sideling. To travel to Scottsdale via the Sideling, leave Launceston through Waverley on Route A3. Continue on this route and pass Mt Edgecombe on your left. Cross the St Patricks River at Nunamara.

On your left is the road to Patersonia, a settlement named after Lt Col. William Paterson. The name was originally held by Launceston itself. About 8 km from the Patersonia turn-off is the right hand turn to Mt Barrow and the Mt Barrow State Reserve. About 5 km further on there is a turn-off to the left, Targa Hill Road, leading to 'Myrtle Bank'. Near the turn-off is Skemps Creek, named for the family who settled there in 1883.

Myrtle Bank was settled by Rowland Skemp and his brother Samuel, who had been born to Rev. Thomas Skemp and his wife in Shropshire in 1863 and 1862 respectively.

Orphaned in their teens, the young men migrated to Australia, Samuel on the *Cassiope* in May 1882 and Rowland on the *Potosi* in June the following year. That year Sam bought, sight unseen, a block of 20 acres at Myrtle Bank, near the prosperous Myrtle Bank Hotel of William Faulkner. Evidently Mr Faulkner had been a dealer in sly grog, and when the Law caught up with him, he turned honest and took out a licence!

Sam and Rowland walked the 20 miles to their new farm, and put up at Faulkner's Hotel. The block had originally been selected by a paling splitter named Boden, but having removed what wood he wanted from the land, he had allowed it to revert to the Crown. His sons, Ran and Jim, were neighbours of the young Skemps.

In 1886 Florence Kearney arrived to teach at Patersonia. She and Rowland were eventually married—after a long and diffident courtship—in 1894. New rooms were added to the hut in the bush. They adopted a child named Leslie after the death of their first child, and in 1900 became the parents of a boy they named John Rowland.

Florence died in 1934, Rowland in 1947 and Sam nearly two years later. They are all buried in Patersonia graveyard.

John Rowland Skemp wrote an interesting book about his family and home, published in 1952 as *Memories of Myrtle Bank* (Melbourne University Press).

Six km and one crossing of the St Patricks River from the Myrtle Bank turn-off, you will reach the Sideling, the steep and winding pass over Sideling Range. Continue for 14 km—most of them comprising hairpin bends. It is about 4 km to the farming district of Springfield. From there it is a further 9 km to Scottsdale.

Bridport Road. Another route to Scottsdale is dealt with in Chapter 5, as Bridport Rd. (If this sounds like an unnecessarily long gap between chapters, well—that's Tasmanian roads for you!)

Early settlement of the north-east

The north-east of Tasmania was first settled along the coastline, which is lightly timbered and provides easy access to the sea. Inland areas were extremely

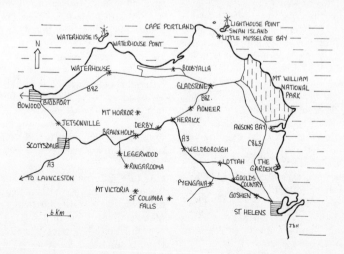

mountainous and had heavy timber through which early pioneers had to force their way. In 1852 the Tasmanian government engaged surveyor James Scott to examine the unknown areas. He and a party of six men set out to investigate. The expedition was successful, and the route taken brought them to Ringarooma. The party camped on the banks of the Ringarooma River, near a rich deposit of tin.

James Scott was born at Legerwood, Earlston, Scotland; the sixth son of George and Eliza Scott. Scott arrived in Van Diemen's Land on board the *Ann Jamieson* in 1832, following two of his brothers, Thomas and George, who had arrived 12 years earlier. Thomas Scott was a surveyor, and he trained James in the same profession. James took over from Thomas in 1838. A kind hardworking and enthusiastic man, James Scott was an expert bushman as well a respected surveyor.

Early Scottsdale settlers

After Surveyor Scott opened the north-east, a man named William Tully surveyed the land around what is now Scottsdale. He called it 'Scotts New Country' as a tribute to Scott. The land was now open for selection, and the first to take advantage was a miller from Launceston named Thomas Cox, who, enchanted with the country, settled in and built himself a tiny two-room man fern house on 200 acres of prime land, by what is now known as Coxs Creek. He occupied this with his daughter Sarah, and was a well-known figure in the district for years. A large man, he was apparently in the habit of riding on a small brown mule, accompanied at times by a large, dressed sheep carcass! Mr Cox's house was both the first building erected on the north-east coast and the first post office.Other settlers followed him, including Thomas Diprose Heazlewood and Thomas Tucker.

Thomas Diprose Heazlewood (1838–192?), arrived in the area from Longford in 1859 along with his sister Jane's husband, **Thomas Tucker**. His brother Joseph followed with his wife Caroline Brumby in 1864. Thomas Heazlewood took up a large selection, which comprised the town area of present-day Scottsdale. In 1863 he returned to Longford and married Mary George. Their journey to their new home was enlivened by the hazardous crossing of a flooded river! The couple had nine children, and between them members of this family supplied many of the street names in the growing town. Thomas Heazlewood opened the second general store in the district, and owned one of the first horses. It is sometimes said of those early days that Heazlewoods owned half of Scottsdale and Tuckers the other half, and the two families often intermarried. As a descendant remarked, at that time they had very little choice! Thomas Tucker and his wife Jane also had a large family, and supplied many more street names. The Tucker family home, known as 'Beulah', is still standing in King Street.

George William Evans was born in England in 1778 and arrived in Australia in 1802. At various times he worked as a farmer and a bookseller, and by 1811 was Deputy Surveyor General of Van Diemen's Land. He died in Hobart in 1852.

Samuel Hawkes was born in the U.K. c. 1846 and arrived in Tasmania in 1876. His wife was born Elizabeth Rankin. Samuel was manager and part owner of the Arba tin mine at Branxholm for 18 years, and lived there for 6 years before moving to Scottsdale.

He built 'Ellesmere House', and later became warden of the then Scottsdale municipality, a Territorial Justice and a Member of the House of Assembly. Some descendants of Samuel and Elizabeth Hawkes still live in the area.

By the 1860s Scottsdale had grown into a small but flourishing township.

Things to see in Scottsdale

After you enter Scottsdale from Lilydale, drive down William Street until it intersects King Street. At the intersection you'll see Number 46 King Street. This is Anabel's Restaurant, a lovely federation-style building and one of the first houses in Scottsdale. It was built in the 1890s and purchased at the turn of the century by George Melville Dinham, a great-great-grandson of George William Evans (see above). George Dinham's wife was the daughter of Samuel Hawkes (see above).

The Dinham family home has been trading as Anabel's Restaurant since the 1980s; it was named in honour of a great-great-grand daughter of George Dinham.

The house and its gardens are classified with the National Trust and registered with the National Estate. Inside many of the original fittings remain and the gardens feature rhododendrons and other flowering trees which are over a hundred years old. Accommodation is provided in six self-contained units, including one two-bedroom family unit. The proprietor, a descendant of George Dinham, recommends a visit when the trees are in flower.

Turn left and drive along King Street. At the top of the hill, you'll see the old Post Office. Recognisable by its high gabled roof, this building was erected in the 1880s and extensively renovated in 1988. Just ahead, on the right, is pretty 'Beulah', the old Tucker family home. Turn off King Street into Alfred Street. 18 Alfred Street is the original Council Chambers, built in 1881. Turn left into George Street, past the Gospel Hall and Roman Catholic Churches. Just before you leave Scottsdale on the Bridport Road, you will see the old Ellesmere courthouse. If you take the last street to the right, you can see 'Ellesmere House', built by Samuel Hawkes.

Scottsdale to Bridport

The Bridport road is Route B84, and Bridport is 21 km from Scottsdale. Pass through Jetsonville to reach the town itself, at the mouth of the River Brid on Anderson Bay.

Bridport—history and a modern tour

Anderson Bay was named after early settlers, Andrew and Janet Anderson, who arrived in the district in 1833. A fishing village, Bridport was surveyed in 1852 Bridport's first recorded white visitor was Thomas Lewis, the surveyor, in 1830. He explored the area and named many features but very few of his names were officially adopted. He surveyed many properties held by early settlers, including 'Bowood', for Peter Brewer, in 1839. Brewer married Elizabeth Harrington Jones, daughter of one of the first settlers at the Pipers River area. Around 12 km north-north west of Bridport, at the mouth of the Little Forester River, and on the Route B82, '**Bowood**' was built in 1838 for Peter Brewer and is the oldest house in the area. Bowood was

'Bowood', Bridport

Bridport

built on the edge of the old Launceston Road, which has now vanished under the grass. The property was granted to Brewer in 1838, some of it being fronted by others, including a man named Thirkell. Brewer named it 'Bowood' in memory of an ancient hunting forest near his former home in England. The house was built by an ex-convict carpenter named James Edwards and a stonemason named Robert Rhodes. Rhodes was an American, and had deserted from one of the many sealing ships of the time. Peter Brewer found him in an area named Sealers Marsh and gave him work. A headstone relating to Rhodes is now near the house. He was from Philadelphia, and died in 1863 at the age of 58.

'Bowood' is a gracious white Georgian house made from local stone and bricks and pit-sawn timber. It was completed in 1844, and the Brewers moved in. The old storerooms have been converted into bathrooms. The thick iron bars put across the storeroom windows to repel bush-rangers still remain. The floors of the fourteen rooms are original, and so are many ceilings.

When we visited it in the late 1980s, we found 'Bowood' to be a beautifully kept and restored private home. Mrs Hirst kindly agreed to show us around, but the house was not generally open the public. A stone wall has been added around part of the garden, as has a fountain, but all additions are harmoniously in character with the house. The original Bridport Post Office was once in the grounds. In the gardens and the surrounding paddocks some of the original trees remain, among them a pear tree and two oaks that are over 150 years old. We remember that Mrs Hirst showed us a beautifully iced cake which the Brewer family had presented to 'Bowood' on its 150th anniversary! These days, 'Bowood' (all 10 000 acres of it!) is a sheep and beef-raising property.

'We have some old diaries', Mrs Hirst told us, 'and in the old days, Peter Brewer made a coffin in the morning and killed a beast in the afternoon! They could turn their hands to anything ...'

Another property first surveyed by Lewis was about 4 km east of present day Bridport. Part of it was selected in 1833 by the Anderson family. In 1858 the property passed to Martin Mowbray Stephenson, who named it 'Barnbougle'. Mr Stephenson married Eleanor, the eldest daughter of Peter and Elizabeth Brewer of 'Bowood', and they had ten children, including Charles Morrison Stephenson who later married his cousin Edith Brewer, a grand daughter of Peter and Elizabeth.

Things to see in Bridport. Bridport offers its visitors safe white sand beaches, a newly built tourist resort complex, a caravan park and golf course, and bushwalking and boating. Drive along Main Street to see the Bridport Hotel, built in 1921.

At the turn-off into Bentley Street is St Mark's Church, whose foundation stone, (if our grasp of Roman numerals is correct) was placed in 1931. All the information on the foundation stone is in Latin, so maybe you'd like to try out your classical scholarship! The outside is pleasing, with a bright stained-glass window above the front entry.

The church may be locked at times, but if you have a chance to go inside, look out for an illuminated cross—a memorial to a well-loved and interesting ex-resident, Rev. William Harold MacFarlane. Rev MacFarlane first came to Scottsdale in 1935, and was rector there for five years. Prior to this he had been in Victoria and had worked as a missionary on Thursday Island. Rev. MacFarlane was a historian and a gifted writer: his collection of articles in newspapers have formed the basis for a fine history of Scottsdale, *Scott's New Country*. After leaving Scottsdale, Rev. MacFarlane was rector at Longford. He retired to Bridport, and continued to be active in church affairs until his death in 1963 at the age of 79.

If you turn into Bentley Street, you can drive along to a right-hand turn where the sign says 'North Pier Beach and Boat Ramp'. There is a charming view of the white-sand beaches, and in the lovely bay you will see the remains of the Bridport Jetty, which burnt down in 1938.

East of Bridport on Route B82 is the Waterhouse Coastal Reserve, and what is left of the township of Waterhouse, which sprang up with the discovery of a gold reef in 1869. Unfortunately the strike proved disappointing and the venture—and the town—folded shortly afterwards. Just off Waterhouse Point is Waterhouse Island, which was named by Bass and Flinders in 1798, in honour of Captain Waterhouse, master of the *Reliance*.

Cross the Tomahawk River and take the next turn to your left to reach Tomahawk, laid out in 1869 and at one time known as 'Ducane' in honour of Governor Charles Du Cane. Back on Route B82 you may cross the Boobyalla River and go on to Gladstone: from which Route C844 takes you to Boobyalla Beach and the Cape Portland area. (Look out for Little Swan Island and Swan Island, which has a lighthouse.)

Alternatively, from Gladstone, you may take Route B43 over the Great Musselroe River to Route B45 and the Mt William National Park and Musselroe Bay Coastal Reserve, or continue on Route B43 to the popular camping area of Ansons Bay. Just before Ansons Bay is a turn-off to the left, on Route B46, which leads to Eddystone Point and the Eddystone Light. Also from Gladstone, Route B82 leads through Pioneer (which was once known as 'Bradshaws Creek' and where a young Joseph Lyons once taught school), and Herrick.

Gladstone

The tin-mining town of Gladstone was first settled in 1870 and was served by the port of Boobyalla.

Far more important than mining these days are tourism and farming. Gladstone has an interesting graveyard, containing some Chinese headstones. At around the turn of the century a coach used to run from Gladstone to Derby.

Cape Portland was first noted by Bass and Flinders during their expedition of 1798. They named it after the Duke of Portland, who was the Secretary of the Colonies at that time.

Scottsdale to Branxholm

Leaving Scottsdale on Route A3, you will see a flora park of endemic species on your right. Later, on your left, you will see a timber mill, a reminder that this is one of the greatest timber areas in the state. You will also see hop poles on either side of the road, hops being another important local industry. Cross the tiny Forester River, and on the right is the Tonganah Road. If you take this road, it is 7 km to the Cuckoo Falls track. A little farther along the main road to the right is the Tonganah clay mine, which produces filler clay for Associated Paper Pulp Mills. About 11 km out of Scottsdale, are more hopfields stretching to the left and right, after which the road is bordered by light bush. At one point, indicated by a sign on the left warning of 2 km of winding road, is a hill known as the Billycock. The story goes that a man walking up the hill in the dark lost his billy cock hat. The next traveller found it and stuck it on a man fern: from this small incident a name was born and passed into common history.

Just before the Billycock is an old building which was known as the old Camp Hotel. This was once a busy coaching inn.

You now enter the **Ringarooma area** (named from an Aboriginal name meaning 'Happy Hunting Ground'). The road comes out into open farming land. Ringarooma district is famous for the production of milk and butter. It also produces timber and indeed the thick bush that used to cover the area hampered European settlement for quite some time.

If you turn off the highway onto Route C 422, you will reach Legerwood. Here, in the 1850s, Surveyor James Scott selected 4000 acres of prime land for his own use. He had a three-roomed hut built there by Thomas Hogarth and William Vestey. A bridge was made over the Legerwood River in 1877, and Legerwood became a farming community in 1862. To reach the township of Ringarooma, follow the road from Legerwood or take the next turn-off from the highway.

Twenty-one km south east of Ringarooma is the **Mt Victoria Forest Reserve**, comprising 3200 hectares of state forest— myrtles, tea-trees and celery top pine. The dolerite and sandstone Mt Victoria rises to 1213 m. Other features in the forest reserve are Cashs Gorge and Ralphs Falls, to be reached by a walking track, and just outside the boundary, is the smaller Mt Albert. From Mt Albert Road a walking track leads to the top of Mt Victoria. The round trip takes around 3 hours. The Mt Victoria area was discovered in 1922 and the reserve gazetted in 1983.

Branxholm

The first town of any size after Scottsdale on Route A3 (The Tasman Highway), is the pretty township of Branxholm, originally a 4500-acre property selected by James Reid Scott, nephew of Scott the surveyor, and named for a hamlet in Scotland. By the 1870s Branxholm had three major buildings, including one on Branxholm Estate, about 2 km north of the town, on the banks of Branxholm Creek. The town grew quickly when tin was discovered in c. 1873 and the Ruby Flat and Arba Tin Mines opened. Four years later, the population was roughly 300. Tin was taken by dray to the ports at Bridport and Boobyalla and in 1883 Branxholm was proclaimed a town.

Early settlers in Branxholm included Samuel Hawkes from Scottsdale, who opened a store and was the first manager and part owner of Arba mine, and James Crichton who, with his wife Elizabeth, came from Victoria and settled at Ruby

Flat, which has now vanished in the encroaching bush. It was about 2 km south of the highway.

Entering the town 26 km from Scottsdale, see more hopfields on the left. The hops were first grown here in 1970, and have since become an important crop. Just inside the town on the left is a tourist information centre. Branxholm is on the Ringarooma River in a valley set among hills.

Just out of Branxholm turn to your left to visit an old cemetery, reached via a small, winding road. In this cemetery some of the Chinese tin miners were buried, and a few of their tombstones may still be seen.

Derby

A few km beyond Branxholm is the old mining township of Derby, once again situated on the Ringarooma River. Tin was discovered in Derby in 1874 by George Renison Bell (see Chapter 16), whose name is commemorated in Renison Street. Two years later the mine, originally called the Brothers Mine, was opened. The name was later altered to the Briseis Mine, in honour of a Melbourne Cup Winner!

The mine continued profitably and was sold to an English company in 1899. This company put in the Cascade Dam, which burst on April 4th 1921, causing disastrous flooding. Derby was inundated, and many lives were lost. The mine closed, re-opened in 1934, then in the 1940s closed permanently, although it was by no means worked out. The township grew rapidly in the quarter century after the discovery of tin. Originally known as Brothers Home, the name was officially changed to Derby in 1897, probably after the Earl of Derby, then Prime Minister of England. By that time, the township had two churches, two hotels, three stores, a bank, a post office, three farmers, a teacher, a baker, a hairdresser and a blacksmith! In our own opinion, it is rather a pity that many of the original place names in Tasmania, bestowed because of natural features or local 'characters' were later changed to honour V.I.P.s who often never saw Tasmania at all.

Since the closure of the mines, Derby's population has dropped considerably; however its charm and the rich local history have made it a popular place for visitors. During the 1950s the Derby Stove began to be produced by Jack Hornby and Jack Wise at Derby. Their company, Derby Products Pty Ltd is no longer based in Derby, but continues to manufacture a number of different items.

Derby is particularly proud of one of its sons, Ken Turner, the sportsman, who has been Australian Badminton Champion eight times.

Mr Turner was born in 1933, and left Derby to go to school in Launceston when he was about 12 years old. He is married with four sons, and the six members of the family have, between them, represented Tasmania over 45 times in Badminton.

On the left, beside the river as you enter Derby is Derby Park and a children's playground. Also on the left, a little farther along, you'll see the old Bank House. This was built in 1888 and is the oldest timber bank building in Tasmania. Just past the park, look for the well-known Derby Tin Mine Museum and Tearooms. Guided coach tours are available here.

Inside the museum building, (once the old Derby School, and built on the site of an old two-storey hotel), when we visited last, we saw such things as a miners' dolly pot, which was used to crush ore samples, scales used for weighing bags of tin, and ore samples taken from round the district. Then there were crosscut saws, an old butter churn and a bullock's yoke used between 1874 and 1940 on bullock teams. In a cabinet was some Chinese money, dating from 1914, old newspapers, maps and photographs, including a large one of the Gladstone dredge, taken in 1905.

'Shanty Town', Derby Museum

'Shanty Town', Derby Museum

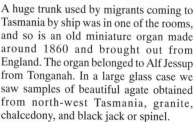

A huge trunk used by migrants coming to Tasmania by ship was in one of the rooms, and so is an old miniature organ made around 1860 and brought out from England. The organ belonged to Alf Jessup from Tonganah. In a large glass case we saw samples of beautiful agate obtained from north-west Tasmania, granite, chalcedony, and black jack or spinel.

Outside the museum was the very interesting exhibit known as 'Shanty Town', with wooden walkways connecting various scenes from the old days in Derby. The exhibit of the town itself consisted of a number of wooden buildings set out exactly as they might have been in earlier times. These included the Briseis Tin Mine registered office, the old butcher's shop, a miner's cottage and a lean-to outhouse. Then there was the general store, tobacconist and hardware. Old Derby gaol, built in 1888 and known as 'the watchhouse' looked very uninviting, but there was a fine old coach and a fully equipped blacksmith's shop, with vintage bellows, anvil, forge and harness. The displays in Shanty Town have been enlarged and updated since our visit, and now include a bushman's hut and printing press as well.

Behind Shanty Town is a lookout view to Briseis mine face.

Moorina

Ten km from Derby is Moorina, once known as Krushkas Bridge, after the Krushka brothers, (Frederick, Charles and Christopher), who walked from Mathinna to search for tin at Main Creek, a tributary the Ringarooma River, and who subsequently opened the Derby mine. The brothers enjoyed life to the full—rather too much so—for the bulk of their money went on horses and gambling. They are supposed have mined tin worth around a quarter a million pounds before selling out to the Briseis Company. Their name survives as Krushka Street in Derby.

The township was later renamed Moorina, after a sister of Truganini. As well as having its own mine, 'The Echo', the township was a distribution and transportation centre. Just before you enter Moorina, there is a turning to the left, Route B82 to Herrick and Gladstone. These days, Moorina boasts a picturesque golf course and an interesting cemetery. Just on the right past the entrance to the golf course is a circular road which leads past the cemetery and out onto the highway again. At the far end of the graveyard, against the fenceline, is a stone which has been erected for the worship of the Confucian religion by the Chinese from the area. At one end is a conical monument, at the other a flat stone telling something of the history of the Chinese people who worked here. At the turn of the century hundreds of Chinese people flocked to the area to work at the tin mines. They were not very popular with the local miners, and there was some competition for jobs. Many of the men went back to China when they grew older, but some stayed on and were buried at the cemetery here. On the left not far from the cemetery is sign warning of seven kilometres of winding road. The road twists up Weld Hill, (elevation 373 metres) through varied forest. Watch for giant tree ferns, myrtle beach, peppermint gums and others, wattles, and blackwoods.

Weldborough

Just after the Weld Hill sign, you reach the township of Weldborough, built on Weldborough Plain. Weldborough, named for Governor Weld who visited the area in 1875, was once a much larger town than it is today, with a school for the 80 local children, a bank, tinsmith and many other shops. It was also Tasmania's first casino town, host to gamblers from all over Australia. On the left you see Weldborough Hotel, which proudly proclaims itself to be the 'worst pub'. If you disregard this notice and enter the pub you will be treated to an 'Irish Menu' which lists such culinary delights as Tasmanian devil, kangaroo tits, maggot mornay, and leeches and cream. There is even a Blarney Stone and a stern warning that it is not to be kissed! The pub was built in 1928, replacing the old hotel which dated from before the 1890s and which burnt down in the early 1920s. The building and its vanished stables were reputed to occupy the only piece of ground on Weld Hill not to be mined for tin! At one time there were 800 Chinese in the Welborough area, but when the tin finished, they left and by the 1940s all had gone, many of them returning to China. According to the memories of one local,

the Chinese mostly got along well in Weldborough, joining with the Europeans and introducing their own customs. The old Chinese Joss House is now in the Queen Victoria Museum in Launceston.

If you can face the Irish menu, go into the pub and enjoy the jokes on the wall and the happy atmosphere. In one room are some interesting photographs, including one of the Chinese leader, Maa Mon (or Ma Mun) Chin, who was Mandarin at the Camp at Weldborough. He and two sons arrived from China in 1875, his wife following in 1881. She is remembered as being a 'very gracious lady'. South of Weldborough is a dam named for Maa Mon Chin. Another photograph depicts John Cummings, who was born in 1841 and died in 1919, aged 78. He had a varied career, being a carpenter, an undertaker, a stage scenery artist—and also the local midwife!

Mt Paris Dam. Just beside the pub is a camping ground, and opposite, a dirt road leads 6 km to Mt Paris Dam. This was constructed in the 1930s, and photographs detailing its building are displayed in the hotel. The dam is a popular destination; a local told me that, despite the fact that there is no official signpost to point the way, he sometimes directs several visitors a week. At the time of writing (late 1996) there are plans to place a proper signpost.

Weldborough Pass. Leaving Weldborough, on Route A3, cross the Weld River, and enter the myrtle forest. The entry to a rainforest walk is clearly signposted. Weldborough Pass, (elevation 594 m) is a 13 km stretch of winding road which brings you down from the Weldborough Plain to the farming valley of Pyengana. The views over the valley are delightful.

Pyengana

Tasmanians think of Pyengana in connection with farming, a waterfall—and

St Columba Falls

cheese! Originally, the cheese was made for purely practical reasons: there was no way of getting the milk to the towns for market. Converting it to butter and cheese made it much easier to transport.

The area which was to become Pyengana was first surveyed in 1863 by the District Surveyor, John Thomas. He noted the superior quality of the soil.

The river on which Pyengana stands is now called Georges River; the local Aborigines had known it as Kunarra-Kuna. The selectors knew their settlement as Upper Georges River or The River. Two rivers meet at the eastern side of Pyengana (an Aboriginal name which probably means 'two rivers'). These are the North George and South George. The South George flows through the valley and spills over the top of the spectacular St Columba Falls.

Early Settlers at Pyengana. In 1828 the Quaker **Francis Cotton** and his wife Anna, with five children, arrived from England. They settled on the property 'Kelevedon' in Swansea. Their son George married an Irish girl named Margaret Connell in 1851, and later decided to investigate the area that

had so favourably impressed John Thomas. In 1875 the family settled on a selection they named 'St Columba'. The Falls take their name from this early farm. Margaret Cotton became the first woman to export apples from the state.

In 1876, the **Terry brothers**—Richard, Charles and William—settled on selections near St Columba. Richard's family home became the St Columba Hotel—now popularly known as 'The Pub in the Paddock'. Other early settlers included William Kennedy of Weldborough, in the late 1870s who built a house called Latara. This is now on the main road on the right, beside the general store. Thomas Coffey, (who married Anna Cotton in 1885), and George Sutton were other early residents. The two major attractions at Pyengana are the St Columba Falls and Richard Terry's old home (the 'Pub in the Paddock'). To reach this, follow the signpost on the right. It is about 3 km to the hotel.

St Columba Falls is claimed to be the tallest waterfall in Tasmania, splashing magnificently down over the rocks from a height of 110 m. To reach it take the St

Columba Falls Road—Route C428. The Falls are 11 km from the turn-off.

Goulds Country, Lottah and Goshen

Leave Pyengana, and bypass a sign which says 'Goulds Country'. About eight kilometres from Pyengana is a left-hand turn into Lottah Road. Two kilometres from the turn is Goulds Country, once the centre of municipality and now the only complete wooden town left in the state. Goulds Country was discovered by geologist Charles Gould, and was settled by five farmers who took up land at the foot of Blue Tier. With optimism, they burnt out the bush, planted vegetable peelings and waited for the crops to grow. Unfortunately, there was a lot of hungry local wildlife which opportunistically ate up the crops as they appeared, leaving the farmers with nothing. They almost starved, but were saved seven years later when tin was discovered on Blue Tier. The town was once known as Kunnarra, and by the turn of the century its population was over 400. A resident, Percy Steel, became the first Warden of the local municipality, known until the mid-1990s as Portland.

Five and a half kilometres farther along the road near the top of the Tier is what is left of the mining township of Lottah, named for an Aboriginal word meaning 'gum tree'. The town was popularly known as 'The Junction', as it formed the intersecting point for three roads.

At Lottah was the Anchor Mine, opened in 1880 and regarded in its day as one of the largest open cut tin mines in the southern hemisphere. Other mines in the area were the Puzzle, the Cambria, the Liberator and the Australian. There were 40 houses at one time, but in 1950 the mines closed and the town was deserted.

Back on the highway, 2 km from the Lottah turn-off, you will cross over the George River

at Goshen. The bridge was built in 1877. Goshen was a centre where stock feed was produced, but now all that is left of the original hamlet are the ruins of the Oxford Arms Inn (closed at the turn of the century) and the old school. There is, however, a scattering of newer houses. 13 km beyond Goshen is a turn-off to the left into Route C843, leading north to Ansons Bay.

Directly after this turn-off comes St Helens.

BIBLIOGRAPHY
Books
BOLCH, Cathie, MUGGERIDGE, Jennifer and WITHERS, Carole, *Bygone Branxholm.*
JENNINGS, J. A., *History of Bridport.*
JENNINGS, J., *Scott's New Country.*
NEWITT, Lyn, *Convicts and Carriageways*, Dept. of Main Roads, 1988.
SKEMP, John Rowland, *Memories of Myrtle Bank*, Melbourne University Press, 1952. SMITH, Theresa H. *The North Eastern Centenary*, 1874–1974.
WEBB, Gwen, *Pyengana: A New Country.*

Pamphlets
'An Introduction to Goulds Country and Lottah'
'Bridport'
'Let's Talk About Ringarooma District'
'Let's Talk About Scottsdale and Bridport'
'Let's Talk About Lilydale District' (Tas Visitor Corporation)
'Lilydale: Tasmania's Country Garden', (The Lilydale Tourist Association)

Maps
Tasmap 1: 100 000 Land Tenure Series: 'St Patricks', 'Georges Bay', 'Forester'.

Information
Thanks to the Brimfield family, Colin and Carol Cook, the late Neil Farrell, the Hirst family, John Jennings, Chris Payn, Yvonne Thorne, Heemskirk Vineyards, National Parks and Wildlife. Additional information from an article by Pamela Kidd.

10. St Helens, St Marys, Fingal and Avoca

Features of this drive

The drive from St Helens to St Marys and across to Fingal and Avoca offers some fine coastal and mountain scenery, historic buildings, a giant bathing beauty, a national park, a huge collection of Scotch Whisky and an award-winning history room. Food, petrol and accommodation are easily available.

Some history of the area. The area in which St Helens is the modern centre, was originally known as Goulds Country after Charles Gould, the first surveyor of the area. It was renamed Portland in 1908, the name being borrowed from Cape Portland, which in turn had been named for the Duke of Portland. It is now known as 'Break O' Day'. In the upper section of the triangular district is the Mt William National Park, reached by travelling along Route C843 until just before crosses the Great Musselroe River. Take Route C845, and follow the first fork to the right. Mt William rises to 216 m. The climate is generally milder than in the north-west and the major industries are forestry, fishing—and tourism.

The Blue Tier— beginning of St Helens

St Helens was first known as Georges Bay, but was given the present name in 1835. It was named after St Helens Point, which had been discovered in 1773 by Capt. Tobias Furneaux, (1735–1781), who also discovered the Bay of Fires. Its first inhabitants were the Georges Bay tribe of Aborigines. Then, in the 1830s, came sealers and whalers and finally, in 1850, white settlers. The first of these were small farmers. St Helens prides itself on its free settler history and complete lack of convicts. People came willingly, seeking free land and settling round the sides of the beautiful bay, and also along the Golden Fleece Rivulet.

The settlement of Goshen, 15 km to the west, was one hard day's walk from St Helens. During 1874, it was discovered that Blue Tier was, in effect, a whole mountain of tin. Hopeful miners arrived, walking the farmers' tracks, through the wooden town of Goulds Country, (settled in 1868), and formed the settlement of Lottah almost at the top of the tier. Soon, Lottah became the biggest local town and the seat of local government called a road trust. On the northern side of Blue Tier was Weldborough. from 1874 till the turn of century there were 3000 people living on the mountain, half of them miners. One thousand Chinese worked the tin, centred in Weldborough. For 20 years the area flourished. There was plenty of tin. The motive power of the mines was water, turning waterwheels to drive the stampers that extracted the tin from the granite. Unfortunately, so much timber was cut by the miners and the farmers that the mountain was left bare. This adversely affected the rainfall. Consequently, each summer there would be no work and soon the mines closed. The ex-mining population converged on the little port of St Helens. In 1900 Lottah had been the official centre of Portland. This was succeeded in 1908 by Goulds Country, and finally, in 1958, St Helens became supreme.

St Helens today is one of the most popular holiday towns in the state, and it is easy to see why. Not only is it beautiful and blessed with a pleasant climate, but it is well placed to be reached in a matter of two or three hours from the north or south. The inhabitants all seem to be friendly and obliging about giving directions, but then we suppose they're used to visitors!

Touring St Helens

As you enter St Helens on Route A3, turn right into Tully St. Along Tully St, you can visit the site of the first Church of England and the old cemetery. Turn right into Cecilia St, the main street of St Helens. Here you'll see St Helens and Stanilaus Roman Catholic Church, built in 1922 and containing the bell from the barque, *Queen of the Sea*, wrecked in 1877. Almost opposite, just before St Paul's, is the old St Helen's Trading Company store, built in 1887.

St Paul's Church of England was built in 1884, the foundation stone being laid by Bishop Sandford on May 24th of that year. The beautiful church is made of hand-made baked apricot clay bricks, and the walls of the nave are built in colonial band: 3 courses of headers and one course of stretchers. The chancel opened in 1929 and the hard red clay bricks came from Hobart. Inside are lovely windows, and on the left as you enter, is the original ground plan of the church. A book is available in the church detailing the first 100 years of this beautiful building—the second church of England to be built in St Helens.

Next to the library, at Number 57 Cecilia St, is the very interesting **Local History Room**. When we visited we found a treasure trove of items relating to the history of the area, all arranged in an inviting and orderly fashion. Around the room were screens depicting stages in the area's history, and a mass of photographs, all with captions. There was also a valuable library, a video recorder, which ran all day, and assorted museum items. One of the most impressive of these was a big bell made from solid brass, taken from the Anchor Mine. We also saw what may have been the last ward case in the state. This arrived on a sailing ship in 1875, in the guise of a portable hot-house bringing English trees and plants to the colony. Next, it was used in a store in Lottah, and finally arrived in St Helens. On top of the case is a black hat, which once belonged to George Avery, a well-known coach driver for Pages, who drove a regular route between St Helens and St Marys. During the late 1800s, Avery had a distinguished passenger—the Duke of Edinburgh—this was the hat he was wearing on this occasion. Descendants of Mr Avery still live in the area.

The History Room staff will give you any information you require about local history walks. You can even arrange for a custom-made escorted tour; a staff member will accompany you in your own car and act as navigator and encyclopaedia combined!

The St Helens History Room is open from 9 a.m.–5 p.m. each weekday, as well as Saturday mornings and Sunday afternoons.

St Helen's History Room

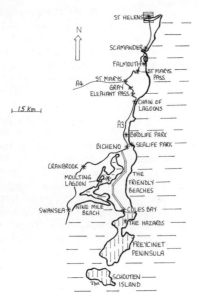

It has been greatly enlarged. Opposite, at No. 11, is a house built in 1890 and formerly used as a shop.

No. 5 Cecilia St is a weatherboard house which was built in around 1870; making it one of the earliest houses in the town. It was the home of a Dr Penny.

No. 1, Cecilia St , occupies the site of the office of the Siamese Tin Company.

The Siamese Tin Company was a London firm that sent an agent to Tasmania in 1930 to investigate the tin deposits at the Georges River. A race was cut from below the St Columba Falls on the South George River to a point on Powers Rivulet. The company established an office in St Helens, but closed down at the start of World War II.

A much more detailed guide to the interesting places in St Helens is available from the History Room.

Many of the streets and features of St Helens have Greek names, bestowed by the classically learned Surveyor General George Frankland in the 1840s. These include Golden Fleece Rivulet, Atlas, Circassian and Cecilia Streets, Dianas Basin and Medeas Cove—not to speak of St Helens itself, whose name put me in mind of the famed Helen of Troy. Maybe lovely St Helens town has launched a thousand ships in her time, too!

Binalong Bay is about 10 km north of St Helens, and is reached on Route C850. Turn off Cecilia St and drive round the coast. On your right, in St Georges Bay, you may see fishing boats and nets. A sandbar across the mouth of the bay causes unwary fishermen some problems. On the right out from St Helens is Humbug Point, a state recreation area.

Two km from Binalong Bay are two turn-offs. The middle road, Route C848, leads to 'The Gardens', an area named by Lady Jane Franklin, who saw the wildflowers when she drove a horse and buggy through

On the corner of Cecilia and Quail Streets, on your left when you leave the History Room, is a magnolia tree which was planted in the 1870s. Opposite the old tree, on the right, is the first hotel to be built in St Helens, erected in 1863.

Number 30 Cecilia St is a shop built in 1888, and on your left between Cecilia and Bowen Streets are a gas light and a memorial to Mr B. Wright, who was a bank manager and who planted a number of elm trees round the streets in 1890.

Numbers 6 Cecilia St and 1 Circassian St were, respectively, baker's shop and bakery, and at the corner of Groom and Circassian Streets is the St Helens District High School, made of apricot brick and built in 1874. A booklet called *Then and Now*, telling something of the school's history, was published in 1974.

On your left, back on Cecilia St, and just before the Esplanade, you will see the Bayside Inn, which was once a tiny hotel called the 'Bay View' and was built in 1866.

St Helens

the area in 1840. Many visitors go there expecting a garden. On the way you will pass Grants Lagoon, Swimcart Beach, Sloop Lagoon, Taylors Beach and Big Lagoon. The bay is the Bay of Fires. The road to the right takes you to Binalong Bay, where you will be welcomed by a large and impressive statue of a bathing beauty. Binalong Bay is a reserve and a popular camping place in summer. The sand here is particularly white, and the bay itself very wide and inviting.

On returning to St Helens from Binalong Bay, turn left into Cecilia St..

St Helens Point. Drive over the Golden Fleece Bridge at Jasons Gates. On your left is Georges Bay, on your right Medeas Cove. Jasons Gates was first bridged in 1881 with a Huon Pine bridge. Just before Jason St, on the right, is the site once occupied by the smelters of tin for the Anchor Mine. The house there was built in 1923, and is called 'Queechy'. Past Jason St, also on your right you will see 'Fair Lea', a graceful brick house built in 1897. To reach St Helens Point, turn left onto Route C851. About 2.5 km along this road, you reach the impressive sand dunes at

Akaroa. It is about 1 km to St Helens Point state recreation ground. South east of Akaroa is St Helens Island.

Interesting features between St Helens and St Marys. St Marys is about 30 km away from St Helens. To get there, you leave the town on Route A3. Just out of town, you may see black swans on your left in the bay, and a little later, on your right, is Dianas Basin. Cross Crockers Arm Bridge over Crockers Arm Creek. Next comes the small settlement of Beaumaris. The mountains well over to your right are Skyline Tiers. After this comes Scamander, another fishing village, (originally called Yarmouth) and the Scamander Coastal reserve, which is low tea-tree scrub and gum, short and stunted, typical of the east coast. Here there are wide peat marshes and lagoons, favourite habitats of the black swans.

Scamander was first explored by the surveyor John Helder Wedge in 1825. Its river has been known, variously, as the 'Borthwick', 'Hansons Creek', and, currently, the 'Scamander River'! Just over Styx Creek, a property called

'**Enstone Park**' may be seen on the left; a big square house with a lot of windows. This house was built in 1867 by John Steel. The property was first settled in 1829 by William Steel, who named it 'Thomsons Villa' and who later became the first known casualty of the St Helens bar when his ship foundered there in 1826 (or 1834). He had been bringing equipment from England to set up a flour mill. The farm passed to his nephew Michael Steel, who leased it to his brother John. It was John's son, Leslie John Steel, who gave it its present name and lived there until his death in 1968.

Choice of Routes from St Helens

Route A3. Past Scamander Reserve, you have a choice of routes. Route A3 turns off to the left and follows the coast in a wide sweep. Until the early 1990s, this was a minor road, but is now a major route. If you take this route, you will be able to visit Falmouth, the holiday resort at Four Mile Creek, and Ironhouse Point (named for the first cottage in the area to have an iron roof), but you will miss driving the St Marys and Elephant Passes and arrive at Chain of Lagoons. The road to Falmouth turns off Route A3.

Falmouth was surveyed by John Helder Wedge and settled in 1829 by Captain John Henderson and William Steel. The town offers splendid views of the coastline, and has some rather interesting modern buildings.

To visit St Marys, Fingal and Avoca from Chain of Lagoons, turn right into Route A4, and drive the several winding kilometres of Elephant Pass. At the top of the pass, follow the signs to St Marys and take up the drive at the end of the following section.

Route A4. Instead of following Route A3 to the left and following the road around the coast, you can turn into Route A4. This is the original route to St Marys and the South East. If you take this route, you will enter St Marys Pass, 7 km of winding road which climbs constantly. This road through the pass has existed since the early 1860s. At the top of the pass is the town of St Marys, at the headwaters of the South Esk River system and close to the Mt Nicholas Range. **The South Esk River** was (in 1892) the first Australian river to be used to generate hydro-electric power, when the Duck Reach Scheme was begun. On 10 December, 1895 Launceston had power.

St Marys. St Marys, a small town with a population of fewer than 1000, is the major coal mining centre in Tasmania, and is also a major depot which distributes hydro-electric power to the east coast. It was originally known as Break O' Day Plains.

In and around St Marys

On your left as you enter the town from the St Marys Pass is the Patricks Head walking track, 2 km through St Marys reserve. St Patricks Head itself is 694 metres high and was named by Captain Tobias Furneaux in 1773.

As you drive through the town you'll see a few older buildings. St Marys Hotel is brick, built c. 1916, replacing a wooden pub which burnt down.

St Marys Hotel

The hospital was built in 1927, and St Marys railway station, which you pass just as you leave the town on the way to Fingal, was built in 1886. It is no longer a working station, but when we saw it in 1996, it had been recently repainted.

Two km west of St Marys, on your left, is Christ Church, built in 1847. The 'Cullenswood' sheep property was granted to Robert Vincent Legge and is still in the Legge family today. Robert arrived in Van Diemen's Land in 1827 and shortly afterwards settled at 'Cullenswood', which he named for his old family home in Ireland. A Roman Catholic church was built near Christ Church, but only the old cemetery remains.

North-west of St Marys is the high conical point of Mt Nicholas, 850 m. above sea level.

Route A4 to Fingal. About 4 km west of St Marys, is a turn-off to the right to a little township called Cornwall. The Cornwall coal mine, discovered in 1886 by George Crisp of Avoca, was reopened a few years ago, and the Blackwood mine is still functioning. Away to your right you can see the Nicholas Range. Just before you enter the town of Fingal there is a left hand turn to Duncans coal mine.

Fingal—history and tour

Fingal, (pronounced fin-GORL), was named by Roderic O'Connor in around 1824, and surveyed by John Helder Wedge. **Roderic O'Connor** (1784–1860), was an Irishman who arrived in Tasmania in his own ship, the *Ardent*, in 1824, bringing with him a Kerry cow and some stud sheep—and the first Irish immigrants to the colony, including his sons Arthur and William, and George Parker and his family. The O'Connors came from Castle Bangan, Westmeath.

A friend of Governor Arthur, O'Connor was one of the most active pioneers in the east, being responsible for the building of a number of important roads and bridges. He was appointed as a Land Commissioner, and later as Inspector of Roads and Bridges, a position he held until 1836. He owned at least two properties: a thousand-acre land grant, 'Connorville', at Lake River (the present Poatina), and Benham, just out of Avoca on the Royal George Road. The original 'Benham House' was burnt down, but 'Connorville' is still standing. Both properties are still in the O'Connor family. Two of the early properties of Fingal are 'Malahide' to the north and 'Tullochgoram' to the south-west of the town. These were granted to William Talbot and James Grant respectively, in the 1820s.

The town of Fingal was established shortly after these grants (in 1827) as a convict station, and gold was found nearby in 1852. Enter Fingal by crossing the Fingal Rivulet, or Township Creek. The highway runs into Talbot St, named for the pioneer William Talbot of 'Malahide', who was a brother of Lord Talbot.

To the south-east is Bare Rock, an intriguing example of natural sculpture. If you look towards the rock in the morning, the figure of an Aborigine can be seen, facing west. In the afternoon you can see a priest with a prayer book, facing east. Cross Pedder and Fraser Streets, and look to your

St Joseph's Church, Fingal

left to see a very old building known as 'Egans'. Turn up Grant St to see the Uniting Church, built in 1882, then turn left into Seymore St. On the corner of Seymore and Victoria Streets is one of Tasmania's oldest schools (1884). Along to the right is St Joseph's Roman Catholic Church (1880), built by a local, Michael Lattin.

The foundation stone was laid in 1887. Inside the church is a memorial plaque to Milo John Reginald Talbot (1912–1973), the 7th Baron de Malahide. The title was originally granted to Hon. William Talbot in 1826.

Back on Talbot St, on your right, is the Holder Brothers Store Building, established in 1859, and on your left, is the old Tasmania Hotel built of stone from the Prison barracks during the 1840s.

Farther west, on your right, are the new Council Chambers building, (1974), the library, and the Historical Society. If you turn right into Brown St, and follow Route B43, you will cross Fingal Rivulet and then reach a Y-fork. The left fork leads to a bridge over the South Esk River, then on to the golf course and right to Mathinna (26 km to the north), and left to Mangana, (10 km north-west). Gold was first discovered at Mangana in 1852. The right fork leads 2 km to 'Malahide'.

Mathinna

Mathinna, (named after an Aboriginal girl) was once a major gold-mining centre and one of the largest towns in the state. There a number of old buildings and a cemetery still to be seen, and a nearby attraction is the Mathinna Falls Reserve. To reach the reserve, take Route C423, north of the town, and cross the South Esk To reach the Evercreech Forest Reserve, drive east on Route B43 and turn left onto Route C430, the Evercreech Road.

Tour of Fingal, continued. Return to Talbot St, and on your left you will see the Fingal Hotel, (once known as the Talbot Arms) which was built in 1844. The hotel has what is reputed to be the largest collection of Scotch whisky in the Southern Hemisphere: 348 bottles have been collected since the war years!

Farther on, across Gleadow St, is St Peter's Anglican Church.

The foundation stone of this church was laid in 1867, but the building was not consecrated until ten years later. Its final completion was greatly due to the determination of the rector, Rev. John Chambers. The original shingle roof of the church has since been replaced with slate.

Old Tasmanian Hotel, now the Tourist Centre

Fingal Hotel Scotch whiskey display

St Peter's, Fingal

The windows inside commemorate some of the pioneers—including Richard Gilbert Talbot of 'Malahide'. Members of early families are buried in the graveyard. Between Gleadow and Short Streets is the railway station (1886) and the Town Hall (1882), which succeeded the Council Chambers built in 1844, is opposite the post office.

Fingal to Avoca. Between Fingal and Avoca, on your right, are Blackmans Marsh and Woodlawn Marsh and, on your left, the intriguingly named Jack the Liars Creek. On your right are the properties of 'Tullochgorum', (granted to James Grant in 1824), 'Rostrevor' and 'Ormley'. The

high mountain about 8 km east of Avoca is St Pauls Dome, about 400 metres high.

'Tullochgorum' estate began as a 2000-acre land grant to Mr James Grant in 1824. Grant came from Nairn, in Scotland, and named his new home after the birthplace of his father (Rev. James Grant), in Invernesshire. James Grant's brother John was also given a land grant, this time of 1500 acres, and more land was added from time to time until the present, when the 'Tullochgorum' property comprises 25 000 acres.

The Grants preferred the Merino sheep to the more usual crossbreds, and this, added to the goods and plants James had cannily

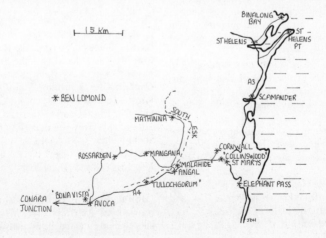

'Marlborough House', Avoca

St Thomas's Church Parish Hall, Avoca

brought with him to Van Diemen's Land, helped to make the family one of the richest and most influential of their day. After the death of James Grant's son, (also James Grant), in 1879, a relative named Henry von Stieglitz took over the property. Towards the end of last century, the original homestead burnt down and had to be rebuilt.

Avoca

Avoca, at the junction of the South Esk and St Pauls Rivers, was originally known as 'St Pauls Plains'. The town was planned and named in 1833 by the ubiquitous John Helder Wedge, who surveyed so much of the district.

From Avoca, you may take Route B42 to Rossarden, (at the foot of Ben Lomond) once the major tin-producing area of Australia. The tin mine there closed down in 1982.

There are interesting walking tracks in the Rossarden area, leading through the State Forest and to the top of Ben Lomond. Rossarden may also be reached from Fingal, via Mangana. The steep hill leading to Rossarden is known as 'Pepper Hill', and is the terror of the local cyclists.

Another route out of Avoca is Route C301 to Royal George, once a coaching stage.

Around Avoca. As you travel west from Fingal, you will be passing the timber mill on your right just before entering Avoca. The main street is Falmouth St.. Look out for the Union Hotel, built c. 1842 on your left. Just past this is the Parish Hall (c.1850). Turn right into Blenheim St to see handsome 'Marlborough House' (1845), which has been used variously as hotel, boys' school, coaching inn and private residence. Close by is St Thomas's Anglican Church, built in 1842. The architect was James Blackbum, who also designed the more famous church at Port Arthur.

To see 'Greyfort Cottage', home of Irish pioneer, Captain James Grey, and one of the first homes in Avoca, take Route B42 towards Rossarden. Cross the South Esk River and, on your right, is the cottage. Captain Grey's brother Major William Grey, lived near the Rockford Cemetery along the Royal George Road, and a cousin, Humphrey Grey, owned 'Eastbourne', about 6 km west of Avoca.

Past 'Greyfort Cottage', there is a turn-off left. This leads to 'Bona Vista'.

'Bona Vista'. Simeon Lord was transported Australia in 1791, and was subsequently granted the property of 'Bona Vista' in 1820. The homestead, begun in the 1830s and completed in 1842, was occupied by Simeon Lord Jr and his wife Sarah Birch, and is now classified with the National Trust. One of the major homesteads of the Avoca area, 'Bona Vista' was built of local stone around a central courtyard. Martin Cash, infamous bushranger, was once a groom at the house. When we visited the Avoca area in 1988, 'Bona Vista' could be visited upon request at the manager's house on the property. It was very large and very dark. We lost our sense of direction and every time we tried to get out of the house we ended up back in the central courtyard! When we returned to the area in 1996, there was a sign on the gate forbidding entry, so ask advice locally before trying to visit the old house.

Another choice of routes!

From Avoca, you have another choice of routes.

West Towards Conara. You can continue west towards Conara Junction, passing Humphrey Grey's old property 'Eastbourne' before you come to a right turn leading to Bonneys Plains. Sally's great-great-great-great-great-uncle Christopher Atkins Bonney had a land grant there which he and his brother Thomas sold to their brother Joseph, who subsequently named the area. From this road it is about 15 km west to Conara Junction.

East to St Marys and the South-east Coast. If you choose to continue your trip down the east coast, you will have to return to St Marys and go back down the Elephant Pass towards Chain of Lagoons.

BIBLIOGRAPHY

Books
MASTERS, David, *St Pauls Plains— Avoca; 1834–1884.*

Pamphlets
'An Introduction To Lottah and Goulds Country'
'A Walk of History Around St Helens'
'A Visitors Guide to Walking on The Blue Tier'
'Places to Visit while holidaying in St Helens'
  (all from the St Helens History Room)
'Notable Tasmanian Homes', St Michaels School, Launceston
'Let's Talk About Fingal Valley District'
'Let's Talk About The St Helens District'
  (Tasmanian Visitor Corporation)

Maps
Tasmap 1: 100 000 Topographic Map Land Tenure Index Series
'Break O' Day', 'Cape Portland', 'Georges Bay', 'St Pauls'.

Information
Thanks to Tony Hendricks, Pat Rubenach, Mrs Cowie and the staff of the St Helens History Room.

11. The East Coast Road to Orford

Features of this drive

If you follow the drive described in this chapter, you'll visit some more of the charming east coast towns, see historic houses and reminders of two local heroines, visit Sea Life and Bird Life centres, see wide and beautiful bays, visit convict ruins on an island, the biggest billiard table in Tasmania, an historic bark mill, some odd rock formations and some pink mountains. You'll also drive one of the most winding stretches of road in the state—the Elephant Pass. There are plenty of sources of food, petrol and accommodation.

A choice of routes

The drive down the east coast is an interesting one: often in sight of the sea and rarely any great distance between towns and settlements.

The climate of the east is generally drier and milder than the west, and droughts can sometimes be a problem.

Instead of going to Fingal, you may choose to stay with the east coast and continue on Route A3 to the Elephant Pass and Bicheno, or of course you may double back from Avoca and retrace your steps to St Marys.

If you have chosen to continue on Route A3 and have by-passed St Marys and the St Marys and Elephant Passes, you'll begin this drive from Chain of Lagoons at the foot of the Elephant Pass.

Elephant Pass. Four km from St Marys on Route A4 is the tiny hamlet of Gray, which, (despite what we said above), has one of the highest rainfalls in Tasmania. It was named after an early pioneering family in the district. Gray once supported a number of farms and a post office and two churches, but these have now vanished. There is a walking track from Gray through the William Appsley Forest Reserve to Bicheno.

To descend to the coast from St Marys, you will now enter the Elephant Pass; 10 km of winding road even more ferociously impressive than St Marys Pass, and first mapped out by a German named William Meinas. Elephant Pass is the namesake of Mount Elephant, which at some angles appears as a silhouette of that animal. Coming into the pass from St Marys you might like to stop at the Famous Mt Elephant Pancake Barn, which was established in 1979. Pancakes are a house specialty.

Route A3 to Bicheno

At the foot of the Elephant Pass is Chain of Lagoons, with a small road turning off to the left to take you to Lagoons Beach. Turn right into Route A3. After a while, you'll pass Piccaninny Point and Long Point on your left. The bay is Maclean Bay. An interesting attraction 7 km north of Bicheno is the East Coast Bird Life Park on the left. Opened in 1981, the park consists of 32 hectares of natural coastal wet land habitat. The animals in the park

Bicheno

are free ranging, and include Bennett's wallaby, forester kangaroo, brush-tailed possums, Cape Barren geese, Tasmanian devils, Tasmanian native hens, bald coots, black swans, cockatoos and pelicans. Feed bags are available at the kiosk, near the souvenir shop. A spacious restaurant overlooks the park, which is open 9 a.m.– 5 p.m. every day. On your left a few km closer to the town is Diamond Island, a wildlife reserve inhabited by penguins.

Bicheno

Bicheno, (pronounced BEE–sh'n–o). is a small town of between 400 and 500 inhabitants, a fishing port since the early 1800s. Sealers and whalers were early visitors to the port, (known at that time as Waubs Boat Harbour), and when coal mining began nearby in 1854, it became a coal port as well. Fishing is the main occupation, and the abalone industry began in the 1960s. Bicheno is a popular spot with fishermen and artists, the whole town being dominated by the wild grandeur of rocks and sea.

The town was named for Mr James Ebenezer Bicheno (1786–1851), who was a Colonial Secretary of Van Diemen's Land. He seems to have been above all for the immensity of his trousers!

Around Bicheno

The Sealife Centre. On the left of the road, just as you enter Bicheno is the Sealife Centre, open daily from around 9.30 a.m.– 6 p.m. Inside the centre are some very well-set-up aquariums, where you may stand practically eye to eye with huge conger eels, crayfish, trevally, giant crabs and even an octopus. Children love it, running backwards and sideways in an attempt to see everything at once. Also on display are some convict-made bricks, around 150-years old.

Outside the aquarium stands the old scow *Enterprise* built at Battery Point in 1902. She was made mainly from local materials, timbers including stringy bark, blue gum and celery top pine. *Enterprise* carried timber for many years, having a lucky escape from St Helens bar in 1958. She had an eventful working life—even being at one stage a film star, and after retirement in 1976 was lovingly looked after by Mr Bill Price, deck-hand in 1919; owner by

The Enterprise *at Bicheno*

1956. Mr Price sold *Enterprise* to the Sealife Centre in 1980, where she is a great favourite with visitors particularly children who swarm around the decks with far more ease than adults.

Also on display is the anchor from the barque *Otago* which was 147 m long, and had a 26 m beam. *Otago* was the only command of the writer Joseph Conrad (1857–1924). She was built in Glasgow in 1869 and traded all around the world, ending her days in Hobart, beached on Risdon graveyard. There is also a huge black funnel salvaged from the steam dredge *Macquarie*, built in Scotland in 1908 for the Strahan Marine Board, and now lying in a ships' graveyard off Betsy Island near the entrance to Derwent Pier. Children enjoy climbing through the funnel.

Two Local Heroines. Past the Sealife Centre, leave the Beachfront Motor Inn to your right and continue on Route A3. On your left is Waubs Beach. The road forks, with the right hand route going on to Swansea and Sorell. Turn left into Burgess St. In the park behind the local hall is the grave of an Aboriginal woman named Waubedebar, for whom Waubs Harbour was named. Waubedebar is a local heroine who rescued two men when their boat was smashed during a storm.

Nearby, opposite the school in James St, is the Old Gaol House, built in the 1840s. During the 1850s, this house was the home of another local heroine, Mary Harvey, wife of the town constable. Mary saved her husband when he was attacked by a thief and then helped with the rescue of a boy whose boat was swamped by high seas. For this Mary was known as an 'Australian Grace Darling'. She died in 1911.

The Gulch, the Blowhole and Rocking Rock. Turn right into James St, then left into the road leading to the Gulch. On your left, facing the sea, is Waubs Harbour, once the tryworks for whalers (1816). Here you'll pass a fish processing plant. Just ahead is the rocky inlet known as 'The Gulch', where the fishing boats come in to anchor.

The boat harbour and the jetty are there as well, and to the left you can see Governors Island. There is a walking track round the Esplanade.

From the picnic area near The Gulch, the walking track continues out over the rocks, marked by splashes of red paint. From the rocks you can see a good view of the famous Blowhole and the Rocking Rock, 80 tonnes of granite making a strange formation which appears to balance impossibly and rocks gently with the waves.

If you drive to the end of the Esplanade, you can climb right down to the Rocking Rock, but be careful; at high tide the area can be dangerous. There are a number of pleasant walks around Bicheno, including tracks to the lookouts on the two hills above town.

Rocking Rock, Bicheno

Freycinet Peninsula— some history and a tour

From Bicheno the way leaves the coast and heads west until it comes to the turn-off onto Route C302. This turn-off takes you to Coles Bay and the Freycinet National Park on Freycinet Peninsula. The Freycinet Peninsula is named after the French explorer Louis de Freycinet (1779–1 842), an officer on Nicholas Baudin's expedition. Baudin (1754–1803) explored parts of the Australian coastline in 1801 and 1802. With two ships, *Geographe* and the *Naturaliste* he sighted the south-west coast of Tasmania in January 1802. The ships sailed up the channel by easy stages, and an expedition under the command of Freycinet sailed up the River Du Nord (now the Derwent) as far as Risdon. Baudin died at Mauritius in 1803.

On the right, 1 km past Bicheno, are the ruins of an old stone house. Cross the Lilla Villa bridge over the Apsley River. After a while you'll see the moulting lagoons, a wildlife sanctuary where the black swans and wild ducks gather. On the left is a turn-off to the Friendly Beaches. Shortly after this turn-off you see Mt Peter on your left and a little farther on, Mt Paul.

The Hazards. As you come towards Coles Bay look out for those pink mountains; the spectacular red granite Hazards which rise to your right.

The Hazards appear to have been named after Captain Richard Hazard in 1924. Or perhaps it was after a Captain Albert 'Black' Hazard? And was he the Master of the *Thalia*, or of the *Promise* or even conceivably of both? And was he really wrecked off Promise Rock, and did he truly abscond with a cargo of whale oil to South America? Goodness knows—but it makes a good story. Or stories.

Individually, the Hazards are named Mount Dove (about 500 m), Mount Amos (about 460 m), and Mount Maysom (about 430 m). Mount Dove is named for Thomas

The Hazards, Coles Bay

Dove M.A., Mount Amos for the Amos brothers and Mount Maysom for Rev. Joseph Maysom, Anglican minister in the area for over thirty years.

Coles Bay. Before European settlement, Coles Bay was a favourite place of the Aborigines. The first Europeans to arrive were whalers in the early 19th century. Chinese tin miners followed, and now the place is renowned throughout Tasmania as a camping area. Fishing, quarrying for red granite, and tourism are the main industries, and there seems to be a truly bewildering choice of places to stay.

The bay and township were named after a man called Silas Cole, an early settler in the Swansea district who used to burn shells on the beaches to make lime. The various beaches are screened by dunes and are full of wildlife: we saw a number of small fish caught in tide pools and even some rather disgusting-looking sea slugs.

The Freycinet National Park is a popular place with bushwalkers. There is a great variety of wild flowers in the area: on a short half-hour walk we noted as many as 15 different species, a number of which we had never seen before. The Tasmanian Field

Naturalists Club, formed in 1904, apparently held an Easter camp there in 1910. The interest and encouragement of the members was rewarded when the area was declared as a National Park in 1916. Around Coles Bay township itself there are walks suitable for small children, scrambles up the rocky hills and the sand dunes along Muirs Beach. In the National Park you can choose from walks ranging from short strolls to a 10-hour trip via Mount Graham to Cooks Beach on the east of the Peninsula. Schouten Island, just across the one km wide Schouten Passage, may be reached by boat. The island was named by Abel Tasman in 1642, after a member of the Council of the Dutch East India Company, and it was once mined for coal.

From Coles Bay to Cranbrook. When you leave Coles Bay, turn left at the sign which says 'Swanwick', continue on the road to the left and soon you will come to a beautiful view of Swanwick Bay and Great Oyster Bay with the Hazards rising way over to the left. Schouten Island is to the far left and the long spit known as Nine Mile Beach is almost straight ahead. Point Bagot is on the tip of the spit.

Leaving the Freycinet Peninsula Road, turn

left and take Route A3 towards Swansea. Cross Apslawn Creek. 'Apslawn' is a property settled by William Lyne in 1826. To your right soon after is the Freycinet Vineyard, and down to the left, just after the vineyard, you can see Great Oyster Bay. Once again you will see the Hazards over the bay. Cross the Swan River and pass the walnut plantation of Vecon. Shortly after this is a turn-off to the right to the property of 'Glen Heriot', owned by a member of the Amos Family. Next you come to the tiny town of Cranbrook where there are a number of historic houses.

Gala Kirk, near Swansea

Gala Kirk and the Amos Family. On the left, soon after entering the town, is Gala Kirk, the Uniting Church which was built in 1845. This is a true country church, complete with a notice asking visitors to shut the door to keep the swallows out! We first visited Gala Kirk in 1988, a further visit in 1996 found it just as beautiful as ever. We turned back to read our original comments in the Visitors' Book, and couldn't think of a better way of putting it! Inside the church is a lovely carved wooden plaque, commemorating Adam Amos of 'Glen Gala', his wife and their three sons, James, John and Adam. Also honoured are John Amos of 'Cranbrook' and his wife and son James, born at Gala Water in Scotland. This plaque was erected on the 100th anniversary of the family's arrival at Hobart.

The Amos families were granted the properties 'Glen Gala' and 'Cranbrook', and through their efforts Gala Kirk was built. Another marble plaque is for Alfred John Amos of 'Cranbrook' (1845–1922). Alfred John was the son of James and grandson of John Amos and was the first child to christened in the church.

There is also a white marble plaque commemorating Rev. Thomas Dove M.A., the first minister of the church and the first Christian minister of the East Coast. Rev. Dove was born in Glasgow, Scotland, in 1803 and arrived in Swanport in August 1844. He died at Swansea in 1882, aged 79. Mt Dove, (one of the Hazards) is named after him.

In the vestry is a collection of old photos, showing the centenary of Gala Kirk in 1945. Also on display is a photograph of Lavinia Amos of 'Cranbrook', the first white baby girl born in Great Swanport. Lavinia was the elder sister of twins, who in 1846 married Henry Cotton of 'The Grange', a property a few km south east of 'Cranbrook'. Henry was eldest son of Francis and Anna Maria Cotton. (See below.)

Gala Kirk is whitewashed brick or stone, and its bell was presented by Richard Cleburne of the Hobart Merchants, on 21 October, 1845.

Just across the paddock from Gala Kirk is the old graveyard, containing several interesting headstones. These include John Banfield, who came from Cornwall, and died in 1858, aged 40, and Alfred Cole, who drowned in 1873 aged 17. Whole families are buried there, including the Lyne family of 'Apslawn', the Robertson family, and also Jessica Barbara Bethune, sister-in-law of James Amos of 'Cranbrook'.

Also commemorated are Rev. H.T. Hull (1858–1933) and Mabel his wife, the daughter of Adam Amos Jr. To the north east of the Gala Kirk is the homestead 'Glen

Gala'. The first house on this site, built in 1821, burnt down in 1827, as did a second house in 1858. The present two-storey house was built in 1860.

Over the Swan River from 'Glen Gala' is Cranbrook House', built of brick in 1833 for John Amos.

Towards Swansea— some interesting sights

Soon after you leave Cranbrook you will cross the Cygnet River, and 10 km past Cranbrook is Swansea, originally called 'Great Swanport' and then 'Waterloo Point'. The name 'Swansea' was chosen by George Meredith, after a town of the same name in Wales.

Between Cranbrook and Swansea is a turn-off to the right. This is Route B34, the road to Lake Leake, c. 30 km away. Look to your right to see 'Riversdale. The flour mill was built in 1828, the homestead 10 years later. 'Riversdale belonged to George Meredith. It is surrounded by a charming English garden. Cross the Wye River.

Shortly before you enter Swansea, cross the Wet Marsh Bridge. Here there is a turn-off to the left, the Swan River Road. If you drive along this road and turn off to the right, you will reach Nine Mile Beach as seen from Swanwick.

Next, cross over the Meredith River: somewhere on the northern bank is the property called 'Cambria', which once belonged to George Meredith (see below) and on the southern bank is the property called 'Redbanks'. On your right is 'Redcliffe House', built in around 1835 and offering colonial accommodation.

Early Settlers around Swansea

The Swansea area was settled in 1821. Early settlers included Lt George Meredith and Adam and John Amos. We have heard

a few conflicting reports about the which of these settlers actually settled where, but the following information should be reasonably correct. We look forward to hearing from any local historians who might wish to suggest any corrections.

Lt George Meredith was a Welsh landowner. He and his second wife Mary came out to Tasmania on the ship *Emerald* in 1821, and settled at the property they named 'Cambria' on the Meredith River, about 2 km north of the present town of Swansea. By 1824, George had established two whaling stations, one on Maria Island and one on Schouten Island. These interests abandoned during the 1830s. George and Mary had several children, including John, (the first white child to be born in Glamorgan), Charles, and Edwin, (who emigrated to New Zealand). Charles married his cousin Louisa Anne Twamley, whose story is told in the book *A Tigress in Tasmania* by Vivienne Ellis. Charles Meredith was Colonial Treasurer and Minister for Lands and Works in 1864. Louisa, who died in 1895, was a writer and gifted artist.

John Meredith—agriculturalist and pastoralist, was born at 'Cambria' on 31 October, 1822. When he grew up, he ran 'Cambria' until 1847, when he went to South Australia. In 1854 he returned to Swansea and bought 'Cambria'. In 1851 he married a Miss Hammond. The couple had nine children.

Adam and John Amos were brothers who landed at Hobart Town on 17 March, 1821 in the ship *Emerald*. The *Emerald* was the first ship to sail from England by private charter direct to Van Diemen's Land. Adam and his wife Mary Tate had eight children, John and his wife Hannah Hardie had nine. Despite this there are only four families of descendants left in the area. Adam and his family settled at 'Glen Gala', while John seems to have settled at 'Cranbrook'. 'Cranbrook House', on Cranbrook Estate, was built in the 1850s, replacing an earlier building, now largely fallen down. Other early settlers included William Lyne, who settled at 'Apslawn' in 1826, 'Edward Carr Shaw, who owned 'Redbanks', Captain King and his family who settled at Piermont, just past King's Bridge over the Stony River, and about 1 km south of Swansea, and the Cottons made their home at 'Kelvedon'.

Edward Carr Shaw was born in Terenure, in County Dublin, and died in 1885. He was descended from an old Scottish family; an ancestor, Captain William Shaw, had gone to Ireland with the army of William III, in 1689. Edward came first to Western Australia and then, in 1840, to Tasmania. In 1835 he married Anne Fenton of Dunlavin, County Wicklow and they had nine children. He later married Emma Goodall, from Birmingham. Edward and a partner, whose name was Orr, bought 'Redbanks' from George Meredith Jr. a son of Lt George Meredith, and lived there for fifty years. He became a J.P. and Coroner. His son, Frederick, (also a J.P.), was born in 1847. He rented 'Redbanks' from his father and later inherited the property. 'Redbanks', (which still belongs to the Shaw family), is situated close to 'Cambria' on the other side of the Meredith River. The population of the Swansea area expanded rapidly during the 1820s and 30s.

400 convicts lived in settlements at Rocky Hills and Waterloo Point, and the barracks housed many soldiers.

Please note; At the time of writing, these older homesteads are not open to the public, but anyone interested should ask locally for up-to-date information, perhaps at the tourist centre below. Some Tasmanian colonial houses do offer accommodation and/or teas and tours, but these are always well advertised at tourist bureaus.

Around Swansea. Swansea township has about 400 inhabitants. Build around Great Oyster Bay, it is one of the prettiest towns on the coast. After you enter Swansea you will see the **Swansea Bark Mill and Tourist Centre** on your right. The mill was established in 1885 by William Morey, with the present building being made by his son Frank during the 1920s. Swansea Bark Mill was built using Oyster Bay pines (indigenous to the area), in the rafters and posts throughout. Also used in the construction was Tasmanian oak and eucalypt. Visitors may watch tanning displays.

In a separate building are displays featuring settlement during the 1820s and early farm machinery. William Morey's mill is the only restored black wattle bark mill in Australia, open 9 a.m.–5 p.m. daily. At one time there was a flour mill as well.

Oyster Bay

Operation of the Mill. Tannic acid (a preservative), was extracted from the black wattle bark to be used in the tanning industry for tanning hides and making leather. Tanning in this fashion was done all over the world, using the bark of a variety of trees, but in Australia and particularly on Tasmania's east coast, the black wattle produced more tannic acid than any other known tree. Consequently, an export market developed and during the seventy year operation of the mill, over 1000 tons of bark were sent out of the area. Morey's mill was set up in the 1880s to break the bark up into chips and dust, which were then put in water so that the acid leached out. Hides and skins were put to soak in the resulting solution. The old plant has now been restored, and skins tanned by this method feel very soft.

The Swansea area has been a wool-producing area since its first settlement and the area now also produces premium wines. The Swansea Wine and Wool Centre, part of the Bark Mill complex, has a combination of both these products on display and for sale.

Historic buildings in town. As you drive along Franklin St in Swansea look, out on your right for Moreys Store, built in around 1850. On your left, shortly after it, is the Morris General Store, an old brick building dating from 1838. Constructed by James Alexander Graham as a general store, Morris's is believed to be the oldest building of its kind in Australia. James Morris bought the store in 1868.

James Morris (1839–1899), his wife Elizabeth and their son Tom sailed from Gravesend, England, in the ship *Fortitude* in 1853. He was so pleased with conditions in Van Diemen's Land that he prompted other members of his large family to follow his example. In 1859, James moved to Swansea to work for James Graham and when Graham died in 1868, the shrewd

Morris Store, Swansea

young man bought the store. It has been in his family ever since.

Past the general store on the right is the Glamorgan Community Centre. The local history museum and war memorial has a unique billiard table, built by Alcocks in 1860 from Tasmanian blackwood and weighing over one ton. Check locally for opening times. In Noyes St on the right, opposite the Glamorgan Courthouse, is 'Rockingham Villa', built in the 1860s. The first occupant of this house was Thomas Watson, who was the first Council Clerk. The Watson family was related to the Earl of Rockingham, and Sir George Farmer, first Police Superintendent of the area, married into that family. Also on your right is 'Meredith House', built in 1853 by J.A. Graham on land purchased from Charles Meredith. During its long history the house has been run as a maternity hospital, a girls' grammar school, a guest house and holiday flats, and has been known variously as 'Laughton House', 'Canberra Guest House' and, since 1987, by its current name. At one time it belonged to James Morris, and at another to Frank Morey! Opposite 'Meredith House' is All Saints Church, built in 1871. Also in Noyes St is the original council chambers, built in 1860 and still in use. There are several other historic buildings and sites in Swansea; a full list is available in the 'Let's Talk About Swansea' brochure.

Beyond Swansea

Spiky Bridge. As you leave Swansea, on the left you will see an old cottage and drystone walls. A few km from Swansea is Spiky Bridge Coastal Reserve and over to the right is the spiky bridge, an extraordinary collection of spikes of basalt standing upright along the edge of a small bridge. There is no permanent waterway: the bridge is actually a 'fill-in' of a small, very steep gully. Originally known as 'La Farelle's Bridge', the rubble stone walling bridge was built in 1843 by convicts from Rocky Hills, at the insistence of Edward Carr Shaw, who is said to have given a doubtful Major de Gillern, (superintendent of road parties) a pointed example of just how necessary the bridge was by driving a gig (with de Gillern as passenger) through the gully at high speed. Walk along the side of the bridge. The spikes were made from local rock which hereabouts has a strange flaky crystalline formation, splitting into sharp shards as if hit with a chisel. On the left is a beautiful view across Great Oyster Bay.

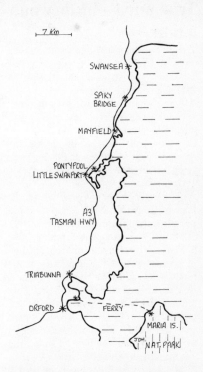

The Cottons of Kelvedon. One km past Spiky Bridge is 'Kelvedon' homestead, granted to Francis (1801–1883) and Anna Maria (1800–1882) Cotton in the late 1820s. The family had arrived on the ship *William and Mary Jellicoe* in 1828. The first Quaker meetings in Tasmania were held at 'Kelvedon', named after Anna Maria's home town in Essex. Francis and Anna Maria had a large family of fourteen children, twelve of whom, (Henry, Francis, Anna Maria, Thomas, Mary, George, John, James Backhouse, Tilney, (his mother's maiden name), Edward Octavius, Joseph, and Rachel), survived infancy. 'Lyings in means laying out', Francis is reported to have said when exasperated by the expenses incurred by such a large family, but his writings show him to have been a loving husband and father.

The Road to Triabunna. To the left is Kelvedon beach, another white sand beach. You can see a good view of Freycinet Peninsula and Schouten Island to the left. Pass 'Mayfield' (settled by the Buxton family) and cross the Buxton River, and soon you'll see a turn-off going off to the left towards Pontypool. Later, there is a long bridge over the Little Swanport River, a narrow stony stream with reed marshes spreading to left and right. In the marshes are black swans.

Look out for a sign indicating a Working Horse Museum. The Little Swanport River flows into Little Swanport, a sheltered inlet. Although the highway leaves the coast after Little Swanport, there are roads leading east to Hermitage Lagoon and Grindstone Bay. You'll be crossing a seemingly endless parade of quaintly-named creeks.

Triabunna—history and a tour

Twenty-two km from Little Swanport is the town of Triabunna, built on Spring Bay. The chief industries of the district are fishing and wood-chipping.

A couple of km before reaching the town, you will pass Rostrevor Reservoir on your left, 'Rostrevor House' and Rostrevor Creek on your right. In the 1880s, this property belonged to George Pitt. For many years it was the largest orchard property in Tasmania.

As you enter Triabunna you will see the Forestry Commission Depot. Drive on until you come to Franklin St, and turn in to see St Mary's Anglican Church, built in 1880. St Mary's is a very pretty little church, built of sandstone and featuring an unusual round window. To see St Anne's Catholic Church, drive on along Franklin St and turn left into Henry St. St Anne's is on the left, on the corner of Henry and Victoria streets. Built in 1868–69, the church was designed by Henry Hunter and built of stone from Okehampton Quarry, south-east of Triabunna, on the Freestone Point road. In 1969 it became necessary to render this church with cement. The bell is of interest, as it was donated to the church by Louisa Meredith. Mention of Louisa and her family has a habit of cropping up in the history of a number of Tasmanian towns, and indeed, her own book *My Home in Tasmania* has many graphic descriptions which bring to life the conditions of those days. If you enjoy reading about the horrors of mutton-bird pillows and the rigours of 19th century travel, get hold of a copy of Louisa's book!

At the end of Melbourne St is Dead Island. Apparently it is possible to walk over to this island at very low tide, to inspect the monuments there. These date from 1848 to 1860. Turn left into the Esplanade and pass a picnic ground and, on your left, the Spring Bay Hotel, built in 1838.

Okehampton and Woodstock. One of the older properties around Triabunna is 'Okehampton' c. 6 km east of Spring Bay, and c. 2 km north of Okehampton Bay. Nearby is Moreys Hill, named for the family that owned 'Okehampton'. Abraham Morey was born in Somersetshire in 1840, and farmed near Evandale for six years.

Just south of Triabunna, across MacLains Creek, is 'Woodstock', which was owned by Captain MacLaine. Mr Samuel Salmon, who was born in Oatlands in 1833, became a tenant of the property and later bought it. In 1880 he married Rachel Cotton. Just past 'Woodstock' is Salmons Flats.

Three km from Triabunna you come to a sign on the left, pointing the way to Route C319, and the Maria Island ferry, 2 km from the main road.

Maria Island

Down at the wharf by the Eastcoaster is the ferry which serves the Maria Island National Park. The island is 15 km away, across Mercury Passage. At the time of writing (1996) the ferry leaves for the island at 10.30 a.m., 1 p.m. and 3.30 p.m. and

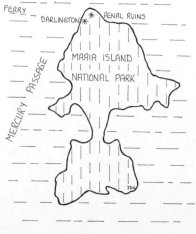

begins its return trips at 11 a.m., 1.30 p.m. and 4 p.m. An extra 9 a.m. service runs in summer and the trip takes around 25 minutes. For more information, ask locally. Maria Island, named by Abel Tasman, is 20 km long and 13 wide at the widest point. It has white beaches, sandstone and limestone cliffs, and a large variety of plants and animals, including the forty-spotted pardalote, which is found only in this part of Tasmania. In the north of the island is Darlington, an historic township settled in the 1830s, and including an old cemetery. Gas and wood barbecues and toilets and fresh water are available for use, and at the Penitentiary is a public telephone; a convenience which might have been much appreciated by early inhabitants! The island was a prison colony before Port Arthur, and the first Commandant, in 1825, was Lieutenant Murdoch. His wage was a princely 7s. 6d. per day! Apparently the 'basic wage' was around sevenpence halfpenny per day. According to one account we read, the convicts found it one of the better places to live, many of them preferring it to working for early settlers. At one time Maria Island was the site of a whaling station belonging to George Meredith, and managed by his son Charles.

In and around Orford

Back on the main road it is only a short distance into Orford, another small fishing town, built on the wide Prosser River. Cross by the pile and timber bridge (built in 1866). From here, Route C320 leads south past Orford Beach and Shelly Beach and Spring Beach and Rehban to Earlham Lagoon, which is a sanctuary. Not far from Shelly Beach is the old Orford stone quarry, opened in 1870. All quarrying here was done by hand, but the stone was reckoned to be first class, some of it even being taken to Melbourne to build the Law Courts there! Unfortunately the supply of good stone ran out and the quarry closed down

in 1890. Below the Quarry is Spring Beach, probably named for the permanent spring in the creek there.

Earlham. Near the Earlham Lagoon, on Route C320, the Rheban Road, is the property of 'Earlham', which once belonged to John Cotton, the fifth son of Francis and Anna Cotton of 'Kelvedon' near Swansea.

John Cotton was born in Great Swanport in 1832, and went to sea at 17 years of age. He married Mary Ann Wills, (a granddaughter of Edward Wills of London), in the early 1860s. The couple had three children, Edith, Howard, and Harold, but their sons died young. The daughter married William Harold Blyth, of Orford. The couple had two children. The 'Earlham' property was named after the home of well-known reformer Elizabeth Fry, a Quaker like the Cottons. The house was built in the early 1860s, using bricks hand-made on the property. The original building has been added to over the years, and stone walls were built around it in 1962. Since 1950 the property has belonged to the Chesterman family. The wool press at 'Earlham' was built by the Cottons, even the thread of the screws being painstakingly carved by hand. The barn which housed it was destroyed, but another building has been erected on the site to preserve the historic press and other pieces of machinery.

Route A3 continues from Orford and turns right to head towards Sorell, 53 km away, and Hobart (see Chapter 14).

BIBLIOGRAPHY
Books
COTTON, Frances, *Kettle on the Hob; the story of the Cottons*, 1986.
EMMETT, E.T. *Tasmania by Road and Track*, Melbourne University Press, 1952
NEWTTTT, Lyn, *Convicts and Carriageways*, Historical Committee of the

Department of Main Roads, Tasmania, 1988.
Cyclopaedia of Tasmania, 1900.
UBD Tasmania Street Directory.
RODGERS, Norah, *Notes on Whaling on the East Coast of Tasmania*.

Pamphlets
'100 Years at Swansea'
'Let's Talk About Bicheno' , 'Let's Talk About Swansea' (Tas. Visitor Corporation)
'The Miller's Pantry'
'Swansea Bark Mill'

'Welcome to Maria Island National Park',
'Freycinet National Park'
'Meredith House History.

Maps
Tasmap 1: 100 000 Land Tenure Index Series:
'Break O' Day', 'Freycinet', 'Prosser'.

Information
Thanks to Ruth Amos, Norah Rodgers, A. Scott and Mrs Turvey and the people of Swansea.

12. From Orford to Tasman Peninsula

Features of this drive

On this trip you'll see a magnificent old church with a fourteenth century window, sundry historic buildings, convict ruins, a gesticulating policeman, museums and hotels, more strange rock formations, a tessellated pavement, a Tassie Devil park, and Port Arthur.

After Orford. From Orford, the road leaves the coast for a while. On the left past the turn-off is 'Malunnah', an old homestead of sandstone, which was occupied by Charles and Louisa Meredith from 1868.
Louisa Anne Meredith (see also Chapter 11), well-known author of *My Home in Tasmania* and other books, was born in Birmingham in 1812 to Louisa (Meredith) Twamley and her husband Thomas, a miller. She was a niece of George Meredith, who became an important early settler in Swansea. In 1838, Charles, one of George Meredith's sons, returned to England and married Louisa in 1839. The couple soon sailed for Van Diemen's Land, and after a number of farming ventures, including a failed partnership with Charles' half-brother Edwin, Charles went into politics, and, before his death in 1880, became Acting Police Magistrate in Launceston. Louisa died in 1895.

The Old Convict Road. There is then a 7 km stretch of winding road with a high rocky cliff on the left and the Prosser River (known at this part as 'Paradise Gorge'), its banks built up with walls, to the right. On the other side the river is the remains of the old convict road which connected Triabunna (then known as 'Spring Bay') with Buckland, (known as 'Prosser Plains'). This road was built some time between 1841, when a Probation Station for newly arrived convicts was established at Buckland, and 1855, when the later Station at Paradise Gorge was closed down. The fire-damaged remains of the Paradise Station still remain in the bush, but are now on private property.

Buckland

It is 18 km south west from Orford to Buckland through Prossers Plains. Just before the turn-off to the right into Brockley Road, ('Brockley' being a pioneer homestead), you will pass Gatehouse Marsh, so named for a prominent early settler. Other features named for the same family are Gatehouse Ridge and Mount Gatehouse, a few km south of Buckland. Near Gatehouse Marsh are Twamley Hill and Twamley Flats, and a road which leads off to the left (c. 4 km) to the property of 'Twamley' itself.

Twamley — the Merediths and the Turveys. 'Twamley' (pronounced 'twomlee'), was built by Chief Justice Sir Francis Smith for his son, William Villeneuve Smith, in the early 1840s. He named it 'Villeneuve'. When the son left Tasmania in 1849, the property was rented by John Mitchell, and in 1856 it was bought by

Charles and Louisa Meredith. Louisa's maiden name had been 'Twamley' and she so renamed the property. The Merediths lived there for nine years, and in 1874 Frank Turvey (born in 1842 and the son of John Turvey, an ex-convict who had been transported for stealing a sheep), leased it. He bought it in 1884, and in that same year a report in the Tasmanian Mail described it as being a fine property of two and a half thousand acres, and spoke admiringly of the good drainage and the plentiful game! The writer also gave it as his opinion that the healthy Turvey family would not die out in the neighbourhood. In this he was quite correct, as 'Twamley' is still owned by a member of the family. It is currently a sheep-raising property.

The house is built of stone, the south and east walls of local material and the north and west of white stone brought by bullock wagon from Kangaroo Point Quarries (at Bellerive). A large barn was also built of the local stone.

Buckland—its history and a tour

Three roads meet at Buckland: the main A3 route, Route C318 to Woodsdale and Route C335 to Nugent and Copping. The area was originally known simply as 'Prosser Plains', but in 1846 Governor Franklin suggested the name 'Buckland' after Dean Buckland, and his suggestion was taken up by the residents. North-east of Buckland is the pioneer property of 'Woodsden', the oldest property in the district. 'Woodsden' was settled in 1824 by a man named Thomas Cruttendon, who built a stone farmhouse and named his home after his old home in Kent. On your way to Buckland you'll pass 'Court Farm' on the left. This old property belonged to the Gatehouse family. The handsome stone house which you see on your right as you enter the town is 'Wincanton', built in 1890 for William Gatehouse. 'Wincanton' was

the last stone house built in the district. Farther on, look away to your right to see the **old Buckland Inn**. The inn was first licensed on 7 October, 1845, the licensee being James Rawlines. The inn has been enlarged since then, but the original bar can still be seen. Just past the road to the inn is a left turn-off at Sally Peak Road, leading to the famous St John the Baptist's Church.

St John the Baptist's is one of the most famous and impressive of the churches of Tasmania. The architect was Crawford Cripps Wegman, and the builders were Andrew Artha Pty. Ltd.

The foundation stone was laid on 12 August, 1846. The building, which is apparently a copy of an English church, is surrounded by a sandstone wall, built in 1887, making it the only walled church in Tasmania. Included in the wall are massive sandstone gateposts. One of these gateposts is dedicated to Silas Alfred Gatehouse (1872–1952), and the second to his eldest daughter Florence Nelson Gatehouse, who died in 1957.

The Gatehouse family arrived in Buckland and were granted land there in 1826: the original property is still owned

Inside St John the Baptist Church, Buckland

by descendants.

Inside the churchyard are old pine trees and some very old gravestones, including that of Samuel Hines, who died in 1864 at the age of 12. The sandstone church is floodlit at night. Just inside the door is a wooden case housing two beautiful old bibles. There are also some photographs of past rectors of this church, including Rev. H.T. Tranmar, who served from 1884 until 1888. The interior of the church is well worth inspecting, with beautiful windows in every wall, including the east window, the precise origin of which is unknown, but which was made between 1350 and 1400. It was probably brought to the church by the first rector, Rev F.H. Cox (1846–48), a reserved man from Sussex, England, who gave no information as to where he had obtained the window. Many interesting speculations have been made—but whether or not the mystery is ever solved, the window remains a beautiful piece of work. Other windows commemorate members of the Cruttendon, Mace, Turvey and Gatehouse families.

At the end of Sally Peak Road is the property known as 'Sally Peak', once owned by William Turvey.

William Turvey of 'Sally Peak', Buckland, was born in Buckland in 1844. His parents were John West Turvey, and Maria (Lyons) Turvey, and he was a brother of Frank Turvey of 'Twamley'. William Turvey died in 1895.

Up to your right as you leave Buckland you'll see another fine old house belonging to the Turvey family. This one is called 'Oakley', and was apparently built for Samuel Lapham, and Assistant Police Magistrate during the 1830s.

Beyond Buckland. As you continue down the Tasman Highway from Buckland there are two hills, known fascinatingly as 'Break-me-Neck' and 'Bust-me-Gall'. Bust-me-Gall's elevation is 336 m. At the foot of the hill, you will cross the tiny Bust-me-Gall Creek. As you approach Runnymead, some time later, you will see a large shearing shed on the left. 256 metres up, just after Runnymead, is Black Charlie's Opening, and opposite the sawmill, a few km farther on is Black Charlies Sugarloaf. Who was Black Charlie? We haven't been able to find out!

Sorell—history and a tour

As you enter the Sorell district, you come to little Orielton. In the 1880s Frank Turvey of 'Twamley' owned 1000 acres of the land around here. Just past Orielton is the town of Sorell, founded in 1821 by Governor Macquarie and one of the Tasmanian features named for Lt Governor William Sorell.

William Sorell (1775–1848) was an Englishman who was Lt Governor of Tasmania from April 1817 to May 1824. He was an effective Governor, suppressing bushranging and causing a number of roads to be built. He was so successful that when his term ended, he was granted a pension from the Colonial Revenues. Port Sorell near Devonport is also named after him.

Sorell tour continued. Turn right out of Cole St into Walker St and drive two blocks to see the Bluebell Inn, (built in the 1860s), the nearby Barracks and, at 15 Somerville St, Somerville Antiques. The building which houses it dates from sometime early

Pembroke Hotel, Sorell

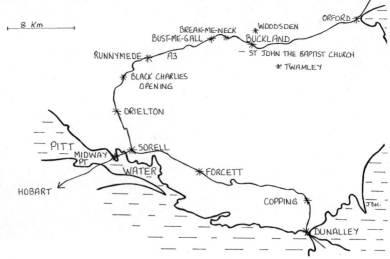

this century, but the range of antiques is fascinating. Other interesting buildings in Sorell include the Pembroke Inn at the corner of Gordon and Somerville Streets, and the Gordon Highlander Hotel in Cole St. Sorell has three old churches, St George's Anglican, St Thomas's Catholic, and Scots Uniting Church. To find these and other historic buildings, ask locally.

After Sorell

From Sorell, you have the choice of continuing on the Tasman Highway or turning into Route A9, the Arthur Highway. If you choose the Tasman Highway, you'll see the very shallow inlet known as Pittwater, which is crossed by a long causeway. Pittwater was named in 1805 by Lt Governor Collins, in honour of the then Chancellor of the Exchequer. During the Second World War Sally's father was stationed near Sorell, and he and some of his mates decided to go for a swim in Pittwater. He reports that they had waded halfway across before the water was deep enough to swim!

At one time two ferries plied across this stretch. Before the causeway was built, the only routes from Sorell to Hobart were by ferry, or 25 miles by road through Ross. The 3-mile causeway was constructed in 1860s by Thomas Oldham, and cost £27 000 to build. It was opened with great pomp in 1874 and has been in use ever since.

An early settler and magistrate, **James Gordon** (who is buried in the old graveyard near St George's Church in Sorell), owned 600 acres at Pittwater from c. 1815. He lent a whaleboat to explorer Captain James Kelly who used it to circumnavigate Tasmania, naming the Gordon River on the way. Halfway across, the causeway reaches dry land on Midway Point, a long tongue of land jutting out into Pittwater. The large island on your left is Woody Island, the much smaller one Barren Island. As you reach the far end of the causeway, you can see Five Mile Beach to your left. Hobart Airport is close by.

East on Route A9

Instead of entering Hobart (see Chapter 14), you may choose to travel the Arthur Highway (Route A9) to the Tasman Peninsula and Port Arthur. If so, drive along

Cole St, Sorell, and out onto Route A9. Dunalley, at the entrance to the Forestier Peninsula, is 25 km by road to the south east of Sorell. The first settlement you will reach is Forcett, and then another 17 km brings you to Copping. Just before reaching Copping you should see some orchards on your right. During World War II, apricots were grown in the Copping area and as they could not be exported, the troops stationed there had quite a feast! At Copping, look out for the Copping Colonial Convict Exhibition on your left. The scene is set outside the exhibition by a gesticulating electric (or is he mechanical?) policeman. One of the exhibits is a cell door from Port Arthur, which was used between 1832 and 1877. Then there are farm implements and a pump (made in 1842), and inside the building, a huge mass of relics, including old kettles, phonographs, flat irons, sewing machines, an ancient pump used at Port Arthur, musical instruments, axes and firearms and virtually everything else relating to early settler and convict lifestyles.

A guided tour of the various working models was available when we visited. From Copping you may go 5 km east to The Long Spit and Marion Bay, and follow the Bay Road alongside Blackman Bay, with a view out to the Forestier Peninsula, or follow the highway 10 km south to the fishing village of Dunalley.

Dunalley. At Dunalley, turn left and follow the sign to see the Tasman Monument, a large rectangular white construction made in 1942. It commemorates the discovery of Tasmania in 1642 by Abel Tasman. The ship's boat, under the command of Pilot Major Visscher, visited Blackmans Bay on 3 December, 1642.

It is said that the Dutch flag was planted by Tasman's carpenter, who swam ashore! Dunalley was once known as 'East Bay Neck', and is the entry point onto the thickly Forestier Peninsula.

Tasman Monument, Dunalley

The Broken South-east

Tasmania's south-east has an extremely shattered and jagged appearance, broken by the wide River Derwent, Pittwater and the D'Entrecasteaux Channel and with the oddly shaped Forestier and Tasman Peninsulas and Bruny Island.

The Peninsulas have a turbulent history. At one stage they were marked off as Aboriginal reserves; later, they became the home of one of the best known of the prison settlements: the 'Model Prison' at Port Arthur.

Forestier Peninsula. Turn left over the Dunalley bridge. This is the 'Singing Bridge' which makes an odd sound as you drive over it. On your right is the Dunalley Hotel, built in 1866. Later on your right you will see Norfolk Bay and Smooth Island, and on your left is Mt. Forestier, 319 metres high. A minor road, (the Blackman Bay Road), leads off to the left, becoming a track that leads right across the peninsula to Lagoon Bay. If you continue on the Arthur Highway, it is about 6 km from Dunalley to the settlement of

Murdunna, once called 'King Georges Sound'.

Tasman Peninsula. At the end of Forestier Peninsula you enter Tasman Peninsula by narrow Eaglehawk Neck, the infamous stretch of ground which was once guarded by a row of fierce dogs, tethered to prevent escape of the convicts. To the left of the Neck is Pirates Bay, to the right is the long narrow Eaglehawk Bay. There is a well-marked turn-off to the left which takes you to see the celebrated tessellated pavement, which has a walking track leading away to the left. If it is low tide, you can climb down to the pavement, which looks almost as if it is man-made.

On the highway again, a sign points off to the left to the rock formations Devils Kitchen, Tasmans Arch and The Blowhole. This road forks, with the right hand road leading 4 km to Waterfall Bay, crossing Blowhole Creek. Take the left fork in the road to see The Blowhole, 1 km from the fork. Climb down nine steps and go along a narrow pathway.

Blowholes are formed when part of the roof of a tunnel is eroded along a weak vein in the rock and collapses. The waves hit the wall of the tunnel and water is forced up through the hole in the roof to form a waterspout. Around the front of this particular blowhole can sometimes be seen the huge horns and fronds of bull kelp. Be careful to stay behind the barrier, for the waves can be unpredictable.

Doo Town, The Devils Kitchen and Tasmans Arch. Take the next turn to the left to see Tasmans Arch and The Devils Kitchen. On the way you will pass the quaintly named Doo Town, where shacks and houses all have names introducing the word 'doo'. Look out for 'Humpty-Doo', 'Doo-Little', 'This'll-Doo', 'Doo-Us' and so on.

Tasmans Arch is a huge arch-shaped formation. The height is 63.9 metres and

Tasman's Arch, Tasman Peninsula

the ceiling of the arch is 52.7 m from sea level. Two hundred metres farther on is The Devils Kitchen, an enormous cleft where rock walls plunge down for a sheer sixty metres to a wedge-shaped bottom. The sea surges in and out through cracks at the bottom. The rocks in which these three formations occur are about 250 000 000 years old, built up of deposits of sand and silt. Beside the Devils Kitchen is a walking track. A 30-minute return trip takes you to Patersons Arch, a 1½-hour walk to Waterfall Bay. This track tends to be rather muddy in winter.

Taranna, Koonya and Saltwater River. Back on the main road, drive along the southern shore of Eaglehawk Bay and down one side of Little Norfolk Bay to Taranna. On the right in Taranna, next to the jetty, is a building once known as 'Tasman's Inn'. The inn was built c. 1842. Drive on to see the Tasmanian Devil Park. Also look out for the Convict Country

Bakery. As you leave Taranna, turn right into Route B37, which leads towards Nubeena. When you reach Koonya, you'll see an old house known as 'Cascades' on your left. 'Cascades' was built in 1841, and served as an out-station of Port Arthur penitentiary. Across the road from 'Cascades' are convict-built cottages, which offer colonial accommodation.

Continue to Premaydena, where a right hand turn takes you to Saltwater River, 7 km from the turn-off. On the right is Norfolk Bay. Saltwater River, (established as a farm to supply the penal settlement in 1841), has several old brick and stone buildings. When you reach a fork in the road, turn right. At Turners Road (on the right) continue straight ahead, for roughly 400 m to see the old convict coal mines. Walk or drive 500 m to the sign that says 'Remains of the old coal mines'.

To prevent accidents, some of the mines have been fenced off, and others have warning signs. The ruins have been stabilised, and these, plus the separate apartments or underground cells, may be visited. Also in the area is a sandstone well shaft. Picnic facilities are available.

Nubeena. Return via Saltwater River to Premaydena and follow the sign which indicates 7 km to the right to Nubeena. Nubeena is the largest town on the peninsula, and is a favourite holiday destination. There is a wide variety of accommodation available. Coming out of Nubeena, cross Parson Bridge and turn right. White Beach is 2 km along this road. On the right, opposite Lagoon Road is a lagoon where swans and other water birds breed. Just past the lagoon, you see on your right Wedge Bay. The small island out in the bay is Wedge island, where colonies of shearwater (or mutton birds) nest. Wedge Bay is a popular fishing bay.

Remarkable Cave. Back along the beach road, continue towards Port Arthur, c. 10 km away. On the way, you will see the turn-off to Remarkable Cave, on Route C347. Remarkable Cave is 5 km from the turn-off. At the end of this road is a viewing platform, and down to the right is a narrow walkway leading down 150 wooden steps to Remarkable Cave. The bluff is a good 50 m in height, and is layered like the rocks at Eaglehawk Neck. The inner entrance becomes flooded at high tide. The ceiling is very high; looking up you can see a vein of lighter coloured rock far above your head. The floor is sand. The seaward side has two openings. Care is needed here as the tide can rise very quickly. Despite all this, Remarkable Cave is truly a remarkable sight, and (if you don't mind a climb) is worth a visit.

When you return to road level, go along to the viewing platform, where there is a coin-operated telescope. Through this, if you are good at focussing, you can see the spiny outline of Cape Raoul, 190 000 000 year old columns of Jurassic dolerite, some 200 metres high. During the 1914–1918 war it is believed that many of the pillars were blasted due to the Royal Navy's wasteful habit of using them for target practice. This stretch of water is called Maingon Bay, and

Due south, Cape Raoul

about 2500 km due south of this point is Antarctica. On a cold day in winter you'll well believe it! Away to the left are Cape Pillar and the lighthouse on Tasman Island, which is one of the tallest in Australia.

Palmers Lookout. As you return from Remarkable Cave look out for a sharp left turn which leads 2 km inland to Palmers Lookout and Gardens. From the lookout, directly in front of you, you see the Isle of the Dead. Down to the left are the buildings of Port Arthur. The long spit you can see ends at Point Puer, (*puer* is Latin for 'boy') where the boys' prison was situated.

Port Arthur

Port Arthur has been represented so often in films and books, photographs and sketches, articles and stories, that we won't go into much detail here. If you visit the ruins you will collect a number of pamphlets and booklets which explain all. Strangely, considering the baleful history of the place, on our last visit we found the atmosphere to be calm and serene. The lovely harbour, the rolling green lawns, and the huge old English trees planted around give more the feeling of a gracious parkland than of a prison. Even the buildings are attractive, with the church being one of the most beautiful we have seen.

Port Arthur was established in the early 1830s as a model prison for habitual criminals. Transportees from Britain did not go there automatically. It was generally reserved for punishment of those who committed further crimes in Australia. At first, bark huts and timber buildings were erected, but later, during the 1840s and early 1850s, more substantial buildings (those remaining today) were built. There are plenty of tales of convicts being sent to Australia for very petty crimes, but many of the 12 500 prisoners who passed through the Port Arthur system were habitual criminals. One in thirteen died while

serving time. Crimes ranged from murder to stealing and embezzling, forgery and horse-stealing. Rather strangely, one man was transported to Australia for life for stealing £17, while another was transported for fourteen years of embezzling £450. Obviously there was no scale of comparison between various crimes and their respective punishments. Crimes involving theft of livestock accounted for the arrival of one seventh of the Irish and one tenth of the British convicts.

Port Arthur was closed in 1877, and was officially renamed 'Carnarvon'. Very soon, curious sightseers began to flock to the site, and, despite the ravages of bushfires, time and weather, the tourist trade has continued.

Isle of the Dead

One attraction at Port Arthur is a cruise to the Isle of the Dead, the burial island out in the harbour. The island was discovered in 1827 by Captain Welsh, master of the *Opossum*. He named it 'Opossum Island' but a convict burial in 1833 sealed its fate. 'Isle of the Dead' it became.

Isle of the Dead

The ferry is the 50-tonne M.L. *Bundeena*. The Isle of the Dead boat leaves regularly for the half-hour cruises and twice a day for the one-hour trips.

The cruise to the island landing stage takes only a few minutes. On the way, look out for a tide marker, cut into the rock in 1841 by Thomas James Lempriere, and possibly the oldest such marker in the world. When you reach the isle, a guide will take you on a tour of the headstones there. Unauthorised landings on the island are strictly forbidden, and so is straying off the marked paths. There are many graves on the island, but comparatively few have headstones. Most of the 81 stones are very badly weathered, as the local sandstone is of poor quality and the damp rises through the stone causing it to flake off.

Convict stonemason, Tom Pickering, made about a dozen of the headstones He had a favourite rope-like border which he carved around many of the stones, and he also favoured flowers and verses.

As well as convicts, 180 free people were buried on the island, on the higher ground. The oldest headstone is that of Joseph Kerr, dated 1831.

There are many communal unmarked graves on the island: one small stretch of level ground containing the remains of over 1000 convicts! These graves were dug to about four metres deep, and the bodies were interred with quicklime to help avert spread of infection.

One convict gravedigger, an Irishman named John Barron, lived on the island, having his rations ferried out twice a week, for 12 years. Descendants of some of the flowers planted on the island at that time still flourish, but the gravediggers apparently declined to grow vegetables in such a place!

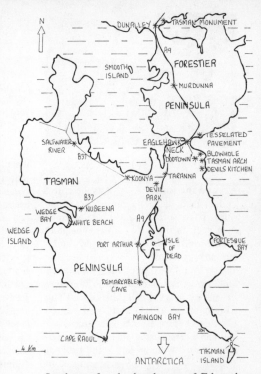

Look out for the headstone of Edward Spicer, a guard on the Southhampton mail coach who stole an envelope containing £17. He was the first convict buried here. Nearby is a memorial to Henry Savery, Australia's first novelist, who died in 1842. He came from a sugar-refining and printing family, but committed a crime of forgery. He was sentenced to hang, but 24 hours before he was due to die his sentence was commuted to transportation. He worked in Hobart as a clerk while a ticket-of-leave man, wrote several newspaper articles for the Colonial Times and also a novel, *Quintus Servinton*.

As it was against the law for convicts to have anything published, Henry used a pseudonym. Finding himself heavily in debt, Henry unfortunately 'home-made' a few banknotes, for which crime he was sentenced to Port Arthur.

Commandant's Cottage, Port Arthur

Around the Ruins. As well as the cruise to the island, there is a guided tour of the ruins. If you prefer atmosphere-at-your-own-pace to organised tours, you may choose to take a plan of the area and wander around on your own.

There is a lot to see, including such buildings as the Commandant's House, part of which was built in 1833. The Commandant at that time was named Charles O'Hara Booth. His successor, William Champ, had a large family, and so more rooms were added to the original

Guard Tower

four-roomed structure. In 1885, the house became the 'Carnarvon Hotel'. It has now been beautifully restored, and guided tours are available.

Not far from the Commandant's cottage is the Guard Tower, a circular tower with turrets around it. It is possible to climb quite safety into the tower—a favourite place for children. It is rather ironic to note that the site occupied by the tower was once offered for sale, although the vendor acknowledged that the existence of the tower building was unfortunate and that it would have to be removed by any purchaser!

Standing away by itself to the right of the rest of Port Arthur is the shell of the lovely church, built during the mid–1830s, altered in 1837 to Lady Jane Franklin's specifications, damaged by wind in 1876, practically destroyed by fire in 1883, the north wall carefully rebuilt during the 1930s and 50s and stabilised during the 1980s!

One of the best features of the church from the visitor's point of view is the spiral staircase inside the walls, allowing one to climb up to enjoy an impressive view. The church served all denominations, including Roman Catholic, until the Catholic Chapel was built in 1857.

There are many other buildings and ruins in Port Arthur, some of which are in very good repair. Wooden walkways have been provided (so you will be able to tour the ruins without falling into any unsuspected dungeons), and, as well as metal plaques explaining the history and use of each of the buildings, a detailed plan of the site is available at Port Arthur. You may also enjoy the ghost tour, fishing or barbecues, shop for gifts in the restored cottage gift shop, eat an excellent cafeteria-style meal, or watch video shows.

The popular lantern-lit ghost tours are available on every night of the year except Christmas Eve and Christmas night, catering for up to 200 people per night.

To fully enjoy Port Arthur, a visit of 5 hours

The Church, Port Arthur

minimum is recommended, and an overnight stay would be useful to allow you to enjoy all the Tasman Peninsula's attractions.

Eaglehawk Neck. On your right is the Bush Mill, Pioneer Settlement and Steam Railway. Presently you will see a sign pointing to Fortescue Bay to your right. This is a fishing area with camp facilities. Nineteen km from Port Arthur is the sharp right hand corner to Tasmans Arch, the Devils Kitchen and the Blowhole.

From Eaglehawk Neck, return up the Forestier Peninsula and over the bridge at Dunalley. Return to Sorell, and, coming out of Cole St, take the Route A5 to Hobart, 25 km away.

BIBLIOGRAPHY

Books and Booklets
EMMETT, E.T. Tasmania by Road and Track, Melbourne University Press, 1952.
LORD, Richard and BOWLER, J.C.S., The Isle of the Dead, Port Arthur.
HEWITT, Lyn, Convicts and Carriageways, Dept. of Main Roads, 1988.
Parish of Buckland Tasmania: Church of St John the Baptist.
Pamphlets
'Isle of the Dead' (Historical Notes), by Maree Anne Stockton. Port Arthur.
Cascades.
Let's Talk about Sorell (Tas Visitor Corporation).

Maps
Tasmap 1: 100 000 Land Tenure Index Series
'D'Entrecasteaux' 'Derwent', 'Prosser',' Storm Bay'.

Information
Thanks to George Farrell, Richard Lord, Maggie and her colleagues at Port Arthur Historic Site, Norah Rodgers, Andrew Simmons, Mr Clark of 'Cascades' the Turvey family and the guide on the cruise to the Isle of the Dead.

13. Bruny Island and Down the Channel

Features of this drive

One of the most beautiful places to visit in Tasmania is the Channel District and Bruny Island. The trip covers some beautiful scenery, and you'll also see a great number of craft galleries and some interesting old buildings, caves, thermal pools, gemstones and fish farms! Cruises and jet-boating, train rides, trout fishing and horseback tours are also available. Ask locally for up-to-date information on these activities.

The way to Bruny Island. Bruny Island is the ideal place to stay for a few days and rest, or walking or swimming, skin-diving or swimming and fishing. You won't find any night-life there, but the residents are friendly and rather easy-going. To reach Bruny Island from the Tasman Peninsula, return to Sorell, and from Cole St take the A5 route to Hobart, which is 25 km away. Continue along the highway to cross the causeway. On your right is the Orielton Lagoon, on your left is Pittwater. At the other end of Pittwater, you will enter the region of Clarence.

Clarence Region

Clarence is partly contained in Hobart City, but also extends over rural land. An important feature of the area is Risdon Cove, suggested by George Bass in 1798 as an appropriate site for the first Tasmanian settlement in 1803.
To reach Risdon and visit Bowen Park, with its display of historical features, turn off to the right just before crossing the Derwent

and drive through the suburb of Lindisfarne.
The name 'Clarence' comes from the original name of Rokeby, 'Clarence Plains', which in turn was named by Captain John Hayes after his own ship, *Duke of Clarence*. Hayes also named Risdon Cove after an officer on his ship.

Rokeby. In Rokeby itself are a number of interesting buildings, including St Matthew's Anglican Church, dedicated in 1842. This was built partly due to the enthusiasm of Rev. Robert ('Bobby') Knopwood, the Chaplain who had been in Van Diemen's Land since 1804.

Rev. Bobby Knopwood (1763–1838) was a very well-known character in early Clarence. He was born in Norfolk, England and educated at Cambridge, being ordained as a clergyman at the age of 26. He arrived in Van Diemen's Land in 1804 with David Collins, who came to take over the settlement established at Risdon Cove by John Bowen. Knopwood remained as Chaplain at the settlement until 1823 before going to Clarence Plains, where, lacking a church building, he conducted services in the school house. 'Bobby' Knopwood, as he was called, is well-known for his various writings, but he seems to have had a novel approach to spelling if his accounts of the 'kangarro' (or 'kannarro') are anything to go by! He died five years before St Matthew's was completed.
Also at Rokeby is 'Rokeby Court', once a courthouse and gaol, built c. 1840, and

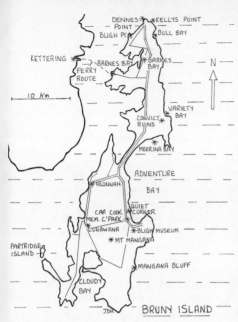

On your right is a sharp right-hand turn leading 1 km to Government House and another km to the Botanical Gardens. Go straight on along the highway, leaving the city centre to your right and continue on the left arm. Drive along Davy St. On your left is St Davids Park.

Kingston, Margate and Snug

Turn left on Route A6 which promises Kingston 11 km away and Huonville 40 km away. Turn left toward Kingston, (leaving the signpost to Huonville to your right) and then turn right again toward Kettering.

Turn left by the sign and drive through Margate on Route B68. Margate Train World is on your left. The creator of Train World has recreated scenes from Germany and some scale model locomotives run round 150 m of track, passing towns and cities, a waterfall and windmill.

Past Margate, you reach Electrona, and then Snug, on the Snug River. This is a pleasant town, popular with campers.

While there you might like to walk to Snug Falls. Just before you leave Snug on the left at C648 Channel Highway is the Channel Folk Museum, which is open on Sundays. Finally, from Snug, drive on to Kettering!

Kettering and the D'Entrecasteaux Channel.

'Down the channel' as this area is known to Tasmanians, is very beautiful, with little hills and valleys and pockets of orchards. Fruit growing is a major industry hereabouts. On a fine day it is a delightful drive. As you reach the top of the small hill in the town, look for a sign pointing left to the embarkation point for the vehicular ferry to Bruny Island.

A few hundred metres down the D'Entrecasteaux Channel, you'll pass Oyster Cove and the marina. Another sign points to the ferry, which leaves regularly

'Rokeby House', about the same age but rather more altered. To visit Rokeby, do not cross the Tasman Bridge but go through Bellerive and Howrah.

Seven Mile Beach. One km from Pittwater, look for a signpost pointing to Seven Mile Beach, 2 km away, and then, on your left, one to Cambridge Airport, which services Hobart and the south. At Seven Mile Beach is a house named 'Acton'. This was built during the early 1840s and was owned by William Rumney, an early settler in the area who gave his name to Mt Rumney, once part of his property.

The Derwent River. As you continue on the Tasman Highway, look for Mt Wellington straight ahead. Drive over the Derwent River on the Tasman Bridge. The Derwent was named by Captain John Hayes in the early 1790s.

Once over the bridge take the lane heading for Hobart (see Chapter 14), leaving the exit to the city of Glenorchy on your left.

several times a day. In calm weather, the trip by ferry takes just a few minutes.

Bruny Island

Bruny Island lies to the east of the port of Kettering, and about 20 km south of Hobart. Its area is 36 210 hectares, making it Tasmania's fourth largest island, following Flinders, King and Cape Barren islands. There are 68 road km stretching north to south, and over 225 km of road all told. The island was named after Rear Admiral Bruni D'Entrecasteaux, (pronounced 'don-tree-cass-toh') who landed there in the 1790s. Originally known as 'Bruni Island' the spelling was altered to its present form in 1918.

In other parts of Tasmania, finding the origins of the names given to features often proved impossible, but the names of Bruny Island are surprisingly well documented.

Bruny's First Inhabitants. The Nuenanne, the Aboriginal inhabitants of the island, called it 'Lunawanna-Allonah'. The two parts of this name have been retained for two different towns. At one time Mangana, who was Truganini's father, was the tribal chief of the island. His name is remembered in Mangana Bluff, on the south-east side. Truganini was sometimes known as 'Lalla Rookh'. She was born on the island in 1812, and died in Hobart in 1876, the last full-blooded member of her race. Many years later, in 1975, her wishes were carried out when her remains were cremated and the ashes scattered in the D'Entrecasteaux Channel.

European Explorers and Early Days. The first known European visitor to sight Bruny Island was the Dutchman Abel Tasman who added it to his charts in 1642, while the first recorded European landing was made by Captain Tobias Furneaux (pronounced 'fern-oh') (1735–1781) who landed in 1773. He was followed by Captain James Cook (1728–1779), by Rear Admiral Bruni D'Entrecasteaux, by Captain William Bligh (1754–1812), by Matthew Flinders (1774–1814), and by Nicholas Baudin.

Present day Bruny is such a peaceful, uncrowded place that it is quite easy to find a deserted beach and stand looking out to sea, and equally easy to imagine that the next wave might bring the great ships *Adventure, Discovery* or *Bounty* over the horizon. In passing, it is rather chastening to notice how young some of these 'great names' were at the times of their deaths: Furneaux was 46, Cook 51, and Matthew Flinders only 40. During the 1820s, whaling stations were established on Bruny Island, and a lighthouse (the second oldest in Australia), was built in 1836. These days, cattle farming and tourism form the main industries. There are also salmon and oyster farms.

Touring Bruny Island

The ferry will land you and your car at Roberts Point on the island. The Roberts concerned was R.A. Roberts, who operated a soap and salt factory in the area in 1825. He also gave his name to Roberts Hill, east of the point. Apollo Bay, which is just south of Roberts Point, is thought to have been named after a ship called Apollo, built in 1826 for Captain J. Laughton. This vessel had a brief career, for it was wrecked on Maria Island the following year.

From the landing stage, turn left to drive to the northern tip of Bruny Island. This tip is known as Dennes Point (pronounced 'denn-ee-s point). Like the island, Dennes Point has changed its name. It was once known as Kellys Point after a Captain James Kelly, who was harbourmaster and pilot. Captain Kelly had a land grant at the point from 1819 until 1845, when he sold it to A. Dennes. The change in ownership brought about the change in name . . . but although Mr Dennes is long gone his name has remained.

On the way to Dennes Point look out for the strange plants known as 'black boys', which look rather like one legged ostriches with upraised beaks. Some of these plants are several centuries old.

The only problem with touring Bruny Island on a pleasant day is the ease with which you become surfeited with natural beauty. The first sight of Barnes Bay, (which was once the ferry landing stage), is inclined to draw gasps of envious amazement: how can a bay be so wide and blue, and how on earth does the sand come to be so white? And why isn't it sardine-packed with tourists?

Dennes Point will probably have a similar effect, and so will Bull Bay, but as you pass Great Bay and Isthmus Bay, which are every bit as beautiful, you begin to feel a bit blasé. It's like seeing a fashion parade: if there were just one lovely garment you would be exceedingly impressed but after a while you scarcely bother to turn your head. At Dennes Point, you can choose to turn south-west and follow the road along Nebraska Beach, passing Point and Killora down to the cemetery. Drive east to rejoin the main road.

Once the road reaches Great Bay, it hugs the western coast of the island for 4 km. Like Forestier and Tasman Peninsulas and Maria Island, North and South Bruny are connected by a narrow isthmus or neck. The Neck was discovered in 1792, and, despite its appearance on the map, you can see only one side while driving along the road. The high central hummock, a bird sanctuary and the dwelling place of shearwaters and penguins, conceals the bay on the other side. Climb to the top of the hummock and be amazed at the view. A cairn to Truganini can be seen at the top of the steps. Ask local Parks and Wildlife Rangers for more information.

At the southern end of the Neck the road divides, with the major branch leading west to Alonnah, and then south to Lunawanna, and the other branch, the Adventure Bay Road, following the east coast around Adventure Bay. The two roads link up with the Coolangatta Road close to Mt Bounty and over Mt Mangana.

Adventure Bay and the Bligh Museum

Adventure Bay, (sometimes known as 'the most historical bay in Australia'), is about 11 km from Cape Queen Elizabeth in North Bruny to Grass Point in the south. It was the landing place of Captain Tobias Furneaux in 1773 and he named it after his command, the *Adventure*. While visiting the bay, stop at the Bligh Museum. The museum building was constructed in 1954 from 26 000 convict-made bricks, dating from 1846 and collected from Variety Bay. Inside are such wonders as a globe of the world made in 1799 and brought out from England, correspondence from and about Captain William Bligh, carved flints, and photographs. There is also a battered piece of wood: all that is left of the so-called Cook's Tree, on which Captain James Cook carved his name and the date in January 1777. Unfortunately, the tree was burnt by a bushfire in 1905. Since 1988 a bi-centennial monument has stood by the place where the tree grew. Close by the monument is a small arm of the sea where we saw a great many different water birds.

Bligh Museum, Bruny Island

Catholic Homes, Cygnet

Catholic Homes, Cygnet

Lockeys Road takes you south of Adventure Bay, and Staffords Road and the Cloudy Bay Road to Cloudy Bay. There are several different places offering accommodation on the island, and brochures available detailing the best walks with their times and distances, and the National Parks and other reserves. Be warned—Bruny Island is addictive! Go there once and you'll almost certainly want to return.

'Down the Channel'

Leaving the ferry at Kettering to begin your trip 'down the Channel', turn left and drive out of the town. Although there are roads crisscrossing this part of the state, most visitors would choose to drive down the Channel Highway hugging D'Entrecasteaux Channel and then up the Huon River to Huonville. On your right, out of Kettering, are apple and pear orchards. The Channel Highway (Route B68) through the Huon district, shows you the largest apple-producing area in Tasmania. The first Tasmanian apple tree was planted by Captain (later Governor) William Bligh at Bruny Island in 1788.

Pass through Woodbridge, Birchs Bay, Flowerpot and then Middleton. There is a very windy road past Long Bay Shoal to Gordon, and a turn-off to the left to Gordon Jetty, which leads to the D'Entrecasteaux monument. Bruny Island is seen for most of the way. The Channel Highway rounds Ninepin Point, next comes Verona Sands.

A well-signposted turn to the right, leads one kilometre to Talune Wildlife Park, including a gallery, orchard, an aviary, koala gardens and the largest Tasmanian devil enclosure in the world. There are barbecues near the Gardners Bay Rivulet, and cabin accommodation and cider and fruit wine sales are available. In the same general area, you'll find Panorama Vineyard, Hartzview Wine Centre, and a local weaving shop.

Return to the highway and take Route B68 to Huonville. On your right is Seymour Orchard and on your left again Port Cygnet and the Huon River.

Cygnet

As you come in to Cygnet, you'll see Port Cygnet, a deep inlet on your left. The settlement extends right around. In the town, opposite the old council chambers building (1913), are a chemist shop and the Schoolhouse Coffee Shop, situated in the original Cygnet schoolhouse.

On the bank behind the shop is St James' Catholic Church and College, which has served the Catholic community of Cygnet, Bruny Island, and Lower Channel since 1864. St James' was built in 1840 and is flanked on either side by the Catholic Brothers and the Catholic Sisters Homes, both beautiful old red brick and weatherboard buildings, two-storied and with gabled roofs and white iron lacework.

Huonville

It is 17 km from Cygnet to Huonville. The Huon River was discovered in 1792 and was named for Captain Hhon Kermandec, a Frenchman and colleague of the river's discoverer, Bruni D'Entrecasteaux. Kermandec's surname inspired the name of the Huon River's tributary, the Kermandie. The Aborigines knew the river as Tahune-Linah: this name is remembered in the Tahune Forest Reserve, 25 km along Route C632 from Geeveston.

The reserve encompasses 102 hectares and includes a pleasant picnic area at the Tahune Bridge. Evidently the Huon area was very uninviting when the first explorers arrived, because it was very thickly wooded.

For many years, however, it has been recognised as the centre of Tasmania's apple industry, producing some 75% of the annual crop. Hops are also grown at Huonville.Huon Pine was first discovered in this region. At one time it was greatly used in ship building: now it is more usually carved or turned for ornamental purposes. It is a beautiful wood and huon pine carvings are much admired.

To the right is a sign to Cygnet Pottery. After Cygnet comes Cradoc, where apricots are grown. To visit Wattle Grove, and the Acacia House tea rooms, turn right at Cradoc at the sign that says 'Acacia House'.

Wattle Grove was first settled in 1838 by George Walter, a friend of Governor John Franklin, and his son James Henry Walter. George's descendants can trace their family tree back to Hubert Walter, who was Archbishop of Canterbury from 1196 to 1203. The Walter family has always been active and influential in church and education circles.

After passing through Cradoc, you will see the Huon River, and orchards of espaliered fruit trees. Go through Woodstock to Huonville.

Franklin

Cross the Huon River at Huonville and head southward on the Huon Highway, (Route A6), toward the town of Franklin, named after Governor Sir John Franklin.

Sir John Franklin sailed with Matthew Flinders in the ship *Investigator*, and governed Tasmania from 1837. He was an honest and humane man, with a well-informed and enquiring mind. He and his wife, Lady Jane Franklin, were probably far more popular with Tasmanians than with the British authorities, who recalled him in 1843. Two years later he led an ill-fated expedition to the Arctic, in search of the North West Passage. He and all other expedition members were lost.

Jane Franklin House in Tasmanian University is named for his wife. Lady Franklin was an enterprising woman. She disliked snakes, and offered a bounty of one shilling per snake's head brought to the police station. In a single season she had to pay out £600, and wisely abandoned the idea of becoming a latter-day St Patrick by casting out the snakes of Tasmania!

In Franklin, look out for the old Commercial Bank building, built in 1904. Farther on, you'll pass Lady Franklin Hotel and Ye Old Franklin Tavern, built in 1853. St Mary's Church and the historic cemetery are also in Franklin.

South of Franklin

To the left, just past the town, look for the long Egg Islands out in the river. Five km south of Franklin is the Huon Showcase, housed in an enormous apple shed. The Showcase contains all sorts of local crafts, including carved apple dolls, and Huon Pine woodware.

Go through little Castle Forbes Bay, and Port Huon which is the depot for Huon River Cruises. Bookings for these cruises may be made at the red brick Kermandie

Hotel, just across the road. The Kermandie Hotel looks a lot like an hotel in Huonville, just before the bridge. They were designed by the same architect and built about 1930. In Port Huon, you'll see the turn-off to Hartz Mountain National Park, 21 km away on Route C632. Activities enjoyed in the park are skiing and bushwalking.

Drive on through Geeveston and Waterloo, after which the Huon Highway leaves the coast, but the Esperance Coast Road, (Route C638), continues on past Police Point and Surveyors Bay, directly opposite Verona Sands.

Geeveston

Geeveston was originally known as Lightwood Bottom and was later named after William Geeves, who arrived from England in 1842 after Lady Franklin requested that someone should come to establish the Church in the area.

It is a small town, and most of the population works in the orcharding or timber industries. Facilities include a swimming pool, and golf, tennis and bowling clubs.

To the west of Geeveston, as well as the Hartz Mountain is Picton Valley, another area popular with walkers.

Dover

If you stay on the highway, you will soon reach Dover, which is about 20 km from Geeveston. Situated at Port Esperance at the mouth of the Esperance River, Dover is a picturesque place, with fishing boats in the harbour as well as the three islands known as Faith, Hope and Charity. Once a convict station, Dover retains a reminder of its past in the old Commandant's Office near the caravan park. Fishing and forestry are the main industries.

At Dover, ask about booking a cruise on the *Olive May*, built in around 1880. For more information, telephone Southwest Passage Cruises on (036) 298 3247. Dover

provides the most southerly accommodation (apart from a youth hostel) in Tasmania, and Anne's Old Rectory, which was built around the turn of the century, offers the 'world's most southern Colonial Accommodation'! If continuing south, it might be a good idea to stock up on food in Dover.

Southport—the end of the highway

After Dover, you'll cross the lovely Esperance River, and drive another 19 km through the tiny hamlets of Raminea and Strathblane, (once thriving timber towns) to Southport. Southport is opposite the southern tip of South Bruny Island and was apparently once known as both 'Mussel Bay' and 'Hythe'.

This little fishing town dates from whaling days, and was once a flourishing timber port.

These days it marks the extreme southern end of Tasmania's highway system, with Route A6 coming to a decided halt. However, the determined southward traveller may choose to branch off to the right 2 km before Southport onto Route C635 towards Hastings Caves, the couple of houses which are all that is left of the town of Hastings, the Lune River, and the thermal springs where you can visit the swimming pool, picnic area and walking tracks, one of which leads you on a 2 hour return walk to Adamsons Falls. The thermal pool remains at a constant 28°C.

Hastings Caves were discovered in 1917 by timber workers. They are impressive limestone caves, with the largest of the three, Newdegate Cave, being named after Sir Francis Newdegate, a governor of Tasmania. It was officially opened to the public in 1939 and continues to attract visitors. To visit the caves, continue on Route C635. Facilities in the pool and cave area include hot showers, picnic shelters, toilets, drinking water, and barbecues. At present (late 1996) there is no kiosk, so you'll need to bring your own supplies.

Things to see at Lune River and Ida Bay. Leave Route C635 and continue on Route C636 to see pretty Lune River and the hamlet of Ida Bay. At Lune River you'll see a fine display of gemstones and fossils at Lunaris Gemstones. The Ida Bay Railway was built to carry limestone but now it sometimes carries tourists instead, on a 6 km trip past Major Honners Bay and Southport Narrows to the Deep Hole which is just across the bay from Southport and in sight of Pelican Island. At the Deep Hole is a good beach, and a forty-minute walk takes you to Southport Lagoon, a reserve area complete with a monument on the bluff to the foundered convict ship George III. You'll need to ask locally about the availability of train rides. Look out for the wildflowers in this area in spring.

South
Around 14 km south of Ida Bay is Catamaran at Recherche Bay. This area is the most southern part of Australia to be reached by road. Recherche Bay was named after the ship commanded by Bruni D'Entrecasteaux, who sailed into the bay in 1792. There was once a sawmill and coal mine in the area, but now it is almost deserted. Before attempting any long walks into the bush and the mountains, adequate preparations must be made and the suitable authorities notified.

At Cockle Creek, south of Recherche Bay, is a ranger station and the trackhead for the long south-coast walk to Port Davey.

North again to Ranelah and Grove

As you return to the north, you might like to turn off at Dover and take the coast road past Police Point. There are plenty of scenic views, and you can also see the ocean fish tanks of Huon Aquaculture. Rejoin the highway about 12 km north of Dover and continue to Huonville. Cross the bridge and go straight ahead, then turn into Route C620 to visit Ranelagh, and the Tasman Antique Motor Museum in Helen St. The museum, which has an impressive collection of Vintage, Veteran and Classic cars as well as old motoring accessories and signs, is open every day. Also in Ranelah is a trio of pretty old churches.

Return to Huonville and turn right. Shortly you'll see the Model Train World on your left. After Huonville comes Grove, with its Apple Heritage Museum and Talune Pottery. Just past Grove, you'll come to a lookout which offers a fine view of the Huon Valley. Continue on Route A6 towards Hobart.

BIBLIOGRAPHY
Books
CHISHOLM, Alec H, (editor) *Land of Wonder*, Angus and Robertson, 1974.
DAVIS, B, *Guide to Bruny Island History*, All Saints Press, Hobart, 1988.

Pamphlets
'Let's Talk About Bruny Island'
'Let's Talk About Clarence'
'Let's Talk About Esperance' (Tas. Visitor Corporation)
'Talune'
'Tasmania's Huon Valley'.

Maps
Tasmap 1: 100 000 Land Tenure Index Series:
'D'Entrecasteaux', 'Derwent', 'Huon', 'South East Cape'.

Information
Thanks to Nigel Ellis, George Farrell, Isobel Geeves, Ruth at Bruny Island, Lunaris Gemstones and the National Parks and Wildlife, Esperance. Additional information from article by Pamela Kidd.

14. Hobart, New Norfolk and Strathgordon

Features of this drive

Apart from the many attractions of Tasmania's capital city, the drives in this chapter cover a wide range of other choices, including historic salmon ponds, the oldest surviving church in Tasmania, a collection of historic sketches, a drowned lake and some true wilderness.

Hobart

Hobart, Tasmania's capital, generally admitted to be one of the most beautiful of the Australian cities, was settled in 1803, and named in September of that year after Lord Hobart, then Secretary of State for the Colonies. Certainly its setting is an advantage, with the lovely harbour, the Derwent, the visible surrounding bushland—and Mt Wellington. In fact, this mountain, 1270 metres high, is one of the things many visitors remember about Hobart. Practically wherever you go around the city it seems to be there, looming over your shoulder.

In winter and spring it is often covered (or maybe scattered) with snow. Hobart is a good place to spend a day or three if you're interested in historic buildings. It certainly has a large share of these, far too many to be covered in the scope of this book. You can drive to some of the attractions, but many of them need to be appreciated at leisure, and that means walking. In September, 1996, we spent a day (9 to 5) walking around Hobart. We emerged, chastened and footsore, to the realisation that it would probably take a week to scratch the surface of the place. If you have the time to spare, you'll find a lot of architectural and historical treasure. It's worth the tired feet!

Mt Wellington

To reach the top of the mountain, drive up Davey St to Ferntree and then turn right, following the signs. Drive with care: Wellington tends to be slippery with ice and snow in winter!

A walk in Hobart

For an interesting walk through historic Battery Point, drive along Davey St to the vicinity of Collegiate School and Anglesea Barracks. We began our walk at Fitzroy Place, just off Albuera and Byron Streets, where parking is easier. Beginning from Fitzroy Place, it's easy to walk through Battery Point, Salamanca Place and the Wharf Area. First, some history of the area.

In and around Battery Point. In 1818, a battery of guns, known as the Mulgrave Battery, was established between Sandy Bay Point in the West and Sullivans Cove in the East. The first occupant of the area was Reverend Robert Knopwood (see Chapter 13). Much of the rest of Battery Point belonged to William Sorell (Lt Governor of Van Diemen's Land from 1817 to 1824), who was granted 90 acres in 1819, but who sold it to William Kermode five years later. In 1930 the farmlands began to give way to buildings, and twenty years later the area had become a flourishing village.

Coming from Fitzroy Place, cross over Byron St and as you reach Albuera St, you can look straight ahead up the hill to see the original army Barracks. Go along Albuera St and turn left into Sandy Bay Road. On your left is the Masterpiece Fine Arts Gallery, open MonSat. This is a good place to visit if you appreciate colonial art, but you will see some modern artists showcased as well. It's a shop as well as a gallery, and we wished we had longer to spend looking at the exhibits. The Gallery is only the first of a feast of antique shops and galleries you'll be visiting on this walk. Cross Sandy Bay Road at the lights, and go into St George's Terrace. St Ives Brewery and Hotel is on your left. As you pass Crelin St, look to the right to see some fine old terrace houses in St George's Terrace. The Terrace splits. Follow the lower level and pass Bath St. Look for oddly named 'Crum Cottage' on your left. Just before you cross Colville St (named for Lord Colville), you'll see the Sandy Bay Yacht Marina ahead to your right.

Turn left into Colville St at the top of the hill and cross Cromwell St. There is a beautiful view over the Derwent from this point. Turn left into Cromwell St. On your left is St George's Anglican Church, the 'Mariners' Church'. The nave of the church was designed by John Lee Archer and the

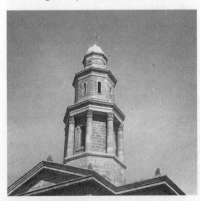

Mariner's Church, Battery Point

tower by James Blackburn. It was opened in 1838, and underwent major restoration in the 1970s and early '80s. The church may be open, but if no-one is in attendance it could be locked as a defence against vandals. On your left as you enter the church is a door leading into a museum. Inside the church the pews are boxed in and you can still see paler marks where the candle holders were once mounted. On the wall is a memorial to William Moriarty, after whom the township of Moriarty in the North West near Latrobe was named. Almost opposite the church is 'Hanover Cottage', built in 1837 by sea captain John Aldridge.

Turn right into De Witt St after leaving the church. On the left is De Witt Antiques and Fine Arts. This is a lovely shop to visit, and the setting is worthy of the stock. The building was erected in c. 1860 by the Holymans, a family of shippers and traders. Since then it has served in many capacities. Inside the main room is a charming ceiling rose.

The gardens of the area are worth admiring: they have been kept beautifully in character with the restored buildings.

At the corner of De Witt St and Hampden Road, on your left, are 'Invercoe' (1883), and 'Barton Cottage' (c. 1850). Turn left into Hampden Road. From the corner of Hampden Road and Waterloo Crescent, you can see the tower of St George's, the landmark known by early mariners.

103 Hampden Road is 'Narryna', built in 1836 and now housing the Van Diemen's Land Memorial Folk Museum.

Return along Hampden Road, pass Francis St and Colville St and turn into Secheron Road to see the Maritime Museum of Hobart , located in 'Secheron House', 1831. The museum was founded in 1974 and features a splendid collection of maritime history from 1804 onwards.

Return to the corner of Francis St and Hampden Road and turn left into Arthurs Circus, a strange little village green,

Arthur's Circus, Battery Point

Salamanca Place

surrounded by gardens and tiny old workmen's cottages, built during the 1840s and '50s. Turn out of the Circus left into Runnymede St. 'Lenna of Hobart' is on your right, at 20 Runnymede St, just after McGregor St.

'Lenna'. This lovely building, constructed during the 1870s and 80s, is now, in the words of a local, a 'rather nice' hotel. It was built by a Scot named Alexander McGregor, who arrived in Hobart as a child in 1831. The site of the house was owned by Captain James Bayley. He sold the property to Alexander McGregor, who married Bayley's daughter, Harriett. 'Lenna' (from an Aboriginal word meaning 'home' or 'hut'), was built to incorporate an earlier house owned by Bayley. It is classified by the National Trust.

Salamanca Place. Turn left out of Runnymede St into Salamanca Place, famous for the outdoor weekend market held there. Most of the stalls are fairly up-market, because the standard is controlled by Hobart Council. Whaling ships used to come in to the docks here, and many of the old warehouse buildings remain, now transformed into art galleries and elegant shops. On your left, just past Aspect Design is an old alleyway leading up to 'Kelly's Steps'. James Kelly arrived on the ship *Queen* in 1790. He married Elizabeth Griffiths in 1812 and later became Captain Kelly. He became famous for a voyage

right around Van Diemen's Land in a whaleboat. Much of Captain Kelly's history is detailed on a board close to the steps, and he is buried nearby in St Davids Park. On your left, a little farther along, is Knopwood's Tavern and Wine Bar, named, no doubt, after Reverend Bobby Knopwood. Salamanca Place has arcades and pavement cafes, arts, crafts and old books. Its a great place to shop, or to watch the world go by.

Walk on until you see Parliament House, the gardens of which are maintained by the Royal Botanical Gardens. Parliament House is a handsome building, a smaller replica of Westminster Palace in London. It was designed by John Lee Archer and built c. 1840, becoming Parliament House in 1856. The formal gardens in the grounds are charming: there are some venerable lime trees and a bronze statue of A.G.

Parliament House

Ogilvie K.C., Premier of Tasmania from 1933 to 1939. In the grounds just after New Year an annual open-air exhibition is held. Walk past Parliament House and look to your right to see St Davids Park, the first burial ground of Hobart. On 27 April, 1804, Rev. Robert Knopwood and Lt Governor David Collins (governed 1804 until 1810), marked out a burial ground 'some distance from the camp'. A number of well-known people are buried there, including David Collins himself (on the site of the first church), and Captain James Kelly of 'Kelly's Steps'. Look out for the memorial to Sir John Eardley-Wilmot, also a Lt Governor, from 1843 to 1846.

Macquarie St

Go back and walk around the wharf. There are a number of harbour cruises available, also lots of fish restaurants. Look out on your left for the Gibsons Flour Mill, a very old building now converted into restaurants and boutiques. Walk around Constitution Dock, where the yachts congregate after the Sydney to Hobart Yacht Race, and go up Elizabeth St. Cross Morrison and Davey Streets and turn right into Macquarie St. Here, you'll see the Town Hall, built in 1864, and the clock tower, built on the site of the original Government House. Beside the tower is the office of *The Mercury* Newspaper.

The Mercury **Newspaper** was founded in 1854, probably by its first editor, William Coote. Another famous bygone editor was Henry Richard Nicholls, from 1883 until 1912.

A short detour to No. 5 Argyle St takes you to the Tasmanian Museum and Art Gallery. Return to the Town Hall and cross Elizabeth St. Franklin Square is on your left. The great oak tree in the square was planted in 1863 to commemorate the marriage of the Prince of Wales (later Edward VII) to Princess Alexandra. In the square also is a fountain, with a statue of

Sir John Franklin (1786–1847) in the middle.

There is also a statue of William Lodewyk Crowther (1817–1885), who was Premier of Tasmania in 1878. A guided tour of Battery Point leaves from the Wishing Well at Franklin Square at 9.30 each morning. Next to the National Mutual Life Building farther on to your right is one of Stephen Walker's sculptures, based on the Antarctic.

Stephen Walker, the well-known sculptor, was born in Balwyn, Victoria, in 1927. He studied at Melbourne Technical College, 1945–47, and from 1942 to 1947 was employed in commercial and advertising art. In 1948 he moved to Hobart and worked as a freelance commercial artist, teaching art at Hobart Technical College 1951–1953. He began producing sculpture, mainly in wood, in 1953, and went to work in England in the next year. In 1956 he returned to Tasmania, and carried out several public commissions. Since then he has studied in Rome, Florence and Prague. Returning to Sydney, Walker won first prize in the Sydney City Council Fountain Competition, and established a foundry and studio at Arcadia, near Sydney, in 1967. In 1972 he returned to Tasmania to execute a memorial fountain and built a foundry and studio at Campania. Mr Walker has won many awards and honours, and his sculptures are widely recognised and popular not only with art buffs but with non-artistic people as well, which must be the greatest triumph of all! He now mainly works in bronze.

The Cathedral and the Barracks. To your right, past this sculpture, is the Anglican Cathedral. The Cathedral's foundation stone was laid in 1892, the 50th anniversary of the founding of the See and the 250th anniversary of the discovery of the island. This stone replaces one now built into the tower, which was erected in 1929. When we visited in 1996, the Cathedral was open to the casual visitor. Inside, is a museum, containing such extraordinary exhibits as stones from many very old British buildings: a stone from the Herefordshire Cathedral, c. 9th century, and one from the Winchester Cathedral, 11th century. We are assured that these stones were voluntarily donated! Also on display are photographs of Bishops and former Deans of the Anglican Church. The church itself is equally interesting, and the comments in the visitors' book provide proof that international visitors are favourably impressed.

As you leave the cathedral, look across the street for Hadley's Hotel. Past the Cathedral, but to the left, you'll see another Stephen Walker sculpture. Also look out for the attractive small Roman Catholic church of St Joseph's. Continue along Macquarie St and turn left into Barrack St,

cross Davey St at the lights, then turn right into Davey St. On the right is Collegiate School and Anglesea Barracks.

Anglesea Barracks, named after the Marquis of Anglesea, is the oldest military establishment still occupied by the Army in Australia. The site was personally chosen by Governor Macquarie in 1811 and the Barracks were built throughout the several years following. A concise history of the Barracks is available in the 'Let's Talk About Anglesea Barracks' leaflet.

Another interesting walk takes in the whole of Macquarie St. Begin at the Evans St end, with the old Royal Engineers' Building and continue to the Cascade Brewery. This walk takes in many fine old buildings and historical places.

Other places of interest in Hobart

It's not possible to give detailed instructions for reaching all the interesting places in Hobart, but fortunately excellent street maps and tourist guides are readily available. The *UBD Tasmania St Directory* is a good one, and so is the R.A.C. map, available from any Tasmanian R.A.C. office. Below is a small selection of the places which might be of interest.

For the kids. It you're travelling with children, you might like to include some of the following in your itinerary. And ask locally for other selections. **The Olympic Pool** is situated in Queens Domain, quite near the Botanical Gardens. The new pool complex was begun in early 1995, and is scheduled for completion by mid-1997. **The Climbing Edge** is an indoor rock-climbing experience situated at 54 Bathurst St. It's open every weekday,

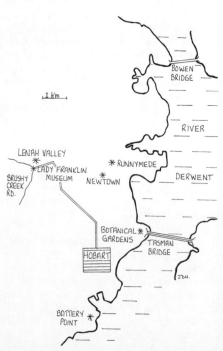

afternoon and evening, and from 10 until 5 at weekends. Instruction is included for beginners, and it includes climbs suited to all ages and levels of experience. **Roller World** is in Collins St, and there's an **Ice-skating Rink** at Claremont. Then, there's the **Cat and Fiddle Arcade** in the city centre, which opens into Cat and Fiddle Square. This is a very popular place with children, who enjoy watching the mechanical cat, fiddle, dog, spoon, dish and cow of the nursery rhyme perform on the hour. **The Model Tudor Village**, often known as 'Tudor Court', is at 827 Sandy Bay Road. The village was made by the late Mr J. Palotta. It has been an attraction for many years; Sally can remember visiting it in around 1969.

The Botanical Gardens. No visitor to Hobart should miss seeing the Botanical Gardens. Just one kilometre off the Tasman Highway, in Queens Domain, the Gardens are situated right beside the fairytale castle of Government House and cover 13.5 hectares. The land was granted by Governor Collins to a man named John Hangan in 1806, and in 1818, after a dispute of ownership with a subsequent purchaser, the land was taken over by Governor Sorell and developed as the Government House Gardens. A much more detailed history of the gardens may be found in the leaflet 'Let's Talk About The Royal Tasmanian Botanical Gardens available on site.

Botanical Gardens , Hobart

When visiting the Gardens, make sure you allow at least two hours; in fact, anyone really interested in such things could probably spend a day just wandering around. Features include a floral clock, (picked out in red and white pansies and hen-and-chicken when we saw it last), a conservatory, an easy access garden, a Japanese garden, a lily pond and a herb garden. There are also displays of cactus, ferns, a section of Tasmanian and mainland species, and a large aviary, containing cockatoos. In the gardens you can also see a number of historic structures, including a wall built in 1829.

'Runnymede' is a National Trust-owned house at 61 Bay Road in New Town. It was built by the first lawyer to qualify in Tasmania, Robert Pitcairn, in 1844. The name 'Runnymede' was given the house by a later owner, Captain Charles Bayle: (the original owner of the 'Lenna of Hobart' property), in 1864. The original *Runnymede* had been the captain's favourite ship!

Wrest Point Hotel-Casino, the first legal casino in Australia, is a popular attraction in Sandy Bay. The famous revolving restaurant takes an hour to complete its circuit, so there is no need to fear flying food!

The Shot Tower, just past Taroona on Route B68, was built in 1870. This sandstone tower is 48 metres high, and you can climb the 287 stairs for a good view of the estuary.

The Lady Franklin Gallery, headquarters of the Arts Society of Tasmania, is at the junction of Brushy Creek and Lenah Valley Roads in Lenah Valley.
This lovely little Grecian sandstone building was built in 1842 and is set in Lady Franklin Park. The Gallery is open only at weekends. It seems that Lady

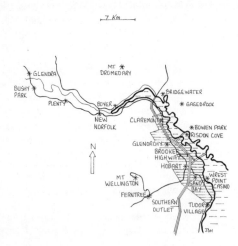

To get there, drive into Bellerive on Cambridge Road, and go around Victoria Esplanade to Gunning St Bellerive has many other interesting sites, several of which are clustered together near Kangaroo Bay. If you go to the Kangaroo Bay Boardwalk off Cambridge Road, you will be in easy walking distance of The Boer War Monument, the Old Post Office (built in sandstone in around 1897), and the Watch House, (early 1840s).

Also very close by is the National Trust classified 'Natone' (1860s) at 4 Petchey St, 'The Villa' (1858), and The Clarence Hotel (1879) which offers a collection of historical photographs).

Franklin purchased 410 acres of bushland here some time prior to the building of her museum. According to one source, the original name of this locality was 'The Vale of Ancanthe'. Take time to enjoy the little courtyard with its sandstone paving. Brushy Creek flows through the park with surroundings of blackwood and wattle.

Ask locally for directions to more places of historic interest, including some lovely old churches and a school house.

The Kangaroo Bluff Forts

The Kangaroo Bluff Forts are at Bellerive. Visit the interesting old fort, (built in the early 1880s) with gun emplacements facing down the Derwent, reminders of the century-old 'Russian threat'. There are lovely views of the harbour and mountain.

The Road to New Norfolk. To see historic New Norfolk, drive out of Hobart by the main road through Glenorchy, leaving Ogilvie Girls' High School on your left. Nearby is an historic Anglican Church, St John's. Along the main road also look out for Hestercombe Church, built in 1833 by Henry Hopkins, and the attractively gabled Granton Roadhouse, also built in 1833, but by George Robinson.

Glenorchy, once a suburb of Hobart, became Tasmania's third city in 1964. The district was first settled in 1809 by farmers, and was then known as 'O'Briens Bridge', after Thomas O'Brien, an early settler. Drive underneath the Brooker Highway underpass, and turn left. As you drive through Claremont, look out for the Cadbury Schweppes factory over to the right. Pass the sign to Chigwell on the left, then turn right where the sign indicates Launceston. Austins Ferry is on the left, and historic 'Austin Cottage' on the right.

Lady Franklin Gallery, Hobart

It is said that the original James Austin stole some beehives from his uncle by prior arrangement, so as to be able to travel to Van Diemen's Land as a transportee, rather than by paying his own fare out! He eventually did very well, amassing quite a large property here. Also at Austins Ferry is the scenic Poimena Reserve, featuring a native garden and spectacular panoramic views.On your left again you'll soon see aptly named Mount Dromedary. On your right look out for more black swans on the river. You may even see some pelicans.

Turn left up towards Launceston on Highway 1. Straight ahead is Route A10 to New Norfolk and Queenstown, while a curve to the right follows Highway 1 north to Launceston.

To visit New Norfolk, 17 km away, take Route A10. It's a pleasant drive in good weather: Mount Dromedary is now almost straight ahead. Until you reach New Norfolk, the Derwent River lies on your right. It is fresh water at this point, but brackish up as far as the bridge. Pass through Sorell Creek. On the opposite bank of the river look for the Boyer Paper Mill.

New Norfolk

New Norfolk's first known European visitor was a man named Lieutenant John Hayes, who was exploring in the area for the British East India Company and who sailed into the Derwent in 1793. The town was established in 1811 by Governor Macquarie, who originally named it Elizabeth Town in honour of his wife. In 1812, Denis McCarty, Irish convict turned policeman, was granted a block of land which is now occupied by the Boyer Mill. He remained in the area until he drowned in 1820. The town was finally re-named New Norfolk in reference to the huge influx of settlers from Norfolk Island.

'Tynewald' and the Oast House. In 1819 John Terry, first miller in the district, established his Lachlan River Mills at the junction of the Derwent and Lachlan Rivers. Some of Terry's descendants are still in the area. Lachlan River Mills was sold to a man named William Moore in 1898. He renamed it 'Tynewald', and expanded and elaborated on the house. It now offers accommodation to guests. Close by is Tynewald Park, once hop fields, but now parkland and playing fields. The turn-off to 'Tynewald' and the park is on the right almost opposite the Royal Derwent Hospital. Close by is the Oast House, converted by John Terry's son, Ralph, into a drying kiln for hops in 1867. In later years more kilns were built, and the whole

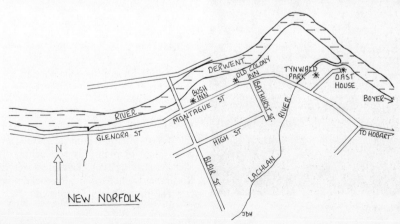

complex is now a museum depicting the history of the hop-growing industry, a gallery for local crafts and a tea room. Cross the River Lachlan, passing Amaroo Motel. Take a left-hand turn from the main road into the shopping area. Turn out of Pioneer Avenue into Bathurst St to see St Matthew's Anglican Church and St Matthew's Close (inspection invited). Lovely St Matthew's is the oldest surviving church in Tasmania, parts of it dating from 1823. The first chaplain, in 1825, was Rev. Hugh Robinson.

The stone floor is an interesting feature, and the windows, displaying a number of different styles, are lovely. These include a 'Parable of the Sower' and a 'Light of the World', both recent additions which blend delightfully with older windows. A very good pipe organ was built between 1914 and 1921, and was rebuilt in 1948. The carved eagle lectern was given in 1881 by a Mrs Sharland.

Around the church is a charming flower garden with anemones, grape hyacinths, hellebore, roses and others. As far as we know, St Matthew's is the only church to have such a garden; most churches seem to attract shrubs and trees rather than flowers.

St Matthew's Close (1866) is the home of the original Sunday School. In front of the Close are the millstones from the Lachlan River Mill, established by John Terry who arrived in 1819 in what was then Elizabeth Town, Buckinghamshire, Van Diemen's Land. Inside the Close is a picture gallery, museum and craft shop.

Turn right out of Bathurst St into High St and pass New Norfolk Hotel on the left. Go round the very large roundabout. The historic information centre is on your right. Go round past the war memorial, turn left into Burnett St, passing Pioneer Avenue on your right. The large cream and green building on your right at the bottom of the hill is the Bush Inn.

The Bush Inn was built in 1815 and began its licensed career in 1825. This makes it the oldest continuously licensed inn in Australia. The first licensee was Anne Bridger.

Turn right into Montagu St to visit the Old Colony Inn Museum and Tearoom at No. 21 Montagu St.

The Old Colony Inn was built c. 1835. It offers accommodation.

Rosie's Tavern. To see an interesting collection of colonial sketches, you may wish to visit Rosie's Tavern. This was originally built as residential quarters for Boyer Paper Mill, but now offers colonial accommodation.

Inside, when we saw it, Rosie's was furnished with red brocade and velvet, and the large sitting room featured an assortment of paintings and prints of sketches made by a colonial artist. To reach Rosie's, cross the Derwent River and turn left. The Tavern is well signposted.

Plenty Salmon Ponds

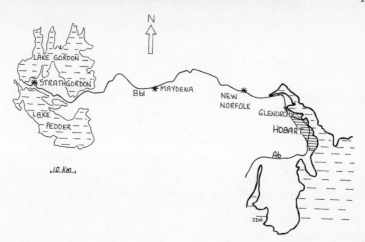

The route to the Plenty Salmon Ponds.
To see the Plenty Salmon Ponds, return up Montagu St, leave the bridge to the right and continue straight up Montagu St or, as it soon becomes Route B62, Glenora Road. The road takes you alongside the Derwent, with sandstone cliffs rising to the left. Pass to the left onto Route C610 to Mt Lloyd. Bushy Park and Maydena (famed for its enormous trees) are straight ahead at the junction and the Salmon Ponds are off to the left.

Bushy Park. In 1812 a mineralogist named A.W.H. Humphrey settled on a property be named 'Humphreyville'. It was later renamed 'Bushy Park'. In 1867 the property was bought by Ebenezer Shoobridge, whose father William had brought the first hops to the colony. Hops have been grown in the Derwent Valley since 1864, and some of the plants are over one hundred years old.

The Plenty Salmon Ponds are maintained by the inland Fisheries Commission for their historical interest.
In May 1864 trout and salmon eggs were hatched for the first time in the Southern Hemisphere. The eggs had been brought from England in an ice chest aboard the clipper *Norfolk*. In Melbourne, they were put aboard HM Colonial steam ship *Victoria* and brought down to Hobart. After that, carried in turn by river steamer, horses and humans, they were brought to the ponds. The fish were used to stock rivers and some were sent to other states and to New Zealand. The graded ponds are long, the fish are enormous, some of them being about half a metre long. The walk along the ponds is lined with labelled trees, including European and English ash, cedars, etc. Some of these trees are the oldest specimens of their kinds. There is also a picnic area, popular with tourists, and a museum and restaurant. From the ponds you can see the rear elevation of Mt Wellington.

A choice of routes

At this point you may choose to go on to Strathgordon or to return to Hobart via the Boyer Road and the Derwent Highway.
To return to Hobart, go back to New Norfolk and cross the Derwent by turning left out of Montagu St into Blair St, then right onto the Boyer Road, Route B10. This route takes you back, hugging the river bank, past Boyer Mills and Mt Dromedary, to Bridgewater.

Rosny. Rosny Historic Centre is on the eastern shore, close to Eastlands Shopping Centre. The centre comprises Rosny Barn (c 1815), Rosny Cottage (c 1850) and the Schoolhouse Gallery.

Risdon Cove. To see historic Rosny and Risdon Cove turn left at Bridgewater onto Highway 1 and then right onto Route B32, the Derwent Highway. Follow this route through the new outer suburb of Gagebrook, past Old Beach and Mt Direction on your left, past Otago and the Bowen Bridge to Bowen Park at Risdon. Pass the Bowen Bridge and the Zinc Works beyond it. Turn right along B32 to Risdon Vale on C324. To your left is Risdon Cove, the site of the first European settlement in Tasmania, where 49 convicts, settlers and soldiers under the command of 23-year-old Lt John Bowen settled in September 1803. Only five months later the settlement was moved to Sullivans Cove by Lt Governor David Collins, and the Risdon Cove site was abandoned.

The road to Strathgordon. If you choose to go on from the Plenty Salmon Ponds towards Strathgordon, you'll be passing through Bushy Park and the hopfields about 7 km farther along Route B62. Go through Glenora and Tyenna, and turn off to the left at Westerway, into the Gordon River Road.

Another 6 or 7 km brings you to the turn-off into Mount Field National Park, 37 km west of New Norfolk.

Strathgordon Dam

Lake Pedder near Strathgordon

Mount Field National Park is the oldest National Park in Tasmania. It was named after Judge Barren Field, a judge of the N.S.W. Supreme Court, who came to Tasmania in 1819. The park is popular with walkers, campers and skiers, with a variety of walking tracks ranging from a simple stroll suited to young children and the elderly to tracks which challenge the experienced bushwalker.

As well as mountains, the park contains many lakes and tarns. A popular feature of the park is the Russell Falls, close to the entrance.

On to Strathgordon. The road goes right through to Lake Dobson. Continue along the Gordon River road, running alongside the Tyenna River. Pass through tiny Fitzgerald. The next town, Maydena, is notable for being the last source of petrol on this road.

It takes around an hour and a quarter to drive the remaining distance from Maydena to Strathgordon. About 17 km from Maydena look out to your left for The Needles.There should be no problems in recognising the features along this road; it

is generously signposted, with arrows indicating the various hills and mountains. Near Pontoon Hill is The Needles picnic area, and 2 or 3 km farther along is Saw Back picnic area.

At this point you should be able to see Lake Gordon.

At Frodsham's Pass, a gravel road turns off to the left, taking you 34 km south to Edgar Dam and Scotts Peak Dam. The last 10 or so km of this road hug Edgar Bay in the 'enlarged' Lake Pedder, passing Mounts Anne and Eliza.

The road gives access for bushwalkers to these mountains, and near its end is the trackhead for Port Davey (about 4 days).

South West National Park is true wilderness. It includes mountains such as Federation Peak, Port Davey, buttongrass plains, Tasmanian myrtle forests, old Huon pine, (*Dacrydium fianklinii*), and many places still largely unexplored.

There are a few marked tracks for bushwalkers, but only experienced walkers should attempt them and must first register with the appropriate authority.

You may, of course, choose to stay on the Gordon River Road, heading for Strathgordon and Lakes Pedder and Gordon. The Serpentine and Gordon Rivers were first navigated in 1958 by Lithuanian-born Olegas Truchanas (1923–1972), a lone explorer and photographer who has left a splendid photographic record of the wilderness as it was before the original small Lake Pedder and its glacial valley were flooded in 1972 to form the present giant lake and dam.

The area is now very popular with photographers, artists, boaters, walkers, climbers and fishermen. The combined Lakes Pedder and Gordon cover over 500 sq. km, forming Australia's largest freshwater storage. The township of Strathgordon itself is much smaller than it was in its heyday when the dam was being built. In the late 1970s, the town was booming, but by 1988 there were only about 25 families living there. By 1996 this had dropped to just fourteen permanent residents.

A couple of kilometres past Strathgordon is the Serpentine Lookout, which enables you to see right down the lake.

The Pedder area has 190 cm of rain a year, drizzling most of the winter; it is hot during the summer, with the temperature climbing to the forties. Strathgordon is in a valley surrounded with wooded hills, and just behind the town is Twelve Trees Range, with a walking track up the side. Past the Serpentine Lookout is the underground power station, the Serpentine and Gordon dams—and the end of the road.

BIBLIOGRAPHY

Books
BACKHOUSE, Sue, *Tasmanian Artists of the Twentieth Century*.
EMMETT, E.T. *Tasmania by Road and Track*, Melbourne University Press, 1953.
The Australian Almanac, Angus and Robertson, 1985
The World of Olegas Truchanas, the Olegas Truchanas Publication Committee, Hobart, 1975.
UBD St Directory.

Pamphlets
'A Guide to The Anglican Church of St Matthew's, New Norfolk'
Bellerive Village. A Walk through History.
Clarence Municipal Council: 'Passive Recreation Areas in Clarence':
'Risdon Cove Historic Site: Site Guide'
'Tasmania's National Parks and Historic Sites', (Nat. Parks and Wildlife Service)
'Let's Talk About Anglesea Barracks'
'Let's Talk About Battery Point'
'Let's Talk About Glenorchy'
'Let's Talk About New Norfolk'
'Let's Talk About The Royal Tasmanian Botanical Gardens'
(All from Tasmania Visitor Corporation and Tasmanian Travel Centre.)

Maps
Tasmap 1: 100 000 Land Tenure Index Series:
'Derwent', 'Tyenna', 'Wedge', 'Old River'

Information
Thanks to Elizabeth Barber, Chris and Kathryn Bramich, Heather Chauncy, June Green, Colin and Rosie Wood, National Parks and Wildlife, the staff at *The Mercury* and Devonport Tasmanian Travel Centre and the City of Clarence Council Chambers.

15. West on Route A10

Features of this drive

Oddly enough, although the west coast was the first part of Tasmania to be sighted by Europeans, it was the last part to be serviced by road, with the four towns of Zeehan, Queenstown, Strahan and Rosebery growing up largely isolated from the rest of the state. Mount Heemskirk and Mount Zeehan were named by Bass and Flinders in 1798, after Abel Tasman's ships. This drive is the one to take if you love wild scenery and mountains. It also offers power developments, some historic sandstone buildings, and a visit to the geographical centre of Tasmania.

The route to the west coast

To reach the west coast from the capital, leave Hobart on Route A1 towards Launceston. On your left, just past the Bridgewater turn-off, is the Old Watchhouse Museum, built in 1838. Cross Sorell Creek, passing Boyer newsprint on your right. On your right on Route A10 you pass the Oast House and 'Tynewald', Old Colony Inn and Bush Inn. On your left are 'Glen Derwent' built in 1820 and once known as the 'King of Prussia Inn' and 'Valleyfield', which is about the same age.

Follow Route A10 towards Queenstown, which is 221 km away. Pass through Lawitta and Hayes, where the prison farm is on the right, and cross Puzzle Gate Creek. Along the roadside are lots of hawthorns, poplars and blackwoods, with very attractive gum trees lining the river. The blackwoods flower during September, and the hawthorns in late October. The road leaves the Derwent at this point. Springs

Creek and Cawthorns Lane to the left run through Macquarie Plains, named after Governor Lachlan Macquarie. The next town is tiny Rosegarland, proud possessor of arguably the prettiest town name in Tasmania.

Derwent Valley Names, Rosegarland isn't the only quaint or unusual name in the Derwent Valley. Here is a sample taken at random; we haven't been able to find out the histories behind these names, but they conjure up all sorts of possibilities. . . Bachelors Flat, Bedchamber Hill, Bedding Hill, Big Peacock, Charlies Hope Creek, The Cockpit, Cobos Creek, Hollow Tree, Little Peacock, Nellys Gully, Norton Mandeville, Officers Bottom, Plenty, The Pound Creek, and Thieving Hill.

Many of the other names argue a heavy concentration of Scottish settlers.

Just out of Rosegarland you'll come to the turn-off left into route B61 to Mount Field National Park, 23 km away and Strathgordon 109 (See Chapter 14).

Shortly past the turn-off comes tiny Gretna with the Gretna Green Hotel and Gretna Store on the left. St Mary's Church, built in 1848, can be seen up Church Road to your right.

A little farther on, you'll see a sandstone house up to your left. This one is called 'Glenelg', and was built in 1878 for the Downie family. The architect was Henry Hunter. It is a private home, and is not open for inspection. Another house on your left is 'Greenwich', built for the Downie family in 1915.

Meadowbank Dam may be reached by route C642 to the left. It is the lowest of the three dams comprising the Lower Derwent Power Development Scheme and a concrete buttress dam, 263 m long and 43 m high. It was commissioned in 1967. The other two dams in the Lower Derwent Development are Cluny (also commissioned in 1967), and Repulse (1968).

Route B110 leads off the Lyell Highway to the right to Hollow Tree and Bothwell (see Chapter 17) shortly after the Hamilton Plains Road to the left.

Historic Hamilton

About 3 km from Hamilton Plains Road you reach lovely Hamilton itself, one of the most charming yet sleepy of the southern towns. It was originally supposed to have been much more important than it ultimately was—the granary and centre for a district. On your left as you enter the town look for St Peter's Church, built in the mid-1830s. The sandstone church has a square tower. Glen Clyde House Gallery is on your right, and then 'Emma's Cottage' (c. 1830), accommodation, a small sandstone cottage. 'George's', another cottage offering accommodation, was built in 1845. Nearby is the Old School House, built in 1856. Historic Hamilton Inn was built in 1834. Coming out of Hamilton, you'll cross the Clyde River, a good place for fishing.

Ouse and the Dams. Fifteen km on from Hamilton you'll come to Ouse, (pronounced 'ooze'), on the River Ouse. On your right is another sandstone church with a graveyard around it. Aside from the churches, there are fewer sandstone buildings in Ouse than in Hamilton, and the towns are curiously unalike.

From Ouse a left hand turn-off (Route

Hamilton

C606), leads about 7 km to Lake Repulse, the Cluny Lagoon and the Repulse and Cluny Dams. These two dams are a little smaller than Meadowbank Dam downstream, and are of a slightly different construction, Repulse being a concrete arch and Cluny plain concrete.

Cross over the Dee River. Fourteen km from Ouse, Route C605 to your left leads to Catagunya Dam.

Catagunya Dam. 'Catagunya' is a Tasmanian Aboriginal word meaning 'black swan'. Catagunya Dam, begun in 1959, and commissioned three years later, was at that time the largest dam of its type in the world. It is now the second largest of the six dams constituting the River Derwent Power Development. Made of pre-stressed concrete, it is 280 m long and 49 m high.

The Nive River and the Lyell Highway

Cross Black Bobs Rivulet and Ringing Creek, and soon you'll come to the Nive River, (pronounced to rhyme with 'dive'). Just before crossing the river look to the left for Route C604 to Wayatinah Power Station. 'Wayatinah' means 'a brook or a creek'.

To the left is a turn-off to Wayatinah camping area, which leads c. 60 km back along the unsealed Florentine Road to Maydena, home of the tallest known hardwood tree in the world. A little farther on, also to the left, is a sign pointing to a steep left hand turn to an observation point and fireplace. This part of the drive is through pleasant bushland with tall gums and ferns along the road. Close by to the left, but out of sight of the road, is Lake Wayatinah with the Liapootah (meaning: 'creek') Power Station.

A few kilometres farther on is a turn-off to the right leading past Liapootah Dam and Lake Liapootah to rejoin Route A10 at Tarraleah, (meaning: a forester kangaroo). About 4 km from this turn-off, Route A10 takes a sharp right-hand turn, with Route C603 going straight ahead towards Butlers Gorge and the lower end of Lake King William, 16 km away.

Turn right, still on A10. Queenstown is now 134 km away. Cross Tarraleah Canal, and to your left look out for Tarraleah Number One Canal. Tarraleah Village is 4 km away.

The Tarraleah Scheme, which uses water from the upper Derwent catchment from the storage lakes of St Clair (almost natural) and King William (man-made), was begun in 1934. Tarraleah village has a permanent population of approximately 500 people. Tourists are welcome, and meals and accommodation are available.

Shortly before you reach Tarraleah, you'll pass a picnic area on your tight and another road leading off left from a second right-angled bend. This is Route C601, Fourteen Mile Road, an unsealed 'shortcut' leading north to rejoin the highway at Nive Plains. Supposing you decide to stay on Route A10, you'll see the huge pipeline leading to Tarraleah. Cross the Nive River, passing Tungatinah (meaning: 'a shower of rain') Power Station on your right.

Tungatinah scheme uses water from the Clarence, Nive, Dee, Ouse and Little Pine River catchments. Hydro staff and their families live at Tarraleah village. The Nive River Scheme, including Tungatinah, was begun in the late 1940s.

Also to the right is Tarraleah golf course. To the left are extremely tall wattles and a very steep downhill run. Just over the bridge from Tarraleah Power Station, a road leads off 3 km to Liapootah Dam. This is the other end of the same road mentioned earlier. There are toilets available in this area.

The road through the Tarraleah area is something of a switchback, but there are magnificent views to compensate and the road itself is well made.

Lake Binney. As you cross Nive Marsh Rivulet you'll be passing Tungatinah Lagoon on your right, and then lovely Lake Binney, named after Sir Hugh Binney, Governor of Tasmania from 24 December 1945 until 8 May 1951. Soon after you pass Lake Binney, the dense forest thins out and is quickly replaced by buttongrass plains to left and right, just about as far as you can see. The next feature on the right is the western shore of Bradys Lake, and then the

Centre of Tasmania

highway loops around past the right-hand turn-off into Route C173 to Osterley, to pass along the eastern shore of Bronte Lagoon.

The Centre of Tasmania. About 50 m past the Osterley turn-off is a stone Surveyors' monument. This monument, located near the geographical centre of Tasmania, was erected in 1983 by members of the Institution of Surveyors to commemorate the early members of their profession who explored and mapped the area.
pic 95
Just past the monument, Route B11, the Marlborough Highway, leads off to the right to Bronte Park and to link with the Lake Highway (see Chapter 17) at Miena, on the western shore of Great Lake about 37 km away. It is 107 km to Queenstown from this point.

Bronte Park was originally a hydro village, established in the late 1940s to serve as a dormitory town for the construction workers of the Tungatinah Power scheme. Like most villages of its type this one has shrunk, but is now enjoying a new identity as a tourist centre offering different types of accommodation, domestic and native animals, fishing, bushwalking and many other attractions. Cross the Nive River once more, on a very narrow bridge, passing through bare and rather barren countryside comprising buttongrass and rocks. Two km farther on you pass the other end of Route C601, the Fourteen Mile Road.

Cross the Clarence River. The mountain you see ahead shortly afterwards is Mt Olympus. The countryside from this point on is fairly featureless until you meet the surprisingly narrow (at this point!) Derwent River at Derwent Bridge, wedged between the upper end of Lake King William and the lower end of Lake St Clair. The source of the Derwent was a mystery for some time until a man named Alexander McKay, a member of Surveyor George Frankland's party, sighted it in 1835.

The 83 km road between Derwent Bridge and Queenstown travels through a World Heritage area: the Western Tasmania Wilderness National Parks Area was inscribed on the 1982 World Heritage List. Without stops, the drive between the two towns will take about one and a half hours in good weather. Be warned: there are no shops or service stations along this route.

Lake St Clair and Surveyor Frankland

Lake St Clair may have been first sighted by W.S. Sharland in 1833, but it was officially discovered in 1835 by Surveyor George Frankland (1800–1838), who was appointed Assistant Surveyor in 1826 and later became Surveyor General. Some of his major achievements included establishing the locations of the Nive, Derwent, Gordon and Huon River systems. It was on this particular expedition that he discovered and named the lake, after a family in Scotland.

Derwent Bridge was frequently used as a base camp for those venturing into the wilderness of the west. After crossing the Derwent, turn right on Route C193 to see Lake St Clair, 5 km away.

At the lake the last time we visited we found a kiosk and Ranger Station, with rangers in attendance at all times. Food was available at the kiosk for the Bennett's wallabies, who would thus become your friends for life—the life of your feed bag, that is! The area about the lake offers walks, including the Watersmeet Nature Walk where the Cuvier and Hugel Rivers meet at Cynthia Bay. This 3 km return walk takes you through tall open eucalypt forest, buttongrass sedgeland and tea-tree scrub. Look out for black cockatoos, wallabies, currawongs and, in the evenings, brushtail possums,

Lake St Clair is over 17 km long, 22 sq. km in area, and at 200 m, is the deepest lake in Tasmania. It is well known as the destination for the Cradle Mountain overland track which passes in its final stage round the lake's western shore. Mount Ossa, Tasmania's highest mountain (1 617 m), is in the 132 000 ha National Park.

A caravan park and cabins, set among the wattles and bottle brushes, are available at the lake, making this an ideal spot for a family holiday.

The Franklin Track

It was from Lake St Clair that the Franklin Track began. In 1838, J.E. Calder and Alexander McKay came through the area to prepare a route for Sir John and Lady Franklin's planned overland journey, due to take place in 1842. The Franklins wished to go to Macquarie Harbour to investigate the possibility of re-opening the penal settlement on Sarah Island there. This settlement had been established by Governor Sorell in 1821, and abandoned in 1833. An account of the Franklins' trip has come down from the diary of David

Burn, who accompanied them. The Franklin Track was used again in 1890 when the overland telegraph line came through.

Mining had begun on the west coast in 1883, and the development of various centres, including Zeehan, persuaded the government of the need for more efficient communication. The main base of the men who serviced the line was at Osterley, and their first day's journey would take them up to the Clarence River. The second day's journey brought them to the Iron Store (near Nevarre River), the next to the Wooden Store (near Scarlett Creek.) and then Lynchford (near Queenstown) and then, finally, to Strahan.

After the telegraph line was finished many people followed that track to Mount Lyell to work at the mine, and the same thing happened again in the late 1920s and early 1930s during the Depression. The Lyell Highway was opened in 1932 and it was then a 6–8 hour trip between Queenstown and Hobart, depending on how your car survived the road! Before the road was sealed, there were patrolmens' huts every 10 miles, lessening the dangers of being stranded in the lonely west. Now there are fewer permanent residents, so care is needed when driving this way in winter.

A Local's Tips for Driving through Snow. If caught in snowy weather on Mt Arrowsmith or other parts of the Lyell Highway, do not stop, and do not touch your brakes, but drive slowly.

Return along Route C193 to the Lyell Highway and turn right towards Queenstown. The Derwent River on your left runs into Lake King William near here. About 10 km from Derwent Bridge look out for Mount Rufus on your right. Mount Rufus was once a popular skiing venue. When new immigrant Australians came to Butlers Gorge in the late 1940s, they used to walk from Butlers Gorge through to the mountain, where there remain two ski huts,

Joe Slater Hut and Gingerbread Hut. They had quite a ski club there and later when the hydro work was finished, they transferred to jobs in Hobart and, with other immigrants, many of them from Switzerland, they formed the Mt Wellington Ski Club which is now at Mt Field. Few people ski on Rufus these days. Shortly after passing Mt Rufus look to your left to see Mt King William 1, seen by Sir John Franklin in 1842. He referred to it as the 'Lion's Head', but it was later renamed as part of the King William Range.

Cross the Navarre River. It was in this vicinity that the Iron Store Depot for the building of the telegraph line was situated, and somewhere around there is still said to be a tree bearing the date 2 April, 1842, carved by a member of the Franklin party. Cross King William Creek. To your right are the Burns Plains, a camping spot named by Lady Franklin after diarist David Burn who travelled with them. The Franklin Track, now overgrown, passes behind Mt Arrowsmith. Once known as Fatigue Hill, Mt Arrowsmith was named in 1841–42 by the Polish explorer Count Strzlecki for a 19th century map-maker. The Lyell Highway goes over the mountain. From this side Mt Arrowsmith doesn't look like a mountain at all; you need to go down the other side to appreciate its height! The names of the early explorers are everywhere: to the right of Arrowsmith is Calders Lookout and to the left McKays Peak. Away to the right is Mt Gell. As you reach the top of Mt Arrowsmith you can just see Gell; a better view may be had from the bottom! Mt Gell was named for Rev. Gell, the son-in-law of Sir John Franklin. On your right is a turn-off to Burns Creek Dam. Straight ahead is the distinctive peak known as Frenchmans Cap.

Frenchmans Cap is 1443 metres tall. Opinion is very much divided on how the Cap got its name. It is often covered with snow, but even in warm weather it retains

Lookout to the Frenchman's Cap

its distinctive white colouring due to its quartzite composition. It is a favourite challenge for climbers.

As you come down Arrowsmith you're virtually surrounded by mountain peaks. The hump to the right is known as The Beehive for the strangely-shaped rocks round about. The Franklin Track went round behind it. Mt Arrowsmith has a reputation for snow; sometimes the Lyell Highway is rendered impassable at this point.

On your left, look out for the aptly named Surprise Valley, a wide vista of the celery top pines, lemon scented tea-tree and sassafras of the temperate forests, the trees all covered with lichen and the rocks with red algae. There is a lookout area marked where you may pull off the road and enjoy the spectacular view.

West Coast Weather and Geology.

Although the west coast of Tasmania has a reputation for rain, (approximately 2500 mm of rain falls annually, with around three hundred days of the year being at least partly wet), the day we travelled the Lyell in 1988 it was brilliantly sunny and very warm indeed—tee-shirt weather in September! By chance we travelled the

same route in September 1996. It was cold, with intermittent rain and some snow, but its splendours had remained unchanged. Be prepared for almost any kind of weather when travelling in the west!

The Surprise River goes through the Valley: if it isn't too windy you should be able to hear it. Beyond is the Lodden Range and Mt Ronald Cross, named after the Right Hon. Sir Ronald Hibbert Cross, who governed Tasmania from August 1951 until June 1958. An information plaque at the lookout area had this to say:

West and East: The watershed above you divided Tasmania into regions strongly contrasted in geology, topography, vegetation and rainfall. Eastwards to your left as you face the plaque), the King William Range is visible on your left and shows dolerite crags capping sub horizontal mudstones and sandstones to the west (on your right) jagged mountains like the Frenchmans Cap are mostly ancient quartzites . . .

Among the features named for the early explorers a more homely character is commemorated in Taffys Creek, which is named for Taffy 'the Bee Man' Huxtable, who camped in the bush and sold honey. A local resident remembers Taffy's consternation when he had an order from America for seventy tons of leatherwood honey !

As you come to the foot of Arrowsmith, flat Wombat Glen is on your right. It was here in 1832, that Surveyor W. Sharland found a skeleton, probably the remains of an escaped convict. Later, in 1840, Surveyor J.E. Calder discovered articles of clothing presumably left by another escapee.

The buttongrass growing here so prevalently is apparently the result of the Aborigines' policy of firing the ground so as to attract game to the new shoots. After several such firings the ground would grow little else.

Near the glen, you will come to a picnic area on the left-hand side of the road. Park here for a short (10 minutes return) nature walk along the bank of the Franklin River. At one stage there was some confusion between the names of the Franklin and King Rivers, but this was sorted out in around 1862. Walk down under the bridge. The nature walk is simple and easy and is bound to appeal to families with young children; and this is your only opportunity to see the famous Franklin River from the road. Every few metres a small information plaque is planted, giving the names and characteristics of such plants as the hard river fern, horizontal scrub, leatherwood (flowering in February) native laurels, mosses, sweet scented sassafras, (flowering in September) and the lovely myrtle beech (*Nothofagus cunninghamii*).

Down to the left of the highway past the bridge is the turn-off to the Jane River Track. The Jane is a tributary of the Franklin, named after Lady Franklin. The Jane River area was the site of the 1930s gold rush.

Three km west of the bridge over the Franklin, the walking track to Frenchmans Cap begins. Fifteen minutes' walk will bring you to the aerial cableway for the crossing of the river. Apparently the walk to the Cap takes about five days return and is suitable only for experienced bushwalkers. To your right is what is left of the Linda Track, cut in c. 1887–1890. The track was used again during the Depression of the late 1920s and early 1930s by would-be workers from Hobart travelling west.

Cross Stonehaven Creek. In front of you here is a fine view of Frenchmans Cap. To your right is Artist Hill, with a convenient lay-by to the left of the highway. It seems that this spot is popular with artists, who like to sit on Artist Hill and paint the view of the Cap!

As you drive on from here, Frenchmans Cap appears to be retreating. Not long after you lose sight of the Cap you'll be rounding a bend. Directly to your left is the valley of the Franklin River. Soon, you'll cross Double Barrel Creek. On your left is a lay-by and the beginning of the track to the Donaghys Hill Lookout, probably named for a Donaghy who was woodcutter. The walk to the lookout takes about 40 minutes return, and is reasonably steep, but well worth the time and effort. As you climb towards the lookout, look down to your left to see the Franklin River almost directly underneath Frenchmans Cap, and down to the right to the Collingwood River, which meets the Franklin here.

Collingwood River

When you finally reach the top, look out over the Franklin-Lower Gordon Wild Rivers National Park. The wooden lookout has handy signs identifying the various landmarks, which include Mts King William I, II and III, Mt Ronald Cross, Mt Mullens and Junction Peak. If you are lucky enough to climb this lookout on a fine sunny day, the view is truly breathtaking— which is just as well, as you will probably feel like a rest before climbing down again! Back on the highway, drive on to cross the Collingwood River. To your left is the Collingwood Range and away to your right the beautifully named Plain of the Mists. Cross Cool Creek and Scarlett Creek, approximate site of the Wooden Store of the Overland Telegraph Line. For the men who inspected the line this Wooden Store was a day's march from the previous base on the other side of Mt Arrowsmith.

The Crimean Connection. Many of the names selected by Gould in 1862 for the rivers hereabouts have Crimean origins— although some of them might seem to refer to a knitwear convention! The Collingwood, the Alma, the Inkerman, the Cardigan and the Balaclava all commemorate either British Generals or battles. On the right of the highway near Cardigan River are the Cardigan Flats, with their fine display of native heaths. From the lay-by here you can see the Raglan and Cheyne Ranges and Camp and Rocky Hills.

As you come over the Victoria Pass, you will see the back of Mt Owen and Mt Lyell straight ahead. To your left is Raglan Range. About 4 km beyond the Pass you teach the Nelson River Bridge. On the other side is a parking bay, marking the beginning of the Nelson Falls Track. Walk back over the bridge, and follow the track leading off to your left. Farther downstream

Nelson Falls

the Nelson River disappears underground! This downstream area is not recommended for exploration, owing to dangerous sink holes, but Nelson Falls is a 20-minute return walk over a good flat gravel track. The falls themselves are spectacularly beautiful and very tall, coming down over black rocks with ferns growing partway up the drop. The falls area is surrounded with ferns and moss.

Shortly after you leave the Nelson River cross Nelson Creek, and then negotiate 2 km. of winding road. Mt Lyell and Mt Sedgewick are ahead to your right. The lake you will see now is Lake Burberry, part of the King River Hydro Scheme. Cross Bradshaw Bridge, and take a few moments to appreciate the majestic ring of mountains before continuing on the final stretch of road to Queenstown.

Lake Burberry near Queenstown

BIBLIOGRAPHY
Books
EMMETT, E.T., *Tasmania by Road and Track*, Melbourne University Press, 1952.
NEWITT, Lyn, *Convicts and Carriageways*. Historical Committee of the Department of Main Roads, Tasmania, 1988.
The Australian Almanac, Angus and Robertson, 1985.

Pamphlets
'Tarraleah Tungatinah Power Development', H.E.C.
'Bronte Park Highland Village'
'Watersmeet Nature Walk', National Parks and Wildlife Service.
'Lake St Clair', National Parks and Wildlife Service
'Lyell Highway'

Maps
Tasmap 1: 100 000 Land Tenure Index Series:
'Tyrenna', 'Shannon', 'Nive', 'Franklin'

Information
Thanks to the late Mr Murfet and Jean Sarson and The National Parks and Wildlife Service.

16. Queenstown, Strahan and Zeehan

Features of this drive

At one time, there was a single route from Queenstown to the north, now there are choices. The distances involved are not great, but you need to allow a fair amount of time to negotiate the roads which are often steep and winding. Outside the towns there are no sources of petrol or food, so stock up before you leave. The drive offers mountains, temperate rainforest, mine tours, river cruises, museums, waterfalls, ghost towns, a 33 km beach, impressive dunes, some fine late Victorian buildings and spectacular views, including some of the most surreal scenery in Tasmania.

The West Coast of Tasmania is a wild and lonely place, with a history centered squarely on mining. Even Strahan, a peaceful and lovely fishing town, had its beginnings as a mining port. Because all the major, minor, ghost and re-animated mining towns of the west share so much of their history, we have not detailed the complicated ins and outs of every mine. For anyone who is specifically interested in the mines and their pasts, presents and futures, we can heartily recommend a visit to the museum in the old School of Mines building at Zeehan, the purchase of one of the many excellent books available, and enquiry at the mining centres themselves, some of which offer tours. Despite all this, and even if you're not at all interested in mines and mining towns, we still urge any visitor to Tasmania to see the west coast. It has a special flavour of its own.

To Queenstown and the West

The King River Power Development's Lake Burberry has submerged the old road which used to lead to Crotty Camp and the North Mt Lyell Copper Co. railway line. This has been replaced by the Mt Jukes Road. Drive through Linda, where the miners from the North Mt Lyell Mine of James Crotty once lived. Up behind the peak of Little Mt Owen is the original 'Iron Blow', discovered in around 1888.

James Crotty was an Irishman from County Clare. He arrived in Victoria c. 1860, and then came to Tasmania, first to the Pieman River, then later to Linda where he met prospector Mick McDonough, and bought out his share of the famous 'Iron Blow', of which he had been one of the discoverers. In 1891 Crotty held a quarter interest in the mine. Here, with determination, luck and good management, he flourished, finally dying in London in 1898, a rich man. The township of Crotty, which was once expected to be as important as Queenstown, lost ground rapidly from 1903 when the North Lyell and Mt Lyell Companies amalgamated.

Linda, in the Chamouni Valley between Mts Owen and Lyell, was once a flourishing mining village. It was complete with houses, Post Office, four hotels, and shops—but, for much of its history, no church. Its life and decline after the Lyell Highway was built is told in the book *Linda, Ghost Town of Mt. Lyell* by Edward John ('Rocky') Wedd, who spent much of his life in the town.

Gormanston, named for Viscount Gormanston, (Jenico William Joseph Preston), Governor of Tasmania 1893–1900, is apparently known to its friends as 'Gormie'. A true mining town, within walking distance of the Mt Lyell Mine, it survived for some time after Linda's decline but is now almost deserted.

Once past Gormanston, you'll soon drive past Karlsons Gap, (probably named for early prospector Steve Karlson, partner of the McDonough brothers). The waterfall you may see on your left has a number of names: King William Falls, Moores Creek—the locals seem to refer to it as the Mt Owen Falls.

From the top of this road, you'll look down into Queenstown, crouching in a valley with its celebrated bare hills looming on every side.

Early history of Queenstown

Queenstown, or 'Queenie' as it is sometimes called, began as a typical mining town in 1896. Situated on the banks of the Queen River, Queenstown is the largest of the western towns. Its history really began when a prospector named Cornelius Lynch found gold in Lynchs Creek, a tributary of the Queen River, in around 1881. The settlement of Lynchford sprouted, for a time supporting two hotels, but has now disappeared. Within months of Lynch's discovery, other creeks around Mt Lyell had been found to harbour gold. These creeks were diligently worked by various prospectors, but it was two years later when the major source of metals in the area, the 'Iron Blow', was discovered at Mt Lyell by Steve Karlson and Mick McDonough. With Mick's brother Bill, the men pegged out 50 acres including the 'Blow', which they considered as the most likely source of the gold in the local creeks. Although the gold concentration in Mt Lyell was not heavy, the Mt. Lyell Gold Mining Company was formed in 1888 and continued for some years. The mine changed hands and the mining of gold gave way to the mining of copper. A new company was formed in 1893, and was greatly assisted by a rich vein of silver which lasted just long enough to get the company 'on its feet'. The shanty town of Penghana, where construction workers for the reduction works and railway terminus lived, burnt down in 1896. The inhabitants moved to establish Queenstown. By 1901 Queenstown had over 5000 people but 20 years later this had declined to 2900.

Queenstown today

Visitors to modern Queenstown may be pardoned for thinking they have accidentally been deported to the moon, for the amazing bare hills have a very surreal

Queenstown today

Galley Museum, begun by Eric Thomas. This museum is well worth visiting; it has a number of old pictures, beds, clothes, telephones and a magnificent collection of china commemorating the British Royal Family.

At **Miners' Siding,** across the street from the Galley Museum, is a huge lump of copper ore, mined from Mt Lyell. This lump of ore bears an impressive description of itself. Also at Miners' Siding is a Mt Lyell Number 3 Engine, an Abt system, mounted on a trestle above water. The engine was built in Glasgow and commissioned at Queenstown in Oct. 1898. It travelled almost a million miles during its working life. The Abt system (rack railway) was part of the line which ran between Queenstown and the port at Strahan from 1896, and until the west coast main road was opened in 1932 it was the only transport link between Queenstown and the rest of the state. Five locomotives operated on the railway, and four still exist. The line was closed down in 1963.

Also at Miners' Siding are eleven bronze relief sculptures by Stephen Walker, depicting scenes from Queenstown's history, and, as the *pièce de resistance*, there is Miners' Sunday, a large and wonderful work depicting a flannel-shirted nineteenth century Mt Lyell miner and his family in bronze and Huon Pine. 'Miners' Sunday' was commissioned in 1983 by the Mt Lyell Mining and Railway Company Ltd to commemorated the Lyell district's centenary. It was cast in Queenstown. On the corner of Driffield and Orr streets is the old Empire Hotel. In its heyday, Queenstown had 14 hotels, but most of them have closed now. Along Orr St is Hunters Hotel, built in 1898.

quality when seen in evening or early morning light. The bareness is the result of a number of factors, including felling of trees to burn in the smelters, the sulphur fumes of the smelters themselves and the twin hazards of fire and reduced rainfall. A few of the hills show signs of returning vegetation, but most Queenstowners who are proud of their unique surroundings.

Queenstown is a town where people seem to go out of their ways to be helpful: a simple request for directions will probably result in an instant offer to escort you to wherever you wish to go, plus friendly advice on the best way to go about whatever you might be planning to do.

In and Around Queenstown. You'll be entering Queenstown on the Lyell Highway, which runs into Batchelor St. At first the town appears to be very small, but soon you'll reach the shopping centre around Driffield St. On the left as you enter Driffield St, you'll see the two-storey

Tourist information can be found Number 1 Driffield St, just across from the Empire Hotel. This is also the depot for Lyell Tours and wilderness walks. The tours on offer include four wheel drive tours of the west coast wilderness, coach tours of the surface of the mine, and underground tours. These should be pre-booked, and any stated conditions as to suitable clothing and level of fitness observed. The current telephone number for bookings (1996) is (03) 6471 2388. Anyone taking any of these tours will learn a great deal about the workings of the mines, past and present, and a fair slice of west coast history.

A walk down Orr St brings you over Sticht St (named after American Robert Carl Sticht, designer of the first Mt Lyell smelters in 1895, whose two-storey house 'Penghana' may still be seen up on the hill) and Bowes St, named after Bowes Kelly a mining investor who bought the then Mt Lyell Gold Mine in 1891. There are plenty of interesting buildings to see along the way. If you drive down Driffield St, you can turn left into Knox St and left again into McNamara St and drive past the hospital and over Alfred St to see the old cemetery. If you have any difficulty finding your way, just ask.

Queenstown to Strahan

To reach the coastal town of Strahan, (pronounced 'strawn'), turn left just beyond Miners' Siding where the Murchison Highway begins. Strahan is 38 km away. Just before you leave Queenstown, you see the Queenstown Chairlift on your left and the Mt Lyell Museum on your right.

The 38 km road to Strahan is rather narrow and winding, but is sealed for the whole distance. During the first part of the journey, the view is dominated by the bare hills of Queenstown, particularly Mt Lyell and Mt Owen, but farther along, you reach thick scrub on both sides of the road.

Things to see in Strahan. As you enter the town of Strahan, you'll see a beautiful view of the Strahan Harbour and great

Strahan Council Chambers

Macquarie Harbour, extending many km away to your left. The Franklin and Gordon Rivers empty into Macquarie Harbour at its southern end and the harbour itself is almost landlocked, with just the very narrow entrance at Macquarie Heads. Strahan is a pretty place, and receives much less rain than the other west coast towns. Visitors may enjoy water sports, beachcombing along impressive Ocean Beach, photography and bushwalking. Turn left into Strahan and drive past impressive Strahan Council Chambers and Library Building (c.1901) and past Hamers Hotel and the depot for Gordon River Cruises.

The Gordon River was discovered, by Captain James Kelly, in 1815 when, with four other seamen, he circumnavigated Tasmania in a whaleboat in 49 days. He discovered and named Port Macquarie, the Gordon River, (after James Gordon of Pittwater who had lent the whaleboat for the expedition), and Port Davey. Cruises up the Gordon River have been popular for 100 years and are offered by several charter-boat firms. The Gordon is Tasmania's largest river.

Some history. Looking at peaceful Strahan and the clear waters of Macquarie Harbour today it is difficult to remember that Sarah (or Settlement) Island in the harbour was

Bank at Strahan

Strahan Macquarie Harbour

one of the most feared of the prison settlements, conceived by Governor William Sorell for secondary offenders. It is a major setting of Marcus Clarke's novel *For the Term of His Natural Life*. Sarah Island was named by Captain James Kelly in 1815 after Sarah Birch, wife of Thomas William Birch Esq. of Hobart town.

The Naming of Strahan. Strahan is named after Major Sir George Cumine Strahan, Governor of Tasmania 18811886. According to Census statistics, the population of Strahan was 561 in 1891, had risen to 1504 in 1901, and then declined in 1911 to 839. Its population in 1990 was around 500. In the late 1980s a large fish factory brought new prosperity to Strahan.

More to see. Drive on round the Esplanade, bypassing the War Memorial to your right, following the coast road. On your left is Peoples Park, a green area with a creek providing good fishing and camping spots. The walking track to Hogarth Falls leads for 30 minutes through rain forest from Peoples Park. This is a well-defined track with identifying plaques for many of the plants. Cross over a small bridge and in sight on your left is 'Franklin Manor', an historical building erected c. 1890 and fully restored and extended in 1988. It is a handsome two-storey house with a stone entrance way and wall. Continue to follow the Esplanade and on your left is the Gordon Gateway Chalet. If you look over at this point you can see the Council Chambers on the other side of the harbour. At Regatta Point, the historic Regatta Point Abt Railway Station has recently been restored. Nearby, in Bromley St, look for the cemetery, with its interesting Huon pine headstones marking the resting places of F.O. Henry and other pioneers.

Retrace your route to the Council Chambers and continue round the Esplanade in the other direction. On your is the elegant old Customs House. Farther round on your right is the large imposing red brick house known as 'Ormiston'.

'Ormiston' and F.O. Henry. Frederick Ormiston Henry was an Edinburgh-born storekeeper who had arrived in Tasmania in 1880 during the mining boom at Heemskirk. Later that year he opened his first general store at Smith Cove and then later moved north to Long Bay, the future site of Strahan. Three or four years later he became the fourth partner in the Iron Blow lease. In 1902, he had a stately home, 'Ormiston', built. There he lived in state in 'his' town until dying in 1919 at the age of 70. Two more Frederick Ormiston Henrys, son and grandson of the original, carried on the family business in several stores, the last of which closed in Queenstown relatively recently.

Beyond Strahan. From 'Ormiston', turn left and then right into Route B27. To visit Ocean Beach and Macquarie Heads, turn left into Route C250. Ocean Beach is 6 km from Strahan. On your left is Mill Bay. Follow the gravel road. On your left Route C251 takes you down Macquarie Heads and Swan Basin, a natural habitat of waterfowl. Macquarie Heads is 10 km from Strahan, and forms the entrance to the harbour. Look across narrow Kelly Channel to see the old homes the harbour master, lighthouse keeper and harbour pilots.

Return to Route C250 and turn left to visit spectacular Ocean Beach, with Lake Strahan a few minutes' walk off the road to the left. In early spring there is a lot of yellow laburnum growing by the road. To see the beach you can drive around a short way or climb directly over the dunes. The beach is extraordinarily long, stretching for 33 km: if you look away to the left you can see the lighthouse on Cape Sorell, and to the right, the Henty Dunes. The sand is rather coarse and greyish, the sunsets are said to be spectacular, and the nearest land to the west is South America!

One route to Zeehan

As you return to Strahan, turn left into Route B27 towards Zeehan. This stretch is known as the 'New' Strahan / Zeehan Highway; prior to its opening you would have had to retrace your route to Queenstown. In contrast to most west coast roads, the beginning of the road to Zeehan is almost dead straight, again coloured in spring with yellow flowering broom, which soon gives way on the right to pines. On the left hand side of the road you'll soon come to a sign indicating the Henty Dunes picnic area. Henty Dunes are over 100 m high, and the area is supplied with picnic and barbecue facilities.

A few kilometres farther on, you'll cross a very narrow bridge over the pretty Henty River, and another over Badger River. The mountains to your right comprise the Professor Range. Cross Little Henty River, and you'll see Mt Zeehan over to your left. Just before entering Zeehan, you'll see the pioneer cemetery over to your right.

Directly ahead, the road branches. The right-hand turn takes you to Queenstown on Route B27 and the left, Route C249, takes you to the town centre.

Another Route to Zeehan

If you choose, you may drive back from Strahan to Queenstown on B24, the Lyell Highway, turn left and then proceed to Zeehan by the Murchison Highway, Route A10. This route also crosses the Henty River, but you need to turn off left at the Y fork, cross Parting Creek, and enter Zeehan from the eastern side.

The history of Zeehan

Zeehan is a pretty but slightly melancholy township, in turn a boom town, with the population peaking around 1901, and then a town in decline, almost a ghost town and now beginning a new life as a residential and tourist town. It was named after Mt Zeehan which was, in turn, named after the *Zeehan*, the smaller of Abel Tasman's ships. Zeehan's period of prosperity began in 1882 when prospectors Frank Long and John Healey found silver-lead at Pea Soup Creek. Many prospectors flocked to Zeehan to mine the silver-lead, and in 1884 John Moyle arrived at the mine as the first manager. He and his friend George Symmons had a large quantity of ore taken to Launceston, and he left after three months. Others were also cautious, and Zeehan grew comparatively slowly. Then, at the end of the 1880s, a silver boom at Broken Hill sparked more interest in the fields at Zeehan, and it began to grow up rapidly. Although the boom died away, by 1894 Zeehan mines were exporting around £300 000 worth of ore. Production dropped

School of Mines Museum Zeehan

Gaiety Theatre, Zeehan

to two thirds of this, but continued steadily for two decades. By 1900 the population had risen to around 8000, finally peaking at 10 000. The town, now sometimes known as 'The Silver City', was thriving. It was the third-largest settlement in Tasmania and had 27 pubs! Prosperity lasted for another decade, but the ore was giving out. One by one, mines closed. Businesses wound down, buildings were dismantled. By the late 1950s Zeehan was the home of fewer than 700 people. When Sally visited the town during the late 1960s, someone had scrawled the words 'Beware of Ghosts' on a wall, but Zeehan is now no ghost town. The population has tripled and it has become a residential centre for the Renison Bell tin mine as well as a popular destination for tourists!

Zeehan has more than mining in its history. Its most famous contribution to the arts came in 1908 when pianist Eileen Joyce was born in King St. Eileen was the daughter of Thomas Joseph and Alice Gertrude Joyce. In 1930 she moved to England, playing with all the major U.K. orchestras. She married Douglas Leigh Barrett in 1937 and had one son. She retired in 1967. Her childhood was covered in novelised form in a book called *Prelude*.

Touring Zeehan. Assuming you have taken the shorter route, cross Shield, King, Gellibrand, Westward, Foweil, Belstead,

and Wilson Streets. Look for the fine old Hotel Cecil. Cross Emma St. On your right is the bank and Zeehan Municipal Chambers. Cross Smith St. On your left is the cream and green Central Hotel. On your right, past the A.N.Z. Bank, is the Zeehan School of Mines and Metallurgy building, established in 1892, now housing the West Coast Heritage Museum. This is open every day including Good Friday and Christmas Day.

The museum contains a very comprehensive range of exhibits, including a dark and dramatic facsimile of a mine, complete with miners. There are collections of bottles, ore samples, samples from core drilling, old books, equipment, and a display of rock drilling through the ages. An interesting exhibit is a railway car (donated by the Mt Lyell Mining and Railway Company Ltd), built by Daimler in 1922 for the personal use of the general manager, who, as the senior official of the railway company, had a free pass for Tasmanian rail travel. Upstairs there are photographs of important people associated with the mining towns—and of the towns themselves.

Next to the School of Mines building is a map of the area and then Zeehan Post Office (c. 1890s), the Magistrates' Court and the old Gaiety Theatre, which, in its time, seated a thousand patrons and was the venue for performances by Nellie Stewart and Houdini. There are many fine old buildings in Zeehan.

Routes out of Zeehan

Trial Harbour, once the port of Zeehan, is 20 km away. To reach it, leave Zeehan on Route C248. Reece Dam, 40 km away, is reached via Route C249. This route eventually joins up with the Western Explorer link road, which comes out near Smithton. We have never driven this road, but have heard that it's necessary to enquire locally before driving as parts of the surface may be in poor condition.

Another interesting place near Zeehan is the ghost town of Dundas. To visit this, enquire at the town.

Zeehan to Rosebery. Leave Zeehan on Route B27, and drive into Route A10, the Murchison Highway, which was opened in 1962. This takes you towards Rosebery. After some time, you'll pass a sign indicating the Battery Mill Historic Walk. Just past this, on your left, is Australia's largest tin producing mine, Renison Bell. This was named after George Renison Bell. Mine tours are organised from Rosebery.

George Renison Bell, son of Sarah and George Bell, was born at Bothwell in 1840. A Quaker, George Jnr became first a farmer, then a prospector. He became familiar with Tasmania's coastline by walking it, and later made friends with James 'Philosopher' Smith. He found a number of mining fields, in the north-east as well as in the west. He died in 1915, and was buried at Devonport. However, his gravestone is now at the town that has his name.

Although the Renison field was discovered in 1890, it was not very productive until the 1960s—just in time to come to the rescue of ailing Zeehan.

Montezuma Falls. This stretch of the highway traverses forest, containing beautiful myrtle beech, blackwoods, heath and ferns on both sides of the road. Just before entering the town of Rosebery, look to your right for Rosebery Golf Club. Poplars and pines replace the native trees, and into sight, overshadowing the town, looms Mt Murchison. To your left is Mt Black. There is a turn-off to the right to Williamsford, 6 km away. This road also leads to the cemetery. Williamsford was once a town supported by the Mt Read (or Hercules) mine, but is now unoccupied. To see the Montezuma Falls on Montezuma Creek, go to Williamsford and follow the old railway for 5.5 km through the bush. Conducted tours to the falls can be booked in Rosebery.

Rosebery

Rosebery was probably named after a gold mining company which, in turn, was named after an English Prime Minister. The ore fields at Rosebery were discovered by Tom McDonald in 1893 at Mt Black, and by Joseph Will in 1894 at Mt Read, and the town grew up during the 1920s when the mining ventures were taken over by the Electrolytic Zinc Company. It is now a medium-sized town with a population of about 3000. It is rather an unusual town in that it exists in pockets among the bush: you can never see the entire town at once! Look out for the booking office for local tours.

Cross over the Stitt River, and enter some more forest, with more of the magnificent blackwoods and myrtle beech. On your right is a turn-off which leads into Lake Plimsoll Road. This road emerges halfway between Queenstown and Zeehan Cross on the old route.

Cross the Murchison Bridge and 7 sq. km Lake Rosebery, part of the Pieman River Power Development. Lake Rosebery is a long narrow lake. There is a right-hand

Mt Murchison, Rosebery

turn-off leading 5 km to Murchison Dam. Pass through Tullah, a small town which rose at the rum of the century to service the Mt Farrell mine.

A turn-off to the right leads to Mackintosh Dam and Tullabardine Dam, 4 and 6 km away. Cross the Mackintosh Bridge over Lake Rosebery. To the left, Reece Dam is 55 km away. This is the other end of the loop of road which leads off from Zeehan. Cross the Farm and Tramway Creeks.

Another route to the north. If you wish to leave the west coast at this point, you can cross the Que River and turn right into Route C132, which leads to Cradle Mountain.

If you take this route, you'll eventually come to a choice of ways. The road to the right leads on to Cradle Mountain and the road to the left leads out towards Sheffield. See Chapter 2 for more information on these destinations.

Continuing on the Murchison. If you wish to continue on the Murchison Highway, cross the Que River, and keep on to cross the Hatfield River, and the Fossey Plains Rivulet, named after Joseph Fossey. Route C191 leads off right to Guildford, and Route B23 goes left to Waratah, Luina, Savage River and Corinna on The Pieman River.

The Naming of the 'Pieman'. The Pieman River was originally known as the 'Retreat'. The story goes that it acquired its present name when Thomas Kent, a baker, was known as 'The Pieman' at the convict settlement. He and his mate escaped, and somehow contrived to cross Macquarie Harbour. They were pursued by Captain Lucas the pilot, who sailed into the Pieman River. He later reported disgustedly to his superiors that he 'couldn't find the pieman', and soon the river became known as the 'river where the Captain lost the Pieman', and the name stuck.

Waratah

Waratah, (pronounced 'worra-TAR') began with the discovery of tin at Mt Bischoff, in 1871, by James 'Philosopher' Smith. Like most of the mining towns, it has had a yoyo history, booming in the 1890s but sadly declined now to a population of c. 400. Mt Bischoff was confidently expected to go on producing the same phenomenal amounts of metal as it did at the beginning, but the forecasts were too optimistic. However, like Zeehan, Waratah has become a residential town for miners from a new mine: this time the Que River Mine.

If you visit Waratah, go to St James Church of England (1880), the first Tasmanian XXX church to have electric light, the Waratah Museum, situated in the old Courthouse building, and the interesting War Memorial outside the Council Chambers. Visitors may stay in the hotel or caravan park, and enjoy fishing for brown trout in the nearby Lake Waratah. ('Waratah' is also the name of a striking red flower, *Telopea truncata*, which grows wild in parts of the state.)

West of Waratah is the town of Luina, another 'revived' mining town which is now the site of Australia's second largest tin mine, Aberfoyle Ltd. Onward again is Savage River, where iron ore was discovered in 1877, but remained unmined until the 1960s.

Modern methods made a large operation, including crushing and grinding plants for the ore and an 85 km pipeline.

Hellyer Gorge. Back on the Murchison Highway, drive a further 17 km, going through an avenue of myrtle beech, where the trees almost meet over the top of the road, and passing through some pines on the way. Next comes some 11 km of winding road, with a steep drop to the left side and myrtles, man ferns and other assorted greenery almost blocking out the sky. This is the Hellyer Gorge, named for explorer Henry Hellyer. The day we drove through Hellyer Gorge there was a thick pea-soup fog. Drive with care, as it is one of the wettest areas in the west, as well as one of the windier roads. Part way through the Gorge, you will be crossing the lovely Hellyer River, with Hellyer Gorge Roadside Park on your right.

Route C101 to the right soon after you leave the Gorge leads to Highclere and Ridgley. As you leave the trees, you are approaching the farming district of Henrietta and the town of Yolla. Wynyard is straight ahead on Route B6 and Burnie and Devonport to the right on A10. Pass the old butter factory at Yolla, and continue to the farming district of Elliott. The Murchison Highway continues a few more km to meet the north-west coast—and the Bass Highway—at Somerset. Turn right to return to Devonport, or left towards Wynyard and Stanley.

Apart from the Cradle Mountain Link Road, there is one other alternative to the drive through Hellyer Gorge. Route C191 links the Waratah district with Burnie through Highclere, Hampshire and Ridgley to Wivenhoe or the town centre.

BIBLIOGRAPHY

Books

EMMETT, E.T., *Tasmania by Road and Track*, Melbourne University Press, 1952.

PINK, Kerry, *The West Coast Story* 1982.

WEDD, Edward John (Rocky), *Linda, Ghost Town of Mt Lyell*, 1987.

WHITHAM, Charles, *Western Tasmania*, 1949.

Various Authors, *Australian Wildflowers*, International Limited Edition, 1976.

Pamphlets

'Let's Talk About Queenstown'

'Let's Talk About Rosebery, Tullah and Williamsford'

'Let's Talk About Strahan and Macquarie Harbour'

'Let's Talk About Waratah' (All Tas. Visitor Corporation)

'Tasmania's Water Power', H.E.C.

Zeehan.

Lyell Tours.

Maps

Tasmap 1. 100 000 Land Tenure Index Series:

'Arthur River', 'Cape Sorell', 'Franklin', 'Hellyer', 'Pieman', 'Sophia'.

Tasmania State Map, UBD.

Information

Thanks to Jean Sarson, and the people of Strahan, Zeehan and Queenstown.

17. Richmond, Bothwell and the Lake Highway

One way to return to the north from Hobart or the south-east, is to leave from Sorell or Bridgewater, tour the historic towns of Richmond and Bothwell, and then traverse the Lake Highway, passing the Great Lake to reach Deloraine. The drive we took turned off the Heritage Highway at the Bridgewater roundabout, then followed route B32 through Old Beach and Risdon Vale to Richmond.

Features of this drive

This is a rather unusual drive, featuring two very old towns, rich with charming old buildings and convict and colonial history, and also one of the less frequented highways in the state. If driving the Lake Highway in winter, (or even spring and autumn) it's a good idea to enquire first at Bothwell, because this is a route that can be rendered impassible if it snows. If there is light snow, however, the scenery can be almost magical. Along this drive you may see the oldest stone bridge in Australia, a historic golf course and golf museum, a beautifully made model village, a toy museum, large freshwater lakes and some quite unusual vegetation. Richmond and Bothwell offer many and varied amenities and accommodation, and there are also places to stay up near Great Lake.

Richmond's History
Richmond, which rejoices in the possession of the oldest bridge in Australia, is one of the best known of Tasmania's historic towns. The district was originally known as 'Coal River', after coal was discovered there in 1803, but Lt Governor Sorell named the township-elect 'Richmond' in 1824. The prosperity of the town is tied up with the history of the highways: until 1872 traffic from Hobart to Port Arthur had to travel through Richmond: in that year the causeway was opened at Pittwater. With this, Richmond's chance of becoming a major modern centre evaporated. The result is a charming town with a great emphasis on history.

Richmond

In and Around Richmond. Just as you come into Richmond, look away to your left to see 'Prospect House', built in the Georgian style by James Buscombe during the 1830s. It is now a restaurant and offers accommodation. James Buscombe was also responsible for many other buildings, including a shop in Bridge Street which has been variously used as a bakery, doctor's surgery, butchery and tea room. 'Oak Lodge', in the same street, was built for James' brother Henry.

On the left just after 'Prospect' is a maze, and opposite this is a toy museum. After the maze comes Old Hobart Town, an historically accurate reconstruction of Hobart as it was in the 1820s. The buildings range from 30 cm to just over two m. in height. Old Hobart Town was developed by John and Andrew Quick over a period of three years.

Next comes 'Ashmore House', built in 1850 by William Ashmore. Turn right and in Henry Street you'll see a colonial cottage, and then the Richmond Hotel.

Turn left into Torrens Street and on your right is the old sandstone school house, designed by John Lee Archer and erected in 1834. On the left is the Richmond Congregational burial ground, 1845. This old graveyard has several unmarked graves. Many of the headstones date from the 1880s. Under a tree at the back of the graveyard is the gravestone Ann Ross and her baby, who died on 6 June, 1846. To the left of Ann's grave is that of Joseph Foote, the Colonial Missionary of this district, who died in July 1848.

St Luke's. Farther along the same street, on the right, is St Luke's Anglican Church (1834). St Luke's is a beautiful church with a large black and gold clock face on the tower. This clock was originally from old

Ashmore House, Richmond

St Luke's Anglican Church, Richmond

St David's church in Hobart, but was brought here to Richmond in 1922. The church is floodlit at night. In the porch are photographs including that of Rev. Arthur Davenport, Archdeacon of Hobart 1880-86. He was rector here in Richmond from 1847–1851.

The foundation stone of the church was laid in 1834, and the church was designed by John Lee Archer, and built of sandstone quarried from nearby Butchers Hill. The story has it that the convict builder was pardoned when the woodwork of the roof was completed. Available inside the church is a small booklet giving the history of the church.

John Lee Archer, architect and engineer was born the only son of John Archer of County Tipperary and Dublin in 1791. He trained in London, and was appointed by Earl Bathurst to the position of Civil Engineer in Van Diemen's Land in 1827.

At the same time he was given the duties of Colonial Architect. He carried out these tasks for 11 years. His works include, in Hobart, Parliament House, Public Offices in Murray St, the Ordinance Stores in Salamanca Place, bits of the Barracks, Old Trinity Church, and here in Richmond, St Luke's. He also oversaw the erection of many bridges, including the famous one at Ross which he designed as well.

In 1838 Archer's office was abolished by Lt Governor Franklin. He was then given the position of Police Magistrate, and lived at Stanley until he died in 1852.

The tour continued. As you turn left into Edward Street, look for Number 15, the old rectory (1831) also known as 'James Gordon's house'. This is the same James Gordon who took land at Pittwater, and after whom Captain Kelly named the Gordon River. The steps leading up to the rectory show signs of long use, and to the left of the steps is a lovely little stone seat. The next building on your right is the Dispensary, built in 1853. Turn right into Bathurst Street, and then left to visit Old Richmond Gaol on your right.

The Richmond Gaol was built in 1825, predating Port Arthur by five years. Built of local sandstone, probably quarried from Butchers Hill, it is unmodified and intact. Enter through the passageway; the heavy lock is still in place. The mens' solitary confinement cells, added in 1835, may be seen, and also a scale model of the gaol. Inside, the walls are plaster over old brick. The floorboards now have large cracks, but huge headed nails still hold them quite firmly together. Inside the cells are records of the prisoners and some of the sentences they received. Out in the exercise yard is a fine old almond tree, probably planted at some time during the 1840s. A pamphlet giving further details about the gaol is available on site, and you can even tune your car radio to hear a commentary!

Peppercorn Gallery, Richmond

The Richmond Arms hotel

Just past the gaol, on the left, is Bridge Inn Mews, containing the Jolly Miller Bakery, plus antique and curio shops. Most of the court is built of red brick, but one building is of freestone. Turn right past the Bridge Inn Mews, and you'll see Peppercorn Gallery (1850), the Bridge Inn (1830) and the Council Chambers, (1825). Just a few hundred metres onward is the Richmond Bridge.

Richmond Bridge is the oldest stone bridge in Australia. It was built in 1823 at the suggestion of Royal Commissioner John Thomas Bigge, using convict labour. Later, extra work was done by John Lee Archer. The first stone was laid on 11 December 1823, in the presence of James Gordon and G.W. Gunning, who were the magistrates.

To the right as you come onto the bridge is a riverbank walk. You can stand on the bridge and look down over the Coal River at flocks of ducks and geese. Down to the left of the bridge a flight of stone steps leads down and under the bridge. You may walk right underneath and look up at the stones above your head.

Drive over the bridge and take the second turn to the left, pass 'Laurel Cottage' and turn left into St Johns Circle to visit the Church of St John the Evangelist, built in 1836, and Australia's oldest existing Roman Catholic church. The foundation stone was laid in 1835 by Reverend Bede Polding, first Archbishop of Sydney. Father James Cotham was the priest in charge.

The ceiling is made from polished brown wood and the church has a wooden spire. Behind it is the original Catholic School

Richmond Bridge

Bridge Cottage, Richmond

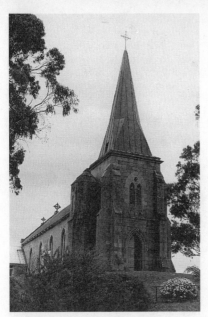

St John's Church, Richmond

building, built in brick in about 1843. Among the gravestones behind the church are those of a baby named Eleanor Moran, who died in 1839 and Margaret Cunningham of Pittwater, who apparently died in 1813. White alyssum and other flowers growing freely in this hillside cemetery makes it an unusually pleasant spot in autumn.

Other Places in Richmond. Other interesting buildings include the village store (1826–36) the Richmond Arms Hotel (1888), (both in Bridge Street), and several houses and cottages, the sites and dates of which are detailed in brochures available locally. Close by is 'Hatcher's Manor' which, despite appearances, was built in the 1990s. 'Hatcher's Manor' offers accommodation and apricot orchards.

Towards Campania. Continue around the circle and cross the bridge again. Turn right just past the Bridge Inn into Franklin Street and continue along the road heading for Campania, about 7 km away. On your way, you pass the property of 'Carrington', owned between 1813 and 1836 by the Lt Governors of the state. First selected by Lt Governor Davey, 'Carrington Park' was raided twice by bushrangers in 1816, first by Michael Howe, and secondly by a gang including men named Jones and Collier and two Aboriginal girls.

Campania

Campania had its birth in around 1816, when a military barracks was built. 'Campania House', the local 'big house', was built at around the same time. 'Campania House' a large freestone two-storey house. In 1884 Campania Estate was owned by H.J. Brock: part of it had earlier belonged to Francis Smith, the father of Sir Francis Villeneuve Smith, Tasmanian Premier May 1857–1860.

By 1914, when the estate was broken up and sold, it totalled more than 4500 acres. 'Campania House' itself now offers colonial accommodation. 'Stratford', another large estate to the north of Campania Estate, has also been broken up, but the original homestead is still occupied. The buildings associated with the barracks were on a small rise on the eastern bank of the river, but have now gone.

After you enter Campania (present home of sculptor Stephen Walker) look to your left for Flour Mill Park, which was developed in 1988 as Campania's bicentennial project. The flour mill was built in 1884 for H.J. Brock, and was used for hay and grain storage and later as a flax mill during the war. In 1949 it became Campania Area School and was then used as a Trade Block by Campania District High. In the park you'll see a Stephen Walker sculpture depicting two school children.

The first school at Campania was 'Enfield

School', run in 'Longford Cottage', 1877–1885. The story of Florence Kearney, the teacher, is told in the section on Lilydale in Chapter 9.

Other points of interest include the Campania Tavern and an old shop in the centre of the town. Estate Road leads out to the right to 'Campania House'. On your right as you leave Campania, is Brown Mountain. On your left, farther on, is the fine Georgian homestead of the property of 'Stockdale', established in 1836. Pass Birmingham Creek, and on your right shortly afterwards is Craigbourne Dam, formed when the Coal River was dammed in the late 1980s for irrigation purposes. The area between Campania and Colebrook is heavily given over to sheep.

Towards Colebrook. On your left as you enter Colebrook is St James' Church of England. Shortly after on your right is the Colebrook Courthouse. On your left not far out of Colebrook is the narrow gravel Lovely Banks Road (route C316) towards Kempton, a good short-cut if you wish to visit Bothwell. This road leads you out onto the Heritage Highway at 'Lovely Banks'.

'Lovely Banks' is the property founded John Bisdee c. 1820. Mr Bisdee was a renowned brewer of beer, Keeper of Hobart Gaol, and was also the man who introduced fallow deer to Tasmania. The property is still owned today by descendants of the family.

Also at 'Lovely Banks' is a masonry arch bridge, begun in 1840. An inn—kept by William Guest from Norfolk Island, and later known as The Mail Coach Inn—was close by, and a convict station was situated at Spring Hill.

To Melton Mowbray. Turn left out of route C316 towards Melton Mowbray, c. 6 km away. Here, you could visit the handsome old Melton Mowbray Hotel, or take route A5 to the right towards Bothwell, 20 km away. If you do this, you'll cross the tiny Jordan River, pass Apsley and cross Little Den Creek. It's a good idea to enquire locally before taking this route in winter—on our last visit we ran into an impressive snowstorm and had to return to the south.

Bothwell's history

Bothwell is said to have been named a man who commented that he and father lived, 'both well', in the district. Another story is that it was named by Scottish settlers. In any case, the region was first known as 'Fat Doe River', and then as 'Clyde'. The area was first visited by Lt Thomas Laycock and his party in 1807, en route from Port Dalrymple to Hobart Town, and was later explored by surveyor J. Beaumont in 1817. According to one source, the first settler, also in 1817, was Charles Rowcroft who arrived from 'The Camp', as Hobart was then known, in February of that year complete with his family, and five gallons of rum—in two bullock wagons. Seven years later the streets had been laid out by Thomas Scott, and Governor Arthur remarked that the area was becoming 'a populous place'.

Another source holds that Charles Rowcroft and his brother Horatio arrived in 1821.

Touring Bothwell. As you drive into Bothwell you will be on Patrick St. On your right when you enter the town is St Andrew's Catholic Church, with, nearby, a plaque showing a plan of the town, and the Anglican Church, St Michael's and All Angels'.

This church was consecrated by Bishop Montgomery in 1891. It was designed by Alexander North, and built by Thomas Lewis. The organ was built by Samuel Joscelyne in 1862, and is one of only two instruments of this type to survive in Australia. The sandstone was quarried locally.

Post Office, Bothwell

Turn right into Market Place and on your right is the old state school, also built by Thomas Lewis, which now houses the Australasian Golf Museum.

Next comes St Luke's Presbyterian Church. The foundation stone was laid in May 1830, and the first service held in March 1831. The church was designed by John Lee Archer, and was built by the colonial government for the joint use of the Anglican and Presbyterian congregations. Lt Governor Arthur told John Lee Archer to alter the rounded windows, which he claimed to be 'unChristian'. Daniel Herbert, a convict sculptor, is said to have carved the heads over the door. Near St Luke's is an old graveyard.

On the left as you enter Dennistoun Road, (named after a Mr Dennistoun Wood), is 'Rock Cottage', opposite St Luke's. It was built by Thomas Lewis in 1864 for Henry Wise, wheelwright. About 1878 it passed to Charles Nichols. He and his family numbered wheelwrights, blacksmiths and About 1.5 km along the Dennistoun Road is the left hand turn-off into Nant Lane. 'Nant Cottage' was the place where two Irish Political Exiles, John Mitchel and John Martin, lived during the 1850s. Mitchel was a journalist, and treasonable writings in *The United Irishman* led to his arrest. Martin was also arrested for such activities: his preferred publication was *The*

Irish Felon. Audacious John Mitchel evidently escaped after handing the local Magistrate what amounted to a letter of his intentions!

With the help of a man named Smythe, he and his family sailed away to America on the *Emma*. Later, he returned to Ireland, went into Parliament, and died in 1875. Near 'Nant' is Thorpe Mill, built in 1822 by Thomas Axford. In 1917 the mill ceased production.

Turn left into Elizabeth Street and on your left a little way down is 'Rose Cottage' (c. 1862). Beside it is weatherboard 'Birch Cottage'. On your right is 'Grantham', where Peter Taylor built a brick house in the 1840s.

Turn left into James Street. At the cross roads on your right is Bothwell Grange, originally the Crown Inn, first licensed in 1846. It has also been known as the Crown Lodge.

Just across the road is the Bothwell Stores (c. 1850) an unusually shaped building of dark red brick, and one of a few that has traded continuously. Nearby is Bothwell Post Office, built in 1891. Turn left into Alexander Street, named for Alexander Reid, of the property 'Ratho'. On your left is the brick Literary Society building (1834–1837) and on your right are identical twin brick cottages, and, towards the end of the block, White's Store, owned since about 1837 by the White family.

Turn right and walk down alongside Queens Square.

Leave Bothwell by the Lake Highway, Route A5, passing 'Ratho' on your right.

'**Ratho**', which belonged to early pioneer Alexander Reid, is a handsome single-storey stone house with interesting columns at the front. Many of the original outbuildings are still standing.

Historic Golf Course. 'Ratho' is also the home of the oldest golf course in the Southern Hemisphere.

The Road to Great Lake

From Bothwell it is 59 km to Miena at Great Lake. On the highway is a left-hand turn to Waddamana, where the first hydro dam in Tasmania was made.

Waddamana Scheme. The first Miena Dam was built in 1916 and a second in 1922. The Waddamana Great Lake Scheme was begun in 1910, and the opening ceremony at Waddamana was in 1916.
Cross Blackburn Creek. Along the sides of the road you can see exceedingly rocky ground, much of it fortunately left uncleared. Cross the Shannon River, on a very narrow bridge, passing a dam on your right. On the left by the bridge is Shannon Lagoon.

Central Plateau and Great Lake

The Great Lake is situated on the Central Plateau of Tasmania, c. 1050 m above sea level. The Central Plateau itself is edged to the north and east by the 1300 metre range known as the Great Western Tiers. In 1978 the Central Plateau was set aside as a protected area. It is very popular with those who enjoy the famous trout fishing in the lakes (which were stocked in 1864), and observing the interesting plants and animals. The Great Lake, on your right as you come into Miena, is 40 km in length and is the biggest freshwater lake in Australia.

The rock around the Great Lake is largely mineral-free dolerite which extends about a metre into the ground. Below that is roughly another metre of good top soil and below that again soft yellow clay. Splotches of surprising orange and white lichens mark the protruding rocks around the lake. As you come round the corner above the top of the lake, you'll see Drys Bluff, marking the north east edge of the Central Plateau over to your right.

Western Tiers from the access road to Great Lake

Drys Bluff was named after the father of Sir Richard Dry (Premier of Tasmania Nov. 1866–Aug. 1869), who lived near Hagley on the road to Launceston. It has been frequently climbed, notably by a party of Aborigines and settlers, in 1831, and by 'Count' Strzelecki in 1835. It is often climbed by bushwalkers now: expect to climb up for three or four hours and down for two.

Leading towards Drys Bluff is a walking track to Liffey Falls. As you drive down from the plateau, you will pass through the Fairy Glade and Stella Glen. At the foot of the plateau, look away to your left for Quamby Bluff (1070 m). Next comes the pretty little settlement of Golden Valley. You will soon come to a turn-off that leads 9 km to the left leads to Meander. Continue 6 km along the highway to Deloraine.

BIBLIOGRAPHY

Books

EMMETT, E.T. *Tasmania by Road and Track*, Melbourne University Press, 1952.

HYDRO ELECTRIC COMMISSION, *Power in Tasmania*.

SMITH, Coultman, *Shadow Over Tasmania*, 1958.

SMITH, Roy, *Early Tasmanian Bridges*, 1969.

STANCOMBE, G. Hawley, *Highway in Van Diemen's Land*, 1969.

Pamphlets

'Central Plateau Protected Area', Lands Department.

'Drys Bluff: A noble peak in the Western Tiers'.

'Richmond Gaol Historic Site'.

Maps

Tasmap 1: 100 000 Land Tenure Index Series:

'Derwent', 'Shannon', 'Lake Sorell', 'Meander'.

Information

Thanks to John and Ismay Banfield, Janet Monks, Leila Watson and Majorie White.

18. Devonport to Burnie, North-west Coast

Features of this drive

The north-west coast features some of the state's most fertile farm lands as well as two cities (Devonport and Burnie) and several large towns. It has both sea and river ports, light and medium heavy industry, and many tempting destinations for the travelling family.

The drive from Devonport to Burnie by the most direct route will take around half an hour, but if you have the time to spare, there are much more interesting ways to go. You can explore caves and waterfalls, canyons, bush tracks, beaches, parks and playgrounds, museums, craft shops, tea gardens, an abandoned mine and a walk among the man ferns, and visit fairy penguins, deer and maybe ostriches. Of course the major towns offer plenty of amenities, but if you decide to take the scenic drive from Ulverstone (detailed later in this chapter), you will need to check your stores of food and petrol first.

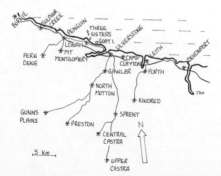

At the time of writing, work is well under way on a new stretch of highway that bypasses Sulphur Creek.

Direct route to Burnie

The shortest route from East Devonport to Burnie is along the Bass Highway. To travel this route, head west through Devonport, driving over Victoria Bridge on the right lane, leaving the route to the City Centre and Spreyton on your left. Go underneath the William St overpass. Cross the bridge over the Don River, and drive through the pretty township of Don.

The highway runs along the coast, and soon you'll see the penguin viewing platform over to your right. This platform was erected in 1996.

Pass Lillico Road on your left. Just past this road are two big houses, just off the road in front of the second of these is a fenced in yard containing two gravestones. Also in the yard is a cement slab marking the site of the first Methodist service in the Forth district, in 1853.

One gravestone is for George Perry Mulligan (d. 1864) his wife Eliza (d. 1908), Mary Elizabeth, their daughter (d. 1877), Thomas Glanvil Trebilcoe (d. 1877) and Adelaide Louisa Trebilcoe (d. 1885). The second stone commemorates James Wilson, from Colvend in Scotland, (d. 1865 at Ellerslieforth Beach) his wife Elizabeth J.N. Wilson (d. 1912) and their daughter Sarah Jane (d. 1888). The gravestones are protected by an electric fence, so take care not to go too close!

Looking ahead to your right, notice the distinctive Dial Range, named for Mt Dial's resemblance to an old-fashioned sun dial. C132, on your left, is one of the routes to Cradle Mountain. A trip to the Cradle is covered in Chapter 2.

Next on your right comes the Turners Beach Junction, and, on your left a sign leading off to Poynton's Nursery.

At Turners Beach, on the west bank of the Forth River, is 'The Gables' (c. 1850). This building began life as an inn, 'The Sailors' Return', but was de-licensed ten years later.

Poyntons' Nursery. We always enjoy visiting this nursery, which is set in a large permanent garden with fruit trees and other flowering trees, shrubs and smaller plants. Poyntons' was laid out in 1949 by Mr Poynton, (who had been a nurseryman in Melbourne), and his wife.

At that time the area was all bushland: to quote Mrs Poynton, it was 'bracken fern, bushland and bull ants', and she often suffered from their bites! Mr and Mrs Poynton did much of the work in the nursery at night, by torchlight, working at other jobs during the daytime. Their house was originally three squares: it is now sixty-four squares, being built up gradually over the years. Mr and Mrs Poynton's son is also at the nursery, and it is still very much a family affair. Mrs Poynton is responsible for the many quaint corners featuring fishponds and rustic bridges.

An interesting feature is the bird tunnel where visitors can walk underneath the aviaries. The bird tunnel was conceived and designed by the nursery owners. The friendly atmosphere, lovely surroundings—and talkative 'Cocky', make this a favourite place with children. On your right, just past the nursery on Clayton Rivulet is Camp Clayton, the Christian Convention Centre, opened in 1950.

Camp Clayton. Christian Youth Centre camps began in Tasmania with small house-party camps for girls in 1944. Camps for boys followed when members of the Christian Brethren church (then Gospel Hall) leased the Old Wesley Dale property near Mole Creek. In 1947 the lease was terminated, and the present 26.7 hectare property purchased.

New accommodation in self-contained units was built in the early 1980s. Camps and retreats are now available for many different age groups.

'Westella'. Next on your left watch for 'Westella', a lovely white house with a grey roof distinguished by a large number of gables. It was built in the 1880s for Anthony Raymond. The Raymond family had come from Nova Scotia. It now offers colonial accommodation. It is reached from the Ulverstone loop road. Immediately after 'Westella' is a fork in the road.

To continue to Burnie, stay on Highway 1. To enter Ulverstone, take the left fork, Route C142 which loops to the left. Westella Drive is on your right as you go through the loop.

A visit to Ulverstone itself is featured later in this chapter.

As you bypass Ulverstone, you will cross the Leven River. Along the sides of the road are young gums and wattles and up on the banks in winter you may see pink heath, white erica and the yellow of prickly moses, or mimosa. The next 2 km are a particularly pleasant drive through the trees, gums and wattles. The highway also bypasses Penguin, but there is a right-hand turn near the traffic lights next to St Stephen's Church which takes you back along the foreshore, past the Giant Penguin and through the town. Penguin will be covered in more detail later on in this chapter.

A left-hand turn leads 14 km to Riana (an Aboriginal word meaning 'dance') and South Riana (19 km).

At the time of writing, work is well under way on the new section of the highway which leaves Penguin at the Penguin Creek Interchange and swings out to the left to bypass Sulphur Creek, returning to the old route at the Howth roundabout.

Sulphur Creek, west of Penguin, is a long township on the narrow strip between the hills and the old Bass Highway, often only two or three houses deep. There is an odd story that Sulphur Creek is really Penguin and Penguin is really Sulphur Creek: it seems that the actual Sulphur Creek was named because of the sulphurous-looking rocks around it and the actual Penguin Creek (the town was once called this) was named for the number of Fairy Penguins which nested there. However, there are sulphurous-looking rocks in Penguin Creek and penguins in Sulphur Creek, so it is quite possible that the two names were accidentally exchanged. Over the Blythe river Route C102 leads left towards the farming district of Natone, and just past this, at Heybridge, you pass the site of Tioxide Australia Pty Ltd, which was a titanium pigment manufacturer. Tioxide began production at this site in 1948 and finished in 1996.

As you approach Burnie you will see the gravel quarry, (Round Hill Stone and Gravel) on your left, and, a long way ahead, look for Table Cape jutting out into the sea.

Burnie was declared a city in 1988. For a closer look at this industrial port, turn to the main article later in this chapter.

Take the turn-off Route C102 (left) towards Wivenhoe, Natone and Stowport. Two km of winding road takes you up Round Hill, at the top of which is a lookout which offers a panoramic view of the city and port of Burnie. Round Hill was named by Bass and Flinders during their 1798/99 voyage, and marks the eastern end of Emu Bay.

Alternative route to Burnie—scenic drive from Ulverstone

To take the less direct but more interesting route to Burnie, follow the highway to 'Westella', then turn off into Route C142 and loop back into Ulverstone. Turn left. The scenic drive that follows is full of waterfalls, caves, canyons, bush tracks and scenery, but short on buildings and straight roads.

Route B15 leads off to the left towards Nietta, Sprent and the Leven Canyon on C128. If you decide to take this route, it can make a very enjoyable day trip. The route could be travelled in half a day, but this would mean missing some of the most impressive sights in the district. To fully enjoy your day, wear strong footwear and tough clothes. Stock up on food and make sure you have enough petrol. There are plenty of picnic and barbecue sites along the way, but though you'll find some toilets and shelters, there's a distinct lack of shops until you reach Gunns Plains!

The Castra Road. Turn out of Ulverstone into Route B15 and drive along the Castra Road. This is a very pleasant drive, through rolling farmland, temperate rainforest, ferns and pines. You'll pass through the hamlets of Abbotsham and Spalford and then reach the small town of Sprent. Before entering the town, look to your right to see an old graveyard. Many members of the Macpherson family, early settlers in the district, are buried here, and some of the stones are beautifully carved. Not far along the road is the charming cream wooden Anglican church of St Andrew, beautifully set off by the giant holly tree in the churchyard. You might see the local school buses lurking behind the church.

Pass the Sprent Primary School on your left, and drive on for 8 km to Upper Castra. Bypass the intriguingly named Ghost Hole Road. There is now a considerably winding

St Andrew's, Sprent

stretch of road to traverse before you reach a left-hand turn into Gaunts Road.

Gaunts Road. A short distance down Gaunts Road is an old picnic area. This marks the entrance to the walking track around the falls of the Castra Rivulet which wanders charmingly around the Nietta district before emptying into the Wilmot River. According to the sign, the circular walking track takes 90 minutes. When we took this walk some years ago, it was a pleasant one, taking in natural rain forest, and several waterfalls. The path was generally good, with a pleasant surface of leaf mould underfoot; however, it was occasionally confusing and best suited to older children and fit adults. It was overgrown in some places and blocked by some fallen branches that had come down in a recent storm. You might like to test-walk a few hundred metres before deciding whether or not to continue.

If you drive on along Gaunts Road you will come out of thick forest into farmland and the 'Gaunts' property, which celebrated its centenary in 1987. The original homestead was burned down some years ago but the new house, like its predecessor, is made from timber grown on the property. 'Gaunts' is a lovely place: the pretty Horseshoe Falls are near its gate and a little farther on is a superb view of Mt Roland. It was first settled in 1887 by T. Oswin Button, (a son of W.B. Button of

Ulverstone) and his wife, who selected 1500 acres of land. They contracted a Mr Nichols, (later M.H.A. for Mersey), to clear the first 20 acres for 28 shillings an acre. This he and assistant George Stephens did, using an axe and a crosscut saw, and tackling quite large trees. It took them two months. The next owners of the property were the three Gaunt brothers, from whom 'Gaunts' took its name. One of the three eventually settled in Canada, and Richard Gaunt, (who seems to have enjoyed pioneering more than most), left the now thriving property to settle in Western Australia, where he was later able to leave 1000 acres of land to each of his daughters! Return to Route B15 and continue along it until you come to the turn-off into Route C128, just past Nietta. The sign indicates 'Kaydale Lodge' and Leven Canyon. Drive past 'Kaydale Lodge' and follow the well-marked signs to the Leven Canyon.

The Leven Canyon is one of the best known tourist destinations in the district, and can be reached from a number of alternative routes. It offers a pleasant picnic area with toilet facilities, and a choice of walks. For those who lack energy, time, suitable footwear or lung power, there is a path leading off past the toilet block to the lookout. This trip is very easy walking, almost on the level and takes about 10 minutes. The lookout is a wire mesh cage perched on the lip of a crag, and offers an excellent prospect of vertigo, and a fine view of the Canyon and Black Bluff. The Leven River is so far down at this point that it appears as a mere silver ribbon winding between the folds of the hills.

The more intrepid may turn off from the lookout path and descend literally hundreds of wooden steps down the hillside, (handrail provided), to intersect another track which leads down to the canyon floor and back up to the carpark. Caution is needed on the lower part of this track: it is steep and rather slippery.

Preston and Upper Preston Falls. Return to Nietta and follow the big sign on your left marked 'Caves 20 km'. There's a short, rather winding drive, then you can take a right-hand turn at the sign marked 'Preston Road'. Continue on this road then take Route C125. Turn into Route C127 to visit the two lovely waterfalls on Preston Creek. The first of the falls, Upper Preston Falls, is very shortly after the turn-off, with a sign post to your right. Follow the wooden steps down to the fall, a rather unusual one, falling clear for half its length before hitting a canted slab of rock and bouncing back at an angle. Behind the falls is an intriguing hollow which is almost a cave. The steps and walkways can be slippery in wet weather, but the fall is well worth seeing.

Drive on a little farther and pull over to the right into the lay-by near the notice indicating the Preston Falls. Follow the walkway down over the creek. Preston Creek is not a very big waterway, but it does plunge very dramatically in a single long narrow tier over a cliff. The walkway ends in a mesh cage which offers an excellent view of this lovely fall. Not only the fall is spectacular; with a fair amount of care it is possible to scramble down the bank beyond the falls to the creek, which continues in a series of short cascades through huge rocks covered with lush growths of grass, kangaroo fern and other greenery. The creek actually flows through a double-ended cave, before disappearing amongst the trees and high ferns. There is another cave hidden among the rocks as well. The only drawbacks of this particular scramble are leeches, stinging nettles and blackberries. Again, the banks and general area can be slippery.

Gunns Plains

Route C127 runs into a T-junction near the Gunns Plains shop, a welcome source of food and petrol. Plains Road, and follow the signs to see the famous limestone caves. Gunns Plains was named after botanist R. Campbell Gunn, who was Private Secretary to Sir John Franklin in 1839. He and surveyor Peter Lette explored the area c. 1860.

Also along this route, you can reach Riana and, as the signpost indicates, the Pindari Deer Farm is 24 km away.

Gunns Plains Caves were discovered when a brush-tailed possum was shot by local farmers earlier this century. The animal fell down a hole, a ladder was let down and the caves discovered. The present entrance of the caves was at that time covered by a mass of timber and a huge fallen tree; this was removed and the entranceway improved with a ladder and later, steps. Electricity came to the caves and these days tours are taken every hour from 10 a.m.–4 p.m. Temperature in the caves is 11ºC all the year round. There is a lot of wildlife to be seen, including small lobsters, platypus and glow-worms.

Upper Preston Falls

Variation. As a variation of this drive, you may choose to go back past Gaunts Road, Upper Castra and Sprent and turn off into Route B16, the Kindred Road. This leads back through the lovely countryside of Forth. The pyrethrum crops are an attractive sight in summer.

Ulverstone

Ulverstone was settled fairly late and grew slowly. The population in 1861 was 15. In the late 1980s it had reached approximately 14 000 Cropping and dairying are major industries, and the mild pleasant climate of the town draws many people to retire there. It is also within easy distance of Devonport and Burnie.

For the kids. If you are travelling with children, Ulverstone is an ideal place to spend a few hours—or days. It might be a bit short on night-life and historic buildings, but it's long on playgrounds, parks, beaches, and places to stay, from caravan parks through bed and breakfast places and motels.

There's a fun and fitness track, a water slide, a bird sanctuary, a dog-exercising-beach and the only dog hitching-rail I've ever seen.

Places to see in Ulverstone. Once in Ulverstone, you should see an information bay to your left. After this, you turn right and then left at the lights to reach the shopping centre. The Baptist Church is on your left and the landmark of Ulverstone's Clock is the centre of a roundabout. The clock, known as the Shrine of Remembrance, is mounted on three columns, representing the three Services. Head west through the roundabout and then up the main street. Pass two red brick buildings, both built in 1903. One is

Back to Ulverstone. Return along the Gunns Plains Road, past the shop, and drive alongside the Leven River, where parks and picnic areas have been laid out along the bank. Continue through the towns of North Motton and Gawler, and return to Ulverstone.

Gunns Plains Caves

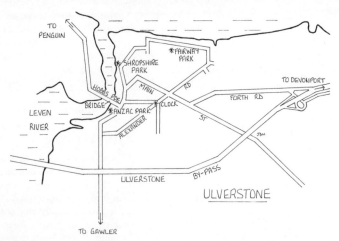

Furner's Hotel. Continue until you come to the Leven River, just past Lancaster House (1923).

On the left of the bridge over the Leven River is Anzac Park, complete with a Space Age Playground for the children, a floral Rotary Emblem, small gardens with names such as 'Prisoners of War Garden' and 'Kokoda Garden' and the Merv Wright Memorial Fountain, erected in memory of Councillor Merv Wright in 1973. In 1990, a seed from the historic Lone Pine on Gallipoli was planted in this park. At the

Space-age playground, Ulverstone

time of writing it has grown into a healthy little tree. Over the river is Trobruk Park.

Route C142 leads over the Leven to West Ulverstone, and Route B17 to Gawler and Gunns Plains. If you turn right before the bridge, or turn and go back over it from the west side, you can drive around the beach road, past Shropshire and Fairway Parks.

These parks offer a giant water slide, a globe of the world, and some very impressive all-age children's playgrounds. All the equipment is kept in excellent condition, there are toilet blocks, barbeques and picnic grounds galore. We used to take our children to these parks when they were young and they always loved them.

The scenic route from Ulverstone to Penguin

On Route C142 continue to the railway line and take the left hand fork to Penguin and Burnie or the right hand fork which is variously known as Hobbs Parade, or the Penguin Road, or the Scenic Coast Road, (Route C240) to Penguin. Pass the caravan park on your right and continue parallel with the railway line. Out to sea are rocky islands, including the Three Sisters and a larger island very close to shore, which is Goat Island. These rocky islands and the immediate foreshore are part of a seagull sanctuary. Overlooking the Three Sisters is the homestead of 'Lonah', built in 1875 for Major-General Lodder, which we are told was later owned by Richard Gaunt of 'Gaunts', Nietta. Just past the Penguin town boundary on your right, you will see gardens of flowering plants and shrubs along the railway line. This is the Max Perry Reserve.

Penguin

Penguin itself is a lovely little town, with a population of about 3000. The Dial Range, (which was first named Dial Mountain by Joseph Fossey, an assistant surveyor attached to the Van Diemen's Land Company in the 1820s, after its appearance), forms its backdrop, with Mt Montgomery (458 m) 2 km to the south. Penguin is another favourite place for children, and not only because of the plethora of penguin symbols in the town. The beach has a fine coating of coloured pebbles, there's a park and it's not far to Ferndene, a charming picnic area complete with creeks and man ferns.

Penguin's history. A few kilometres away is Preservation Bay, a landing place of Bass and Flinders. Penguin was originally

Islands off Penguin

named Penguin Creek by botanist Robert Campbell Gunn in 1861. It was one of the last parts of the north-west coast to be settled, because of the extremely dense and luxuriant bush. Some settlers from Canada brought along with them their method of ringbarking trees: this enabled the pioneers to clear their farms by ringbarking the trees, waiting until they were dry and then burning them. The clear ground was then ready for homesteading. It sounds rather shocking to our modern sensibilities, but the pioneers saw the trees as heavy and immovable objects that were parked on the land they wanted for buildings and farms. Some people were grateful for the heavy timber when the gold rush and the growth of Melbourne caused a demand for palings throughout the 1850s. This activity led to the building of a wharf, and a number of ships sailed to and from Melbourne taking timber split in the Penguin district.

Well-known sailors included Captain Dan Jens, Captain Christopher Anthon, Peter Gowans and the Taylors. Some of the sea captains retired to Tasmania and the graves of a number of them may be seen in the cemetery.

The first major settler in Penguin was Mr Edward Joseph Beecraft.

Edward Beecraft must have had a taste for pioneering; he was also the first pioneer of Ulverstone! He acquired 167 acres in Penguin in 1861. He arrived in Launceston with his widowed mother and the rest of her family in 1836. When he sold his place in Ulverstone, he moved to Forth where he managed the estate of Dr C.G. Casey, the grandfather of Lord Casey, one-time Governor-General of Australia. In 1876 Beecraft married Barbara Emily Thomas, a daughter of the magnificently named Samuel Henry Leipsie Thomas. From Forth he moved on to Penguin and built a ketch called *the Penguin* which he sailed as its master. Captain Beecraft's land passed to Mr G.C. Walker and then to Alexander

Clerke. At that time it became known as the 'Coroneagh' Estate. He is buried at the Pioneer graveyard at Forth,

Other settlers of the early 1860s were J.M. Dooley and Anderson Cummings. The first silver in Tasmania was discovered at Penguin by James 'Philosopher' Smith, in 1858. He also found some copper.

James 'Philosopher' Smith was born in 1827 at George Town and later became a flour miller's apprentice in Launceston. He went mining during the gold rush in Castlemaine in 1851 and moved to forth near Clayton Rivulet, onto a property called 'Westwood'. He continued prospecting, finding small traces of various metals in the area, but his major discovery was of tin at Mt Bischoff, (named for V.D.L. Co. director James Bischoff), in 1871. Two years later the Mt Bischoff Tin Mining Company was started, but a change of personnel caused Smith to sever his links with this venture in 1876. However, he was honoured for his discovery and awarded a lifetime pension. He died at Forth in 1897.

Around Penguin. On your left in the main street is the Tourist Information Centre. Opposite is the War Memorial and the Giant Penguin. The town abounds with penguin emblems; even the rubbish bins are shaped like the town's favourite bird! Down on the beach beyond the picnic area are the unusual pebbles for the rockhounds and a pleasant play area for children. Continue along the street past the Tasmania Bank to see the Uniting Church on your left. This is a most attractive building, and was erected in 1903, replacing an earlier church on the same site.

Cross over the railway line, and on your left is little shingled St Stephen's Anglican Church, built in 1874. St Stephen's (open daily) is charming. It has National Trust classification as an Historic Building. It is furnished inside with blackwood, and care has been taken to retain its simple charm.

St Stephen's, Penguin

In the church is a memorial to Geoffrey Hugh Brown of the Imperial Tasmanian Bushman, who fought and died at the Transvaal in 1900, and behind in the churchyard is the grave of Alexander Clerke, who died in 1877 at the age of seventy-five. An Alexander Clerke was Chairman of the Penguin Road Trust in 1883, but this cannot, (for obvious reasons) have been the same one!

To see the Penguin Cemetery, drive over the Bass Highway at the lights and continue past the turn-off to Gunns Plains. On your left is the George Hooper Reserve. Just past that, on top of the hill at your right, is the cemetery, containing a number of interesting old graves, including that of Thomas Moriarty Clerke, (1837–1891); we wonder if he was a connection of Alexander's? Also the grave of the splendidly named Featherstone Ockerbie, who died in 1916. Near this is the headstone of the wife of Captain Edward Taylor, who died in 1895. Also buried in the graveyard are descendants of pioneers named Sushames and Yaxley.

The road to South Riana. The highway runs just beyond St Stephen's Church. Not far back on your left as you face the highway, is the sign indicating South Riana. If you enter this route and drive along Pine Road, South Riana, you can follow the signs to Pindari Deer Farm and licensed restaurant. You may also be able to visit the Beltana Ostrich complex which, at the time of writing, is due to reopen in late 1996.

Walking Tracks. For the energetic, there is a walking track up Mt Montgomery, named after a Mr Montgomery who purchased some land sight unseen—and discovered it included the mountain! To reach it, turn left off the Esplanade into Crescent St and then left again into Ironcliffe Road. Mt Montgomery Road leads off from this. For another pleasant and less strenuous walk, continue along Ironcliffe Road to Ferndene. Maps showing more walking tracks may be obtained from Penguin Council Chambers.

To Ferndene. To visit the Ferndene Reserve, turn off the Esplanade into Crescent St, then take the first turn to the left, into Ironcliffe Road. Pass the Baptist Church on your left. It is c. 6 km to Ferndene. Pass Penguin Primary and High Schools on your left and the Penguin Sports Centre. Soon, on your right-hand side, Ironcliffe Road turns sharply right and down and the road winds for some way down the hill to The Ferndene Gorge State Reserve. Drive over a wooden bridge across the creek and park on the left near the barbecue area.

From here, a walking track leads to Thorsbys Tunnel, Mt Dial and Mt Gnomen. It takes 15 minutes of brisk walking to reach Thorsbys Tunnel, which is just that; a dark tunnel in the hillside. This is a fairly easy walk, mostly on level ground, among mossy giant tree ferns and dogwoods, crossing and recrossing the creek via a dozen wooden or tree-trunk bridges. The track is narrow and a bit stony, but even small children seem to have no problems with it. The walk to the mountains is much longer, taking about 2 hours.

Thorsbys Tunnel was named after a mine manager. The tunnel, (a galena or silver-lead mine) was made during the 1880s or 90s and extends c. 90 metres into the hillside before dropping steeply to a lower pit which is now fenced off. The tunnel is in surprisingly good condition and is quite dry. Any would-be explorer is advised to bring a torch, and to watch out for leggy cave spiders.

The end of Ironcliffe Road runs into the gravel Forestry Road Hales Road, which passes the mountains and ends up at Riana. This road is very rough and difficult, and it's much simpler to visit Riana from the highway turn-off.

The V.D.L. Co. at Emu Bay (Burnie). The site of Burnie was chosen by the explorer Henry Hellyer in 1827 when a port was needed to link Surrey Hills with the coast. Hellyer was a popular and able man who is classed as the greatest of the Tasmanian explorers. His suicide in 1832 shocked those who knew him.

Although the Inglis Estuary was preferred by Van Diemen's Land Company man Edward Curr, Hellyer chose Emu Bay and had a road constructed from there to Surrey Hills, where a stock settlement was established the following year.

The V.D.L. Company pastured cattle through the region during these years, and sheep were added in 1829. However, a very harsh winter and the depredations of Tasmanian tigers, (Thylacines), drastically reduced their numbers. All attempts at sheep farming there ceased in 1834.

The beginning of Burnie

The first private settler in Emu Bay, (a Mr Romaine), arrived in 1841. Romaine Creek and the farming area behind Burnie were named after him. Burnie is an industrial city/port, traditionally the jumping-off point for the far North West.

Nomenclature in Burnie. Other settlers quickly followed, and the township of

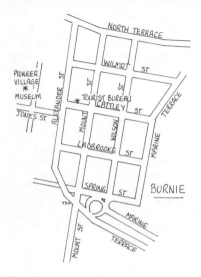

Burnie was surveyed c. 1841. It was named after William Burnie, who had once been a director of the V.D.L. Co. The early influence of the Company is still strongly present in Burnie in many of the street names; Cattley St (after John Cattley), Ladbrooke St, (after Felix Calvert Ladbroke), Alexander St (for Henry Alexander), and Wilson St, (for Francis Wilson). Old Surrey Road was originally known as Surrey Hills road, and marks the earliest part of the city. However, Spring St was named because the Catholic Church there had a spring behind it. The town grew slowly, and in 1863 the population consisted of a mere 50 people. By the 1880s Burnie was still a small place, with activity centred on Marine Terrace. In 1887 it was resurveyed, and from then on began to grow rapidly. Wilson St became the new trade centre.

Noted early citizens included Mary Morris, an Irish widow who became the school teacher in Burnie in 2862, Captain William Jones, prospector William Bell, a son of Robert Bell after whom Bells Parade at Latrobe was named, and John Stammers who built the Town Hall, the (present) National Australia Bank, the Bay View Hotel and other buildings.

Captain William Jones (1842–1907), at one time had interests in most of the businesses in Burnie and was known as 'King of Burnie'. He was born in Newborough, Anglesey, North Wales and arrived in Australia aged 19. He was employed by his uncle, another Captain William Jones, as a crew member of the *Dove*, which plied between Table Cape and Melbourne. In 1866 he and his brother, Captain John Jones, were in command of the *Margaret Chessell*. In 1869 he had the schooner *Onward*. Three years later he retired from the sea and bought the Ship Inn. This was demolished in 1874, and he then built the Bay View Hotel. This he sold in 1876 to buy John Byrne's property 'Uplands' at Cooee Creek, (named after Aborigines were heard 'cooeeing' there in the 1820s). Here he established a brick factory, a jetty and a cordial factory, a bacon factory and the butter factory.

By the late 1980s, Burnie had a population exceeding 21 000, and is now Tasmania's major overseas cargo port.

Around the City. We had an interesting time searching for historic buildings in Burnie, being informed, (with what seemed like a certain gloomy satisfaction), by several residents that there weren't any! Certainly many of the original houses and shops have been either relocated or pulled down since Peter Mercer's books about the city were published in the 1960s.

For example:

Burnie Inn, (once situated next to present Burnie Hotel and behind a shop built in the 1890s) was built in 1850 by shipbuilder Thomas Wiseman. He managed this until his death in 1876 when his widow, Grannie Wiseman took over until she died in the early 1900s. Since 1973, the Burnie Inn has graced Burnie Park. It is now restored.

Marine Terrace was the site of many early buildings, including an old house built in the 1850s for Mrs Michael Mylan next to Page's store. She had arrived in 1848 from Herefordshire, and her son John became the first blacksmith and undertaker in Burnie in 1868. This house has also gone. Now—from what is not to what is.

As you enter Burnie, look to your left to see the Associated Pulp and Paper Mills, (A.P.P.M.), established in 1934. Also to the left is the turn-off to Fern Glade, two km off the highway. Fern Glade is a beautiful reserve of man ferns on the Emu River. Follow the signs into the town centre and head up Mount St on Route B18 until you reach the suburb of Hillcrest and Aileen Crescent.

Number 9 Aileen Crescent is 'Glen Osborne', a big two-storey brick house with white iron lace trim. Built in the 1880s, 'Glen Osborne' belonged to William Bell. It stands today in an old established garden. Little of the house can be seen from the road owing to the screening trees. The Olympic Pool is close.

Return down Mount St, crossing the lights. Cross Ladbrooke St, with the Uniting Church on the left. On your right a little farther on is the Baptist Church and, on the left at 56 Mount St is the office of *The Advocate* Newspaper.

The Advocate had its beginnings in 1890 when Robert Harris and his two sons Robert Day Harris and Charles James Harris, established a twice weekly paper called *Wellington Times* at an office in Cattley St. For a time a separate branch paper was published in Devonport, but the papers merged and in 1916 became known simply as *The Advocate*. It is still run by descendants of the Harris family.

A walk through Burnie. Park your car somewhere near the Advocate Office, as there are now several interesting places in easy walking distance. The Tourist Bureau is on the corner of Cattley and Mt Streets. To see the Pioneer Museum, turn out of Cattley St left into Alexander St. There you should see the red brick Burnie Supreme Court. Turn right up Jones St, and, just before you reach the overpass, turn right. On your left is the low brick building housing the Pioneer Museum. Just past the museum is a brick wall with the crest of the Van Diemen's Land Company 1825 on it. The crest incorporates a sheep, a crown, a ship, a sickle, sheaf of wheat and some vines. This wall was a feature of the Van Diemen's Land Company building, once a landmark sited at Marine Terrace, overlooking the Port.

On this side of the museum is a mural depicting gum trees. Inside the museum the last time we visited were replicas of many of the original businesses in Burnie, comprising in part a general blacksmith and farrier, established 1868 by John Mylan, who was born in Herefordshire in 1839. His son Hugh Mylan continued the business, sited at the lower end of Ladbrooke St, into the 1930s.

Next to it was a saddler's, established 1885 by E. Evans. An interesting feature was a harness and saddlery sewing machine dating from around 1870. Next was a grocer's shop and a bookseller's (run by J. Dudfield, Wilson St), the office of the

Outside Pioneer, Museum, Burnie

Wellington Times, forerunner of *The Advocate*. Next was the Emu Bay butter factory, run by William Jones, after whom Jones St was probably named.

This factory became the North West Co-operative Dairy Company. Beyond these was the general museum area with cards, clothes, dolls, etc.

Past the Museum. Walk on past the Pioneer Museum. To your left is a fountain, to your right is the rear of the Hellyer Regional Library. This narrow one way street is Little Alexander St. At its end, turn left down the path to the Civic Centre and Art Gallery. The gallery was opened in 1978 and houses its own collection of 500 items as well as other exhibitions on occasion. Upstairs in the Civic Centre is the theatre. The ground floor comprises three galleries.

Walk down Wilmot St, cross Mount St and go into Wilson St to see the one-time residence of the Loucado-Wells family, a large square Edwardian brick house with a handsome wrought iron verandah, opposite the Gospel Hall. It was built in 1907.

Return to Mount St. Opposite K Mart is the Plaza Arcade, worth a visit for its interesting shops.

Burnie Park

To visit Burnie Park, drive down Mount St and turn left into North Terrace. The park is on your left. **Burnie Park** was once part of the property leased by the V.D.L. Co., first to Henry Hastings and then to John Swain. In the late 1880s it was sold to landowner William Oldaker, who called it 'Avon'. It was bought at auction by the Burnie Council in 1928.

The park is a pleasant place to visit, featuring extensive rose gardens; the war memorial; a music bowl; a wildlife sanctuary with a resident emu, peacocks, black swans, a cockatoo, a turkey and wallabies; playground; the old Burnie Inn, identified trees and a walking track to the Oldaker Falls. The Burnie Inn is classified with the National Trust of Australia.

Waterfalls. Apart from the above-mentioned Oldaker Falls, Burnie area has more than its fair share of waterfalls. The best known of these are the Guide Falls, but many of the others are equally beautiful: *if* you can find them!

To reach the Guide Falls, drive west along the Bass Highway. Veer left to Ridgley (named by Henry Hellyer in the late 1820s) on Route C18 with Parklands High School up on the hill to your left. When you arrive

Loucardo Wells, Home, Burnie

Burnie Inn, Burnie Park

in the township of Ridgley, you will see a signpost to the Guide Falls (1 km). On your left, you'll notice the big Pet Dam, the water supply for the city of Burnie. The distinctive mountain ahead is Valentine Peak.

Turn right into C104, the Guide Falls turn-off. There is an abrupt turn to the left into the Guide Falls Reserve (open Nov.–Apr. 9 a.m.–8 p.m., Apr.–Oct. 9 a.m.–5 p.m.). In the Guide Falls Reserve is a picnic area with toilets. If you drive along the road to the left you'll go a short way under blackwood, wattle and assorted gum trees, to the top of the falls.

The Guide Falls (on the Guide River) are a double tier falling down very steep black rock. The top tier is only a metre or so high, the second one much more impressive. The rock around here has an unusual cobbled appearance and, as at Mole Creek (See Chapter 3), lumps of it show through the ground. There is a 5-minute walk down past the falls to the picnic area. Go down a steep set of winding steps. On the right is a beautiful mossy bank, with kangaroo fern growing on top. Steep slabs of rock look as if they have been carved out deliberately. A couple of hundred metres down the track is another part of the falls, and a little farther along are some man ferns. This is an easy walk, well within the range of most

War Memorial, Burnie Park

families, even those with small children.

To see Sandersons Falls, turn left as you leave Guide Falls and follow Route C105 to West Ridgley. When you reach a T-junction, turn left. Shortly afterwards, turn right into South Prospect Road, bordered to the right by young gum trees. Drive about 1.5 km along this narrow gravel road until you reach a culvert with a wooden fence to the right. Climb the fence and walk up and across the hill to your right. Caution: this paddock is on private property so take care. From the fence you can look back toward Sandersons Creek and see the very steep falls.

Also around the Ridgley district are the Darling, Pet, St Georges, St Josephs and Serpent Falls. Many of these are quite inaccessible, and even with a local guide and the aid of two maps we failed to find the St George Falls among the spaghetti junction of Forestry Roads. Around this area you will find several tea-gardens, craft studios, display farms and other such attractions. Just follow the signs to any that take your eye.

Return to Burnie via Route C105: any attempt to deviate from this tends to bring you through attractive rural scenes to all kinds of dead ends.

On your way you will see a sign (right) pointing to Tewkesbury. At Tewkesbury is a potato research station. Potatoes were once very important in the Burnie area, forming the major export from the port for its first forty years.

If you return from Burnie towards Devonport, leave on the Bass Highway and pass the A.P.P.M. mills. The turn-off to Lactos cheese factory leads off to the right, 3 km up Old Surrey Road.

Lactos Pty Ltd was established in the mid 1950s by Milan Vyhnalek, and now produces a wide variety of speciality cheeses, including Camembert, Brie and Gouda. In 1988 exports reached 65 000 tonnes.

Choice of ways

You may now wish to return to Devonport, and a pleasant alternate route is given below. If you prefer to continue to the far north-west, turn to the next chapter now.

Forth detour

On your way back to Devonport, it is interesting to detour around the town of Forth.

The route to Forth is B19 to the right, opposite Turners Beach. Go through the roundabout, over the overpass, through another roundabout, through part of Turners Beach, and you'll reach the town. A pretty place, particularly in spring when the blossoms are out, Forth is situated in a valley, on the Forth River, and surrounded by red soil farmlands. The soil type is Krasnozem, the rainfall about 1000 mm, and the average size of farms 40 to 60 ha: for stock grazing a hectare of land can support 1 dairy cow or 2.5 beef cattle, or 10 prime lamb ewes, and can produce 5000 kg of meadow hay, 56 000 kg of green peas, 22 500 kg of potatoes, 3600 kg of wheat or 3150 kg of barley. All kinds of vegetables are grown.

Just before you enter the town, you'll pass the Forth graveyard on your left. Like many country cemeteries, this is a peaceful place, given over to long grass and wild flowers. Most of the graves date from the early twentieth century. If you walk to the rear of the graveyard you can see the Forth River.

On your right, just past the graveyard, is the turn-off to 'Westleigh', near Wensleydale Arabian Stud.

'**Westleigh**' itself, a few hundred metres off the road, is a white two-storey weatherboard house with a tall chimney and red roof. Wysteria climbs over the porch. In the front garden is a flagpole, complete with flag.

'Westleigh' was built for Edward J. Beecraft, who arrived in Forth around 1833. He lived there with his wife Barbara and is buried in the Pioneer Graveyard at East Forth.

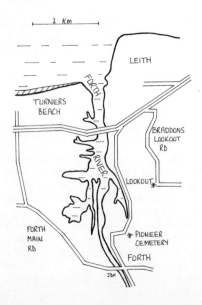

Back towards Devonport. Shortly after leaving 'Westleigh', you come to a turn-off to Route B16 to Kindred, and Sprent on B15. It is now about 12 km to Spreyton. Pass the little Forth shopping centre, and the Forth Uniting Church, half hidden by the massive weeping willow trees. Coming towards the river watch for the attractive cottages and the Recreation Ground to the left. Pass a turn-off (right), Route C132 to Wilmot and Cradle Mountain. Cross over the Forth River. On your left is the Bridge Hotel, a very handsome black and white building. From this point you may turn left to visit the seaside township of Leith at the mouth of the Forth River, perhaps calling in at the East Forth Pioneer Graveyard as you go. Under a tree there is the grave of pioneer Edward Beecraft.

If you choose to go straight ahead rather than turning left to Leith, next you will pass the Forth Post Office and begin a long winding climb up out of the valley. Just past the end of the speed limit sign is a signpost indicating a scenic point.

Turn off at C145 to Melrose and Lower Barrington or continue on B19 towards Spreyton.

Braddons Lookout. Turn off to the left on Route C189 to visit Braddons Lookout at the top of the hill. Turn right into Braddons Lookout Road. Down to your left as you drive along you'll see a beautiful view of Forth spread out in its valley, and the Forth River right down to the sea. This road is sealed, and although it has a few sharp bends, these are well signposted. Braddons Lookout itself is contained in a little grove of trees, and has barbecue facilities and picnic tables.

The lettering at the lookout reads: 'To the memory of Sir Edward Braddon, K.C.M.C.P.C., Premier of Tasmania, a member of the first Federal Parliament'. The cairn was erected on the property which was his home to commemorate the hundred years of government in Tasmania from 1856 to 1956. It was unveiled at Forth by the Honourable G.H. Green, President of the Legislative Council, in 1956.

If you look down to the left you can see Forth and the Forth River, and to the right you can see the Dial Range ahead and right out to the west as far as Table Cape. You can continue along the same road to come back out on the Bass Highway, or else return to B19 towards Spreyton.

If you take the latter route, Lillico Road on the left runs down to the coast. Come over the crest of a hill and on your right is Bells Strawberry Farm and then Vecon Pty Ltd. Pass Cutts Road on your left, and there is

another fine view out to sea straight ahead. Spread out in front is the township of Don, (see Chapter 1). On your right are Riverview Nurseries. Go under the bridge and out past Don Railway on the left, Don Memorial Hall on your right, and the Post Office on your left. Cross Highway 1 (to Burnie and Launceston) pass St Olave's Church and follow the road around towards Spreyton. There is a turn-off to the left which takes you back to Devonport.

BIBLIOGRAPHY

Books
FENTON, James, *Bush Life in Tasmania*.
MERCER, Peter, *Burnie . . . Its History and Development*, 1965.
MERCER, Peter, *The Story of Burnie— 1823 to 1910*, 1963
The Story of Penguin
U.B.D. St Directory

Pamphlets
'A City is Born'
'Burnie Park and Tree Guide', (Burnie City Council)
'Let's Talk About Burnie'
'Let's Talk About Penguin'
'Let's Talk About Ulverstone' (Tas. Visitor Corporation)

Maps
Tasmap 1: 100 000 Land Tenure Index Series:
'Forth', 'Hellyer'

Information
Thanks to the staff at *The Advocate*, Anne Heazlewood, Norma Hudson, Viv Kranenburg, Mrs Miles, Mr and Mrs Poynton, Gerwyn Wright, and the guide at Gunns Plains Caves.

19. The Far North-west

Features of this drive

The area west of Burnie, often known as 'Cape Country', has more than its fair share of scenic wonders, just a few being the famous Stanley Nut, Table Cape, Fossil Bluff, Rocky Cape, Boat Harbour Beach and the Dip Falls. If you're fond of impressive scenery, cliffs, lush pastures, arts and crafts and cameras, this is the trip for you. As a bonus you'll visit the pretty towns of Stanley, Smithton and Wynyard, and several historic houses and villages along the way.

Towards the far north-west

After leaving Burnie Park, drive through Cooee, cross Cooee Creek and go through the 'Golden Mile' where much of the local business is conducted. Cooee Primary

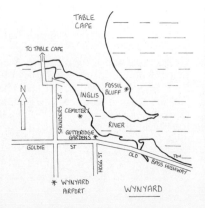

School is on your left, and farther on is Burnie High School.

To the left is Route A10 to Tullah and Queenstown, just as you cross over the Cam River coming into Somerset. Until 1996, a trip to the far north -west meant another reverse trip coming back, but now Smithton in linked with Queenstown via the road known locally as either (officially) the Western Explorer or (unofficially) the Tarkine Road. We haven't driven this road, but it's currently unsealed, and we have heard that it's best to enquire locally before setting out in wet weather. This is the same road whose beginning you met in Zeehan in Chapter 16.

The Cam River, named by Henry Hellyer, was a flourishing port during the 1860s, '70s and '80s. The area was first settled in 1858, when Captain David Thomas Lewis, a Welshman, bought some land from the Van Diemen's Land Co at the east bank of the Cam. He built and had licensed the Ferry House Hotel that year, and also ran a ferry. Two years later he went into partnership with Captain John Gibson, who also built a home for his family at the Cam. In 1864 Thomas Dodd Wragg, his wife Emily and their family moved in on the west bank of the river, setting up the first house, school and church, and probably naming Somerset. The next turn-off is Route C241 (left) to lower Mt Hicks. The headland on your right just before you come into Wynyard is Doctors Rocks. Just after Doctors Rocks turn right into C240, the old road into Wynyard.

Wynyard's history

Wynyard is a pleasant town with a population of over four and a half thousand. It's well supplied with walks and parks, beaches and scenery.

The European history of Wynyard really begins in 1798 when George Bass and Matthew Flinders sailed past and sighted and named Table Cape. Other explorers of the coastline included Lt Charles Robbins in 1802, Captain James Kelly in 1816, Captain Charles Browne Hardwicke in 1823 and James Hobbs in 1824. It was left to explorer Henry Hellyer to discover and name the Inglis River in 1827.

The major settlement in the district was made where Burnie now stands, and Wynyard was settled by people such as John King, in 1841 and the Alexander brothers in 1851.

John King became the first settler at what is now Wynard when he selected two blocks of land, totalling 1280 acres, in 1841. He was an industrious man, and within 3 years he had built a comfortable house and cleared much of his ground. Unfortunately, he died soon afterwards, and his land was later bought by James Percy, descendants of whom still own part of the property. King's first neighbour, Frederick Wilbraham Ford, later married one of the Misses King.

As in Penguin, the paling splitters moved into this area during the 1850s, and the embryo settlement was named Wynyard after Edward Buckle Wynyard of the New South Wales Corps.

Until the discovery of tin at Mt Bischoff, Wynyard was the principal port of the North West. In 1870 it had overtaken Burnie and had a population of approximately 900.

During the 1890s a butter factory and a flour mill were established. In 1915 electricity was installed. The aerodrome opened in 1936.

Wynyard today

Wynyard in the late twentieth century is a thriving residential town, servicing the fertile dairying and cropping district of Circular Head.

Attractions include the Scuba Centre in East Wynyard and Western Aviation at 76 Dodgin St, where chartered flights over the scenic Cape Country (as the North West corner of Tasmania is now known), are available.

Things to see in Wynyard

Pass Seabrook Golf Course to your left as you enter Wynyard; Table Cape is straight ahead. The other golf course in the area, the Wynyard Golf Course, occupies the land once owned by settler John King. To your left, just past Martin St, is the hospital near Camp Creek.

Wynyard is a pretty town, with lovely gardens. And, as an enthusiastic resident says: 'Within a few minutes you can get out into the bush . . . '

As you enter Wynyard past the building known as the old Spencer Hospital, stay on Goldie Street. Richard Guttridge Gardens, on the corner of Hogg and Goldie Streets, have been a pleasant park in Wynyard for over 40 years. The gardens contain a lily pond and stands of tea-trees

Guttridge Gardens, Inglis River, Wynyard

The old cemetery, Wynyard

Table Cape, Wynyard

and native shrubs, as well as a raised walk through ferns and shrubbery, but their chief charm lies in the extensive green lawns leading around the east bank of the lovely Inglis River. Fifty years ago the gardens contained formal terraced gardens.

At the far end of the gardens, walk past the War Memorial and the boat ramp to see the old cemetery. Several young native trees were planted at the cemetery during the mid-1980s, and the quiet peace of the place attracts many birds. On a recent visit, we saw three fat galahs. Wild galahs are rather uncommon is Tasmania, although large flocks of them thrive on the mainland.

Buried in the graveyard are James Pringle, 1894, Joseph and Mary Anne Thunder, 1903 and 1921, Thomas Brewster, 1887, John Fleming, 1861 and his wife, 1868, and many other members of the Fleming family, who came originally from Cahirconlish, County Limerick, in Ireland. It is possible to walk right out to Fossil Bluff if you cross the river at the bridge near the picnic area and then walk back around the river road. However, most people prefer to drive there.

Fossil Bluff is an amazing geographical formation across the bay to the east of Table Cape. The bluff sits on Permian Tillite, which came down on the glaciers and

became cemented with mudstone. This material underlies the whole of Wynyard. Fossil Bluff is composed of three major layers: Permian Tillite at the base, then sandstone, (an estimated 30 000 000 years old), and then a cap of basalt (an estimated 12 000 000 years).

To visit the bluff by car, go back through one roundabout, and at the second roundabout, turn up Saunders St, past the Wynyard Bowls Club. Follow Route C234 2 km towards Table Cape. Cross the bridge and turn right, following the sign. Turn left into Freestone Crescent. Then there is a brief scramble down the grassy bank to the beach, which is strewn with rocks that look like a cross between Swiss cheese and chewed chewing gum, and the bluff itself.

Table Cape. To visit Table Cape continue on Route C234. The Cape is an almost circular volcanic plug of about 1.5 km diameter. The sea face is about 170 metres above sea level, and the rest of the feature rises some 70 m above surrounding land. Drive west towards Table Cape, turn right onto the Cape Road, past Alexandria, (where the Alexander Brothers had a hotel in 1851), and through rich land where crops of oats, peas, barley, potatoes and oil poppies flourish. On your left, you'll see the tulip and bulb farm—a glorious sight

Fossil Bluff, Wynyard

in spring. Drive onto a gravel road and look for the lighthouse in view to the left. Turn left to the lighthouse (1 km).

The lighthouse was established in 1888. The original light source was an oil wick lamp which was converted first to acetylene operation and then in 1979 to mains electric power. The tower height is 25 metres and the elevation 180 metres.

Directly in front of the lighthouse is a climbing track (caution: literally climbing!) where, with a certain amount of care it should be possible to get down the face of the Cape. At one point the face is so sheer that wire rope has been strung between two trees.

The Alexanders. There were three Alexander brothers, Joseph, John and Matthias, all three of whom were transported to Van Diemen's Land as convicts: Matthias and Joseph for taking part in a riot and John for stealing a pig. Having been granted their freedom, the brothers arrived at the Inglis c. 1840. In 1851 Joseph and Matthias opened the Table Cape Inn. They also had a store, and John eventually became a large landowner.

To see another lookout on the Cape, drive on past the lighthouse turn-off towards the sea. Just ahead is a flight of steps down to the lookout.

At the head of the steps is a memorial to another Alexander—Frederick Matthias Alexander, (1869–1955), who was the founder of the Alexander technique. Apparently this technique relates to functional human movement.

Tollymore Road. If you wish, you may continue over Table Cape on Tollymore Road (Route C232), which soon rejoins the highway. Tollymore Road is named after the home of George Shekelton, an Irishman who settled in the Cape district in 1853 and went on to become a magistrate. It's a very pretty drive, offering more splendid views. Otherwise, you can return down Saunders street, turn right into Goldie Street and rejoin the old Bass Highway, Inglis Street, on Route C240 passing; the United Milk Trading cheese factory to your left as you leave the town.

The old Bass Highway rejoins the new one near the turn-off to the left into Godwins Road, just before you cross over the Inglis River.

The next turn-off is Route C229 to Flowerdale, a farming district on the Flowerdale River. Poet and author Barney Roberts lives at Flowerdale. Also on that road is Preolenna.

As you continue on the highway, you'll pass a great many shops specialising in arts and crafts and local produce. On a recent visit we saw leather work, stained glass, herbs, pottery and woodwork. Much of the work is done locally.

Boat Harbour

Boat Harbour Beach

About 6 km on, you will arrive at the township of Boat Harbour, and a little farther on at the turn-off into Route C232 to Boat Harbour Beach. The first settler at Boat Harbour was named Roastplate Lane! The road is sealed, with farmland on both sides. A sharp elbow bend to the left brings you to the turn-off to Boat Harbour at the end of 1 km of winding road.

Boat Harbour is one of the most attractive and easily accessible of the north western beaches. It was originally known as 'Jacob's Boat Harbour', and may have been named after a seafarer of the 1830s, Captain John Jacobs, or after Van Diemen's Land Company Director of the same name. Boat Harbour is no longer a shipping centre, but the township surveyed there by the Lands Department in 1866 became a popular holiday place during the 1920s. The safe and sheltered white sand beach is popular with swimmers and skin-divers. It is quite a busy holiday centre with Caravan park, camping sites and a general store. Motel accommodation is also available.

Sisters Beach. Route C232 forks, with Route C233 leading on to pretty Lake Llewellyn, along Sisters Creek to the hills known as the Two Sisters, and to Sisters Beach, 9 or 10 km from the highway. The road is sealed right through. Lying about 1 km offshore to the north is Sisters Island. This is the road from which the Postmans Track departs, and also provides access to the Rocky Cape National Park. It takes an hour to walk down to Sisters Beach.

Lake Llewellyn comes as rather a surprise, nesting down among the hills. Boating and water skiing are allowed from around ten a.m. until five p.m., but check by the signs for the Dos and Don'ts.

Sisters Beach is a peaceful holiday town, with attractions such as a visit to Birdland, boating, swimming and walking.

Return to the Bass Highway to pass through the hamlet of Sisters Creek, with the Sisters Hills to your right. A walking track leads about 2 km to Breakneck Point.

First Settlers at Sisters Creek Beach. The settlement of Sisters Creek Beach came remarkably late in the history of Tasmania when the intrepid Irby family moved there from Hobart in 1933. Land had been selected there by J. Alexander in 1872, but he left soon afterwards.

It was in 1841 that Edward Irby and his

family left Lincolnshire to come to New South Wales on the *Flora Kerr*. Edward bought 100 000 acres called 'Bolivia Station' there. The Irby who came to Tasmania was Llewellyn George, born in 1883. Young Llewellyn became a botanical collector, and walked 400 miles through Tasmania. In 1920 he became Tasmania's first Conservator of Forests. Then in 1933 he decided to prove that some of the so-called wastelands of Tasmania could become productive.

There was no road to Sisters Creek Beach, so Llewellyn and his family made one. They cleared some land, built a cabin and grew vegetables. They fished and hunted rabbits. The family has made its mark on the land all right. Anniversary Point at Rocky Cape was named by Llewellyn's daughter Betty when they visited it on her parent's 22nd wedding anniversary, and Llewellyn s name was given to two species of tree: *Melaleuca irbyi* and *Eucalyptus irbyi*. Ken Irby, one of Llewellyn's sons, remembers those days with affection and has written about them in his book *In the Beginning*.

Note for the Adventurous. Although the far north-west offers many scenic routes through the fertile countryside, it also offers plenty of chances to get lost! For the adventurous—turn off at Flowerdale into Route C229, travel down between the Inglis and Flowerdale Rivers through Moorleah and Preolenna, cross over the Flowerdale River, go through Meunna, then turn north towards Milabena, detour to the left to see the Detention Falls, return to Route C229, detour right to Lapoinya, then go up to Myalla and Sisters Creek. From Sisters Creek the landscape becomes very hilly. Drive west along the highway past Montumana Road. Over to your right are the rounded hills of the area known as the Rocky Cape National Park. Just past the Montumana turn-off, you will see your first view of The Nut.

Rocky Cape National Park

Rocky Cape was named by Bass and Flinders in 1798. Rocky Cape National Park consists of over 3000 hectares of land with coastal heath vegetation, bird-life and Aboriginal middens. The Park was first proclaimed in 1967, and was enlarged in 1975. The park has walking tracks laid out, ranging from a 7 minute walk to North Cave to a 6 hour trek. North Cave and South Cave are at the northern end of the Park. Below Anniversary Point, closer to

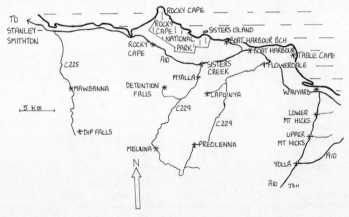

Sisters Beach, are Lee Archer Cave and Wet Cave. An entry fee applies, and permits can be obtained from the Rocky Cape Roadhouse which is situated at the turn-off. Walking track maps are available which details walks ranging from twenty minute strolls to full-day excursions.

The Postmans Track. Of note for bushwalkers is the opening during the late 1980s of a section of the Postmans Track, at the east end of the park. The Postmans Track is part of the original route surveyed by Alexander Goldie and Joseph Fossey for the use of the Van Diemen's Land Company. The track was used again during the 1850s for the first mail run, made by a postman known as Paddy the Tinker. Not only people with legitimate business in the area made use of the track in the early days. It was also travelled by bushrangers Bradley and O'Connor. To reach the re-opened part of the track, drive to Sisters Beach, cross Sisters Creek and drive along Irbys Road to the car park. Walk a few hundred metres down the road to the sign indicating the Postmans Track; the track takes you on a 45-minute walk to Sisters Beach.

Early settlers at Rocky Cane included the Hogarth, Walker, Dallas and Boys families. Cross Wilsons Creek, and drive through the township of Rocky Cape. Not far past the turn-off to Rocky Cape Siding, you will go through a gully and see another excellent view of The Nut. About 9 km from the Montumana turn-off, Route C227 (Rocky Cape Road) leads right from the highway, and about 5 km through the strange landscape of low-grassed and scrubbed hills brings you to the Cape itself.

Where the road forks, there is a map of the area on a large noticeboard. Take the left fork to the boat ramp or the right to North Cave and the lighthouse, built by S. Luck. If you stand near the lighthouse on the cape, to your right is Cave Bay and to your left the long Forwards Beach. Walk out on the

North Cave, Rocky Cape National Park

rocks and to your left you can see The Nut and to the right, Table Cape and, closer by, North Cave. The rock at the cape is a strange pinkish grey, and there are lots of little pockets of tarns and moss among the rocks.

In 1889, the S.S. *Southern Cross* sank off Rocky Cape. An onlooker was lucky (or unlucky!) enough to get a photograph of the vessel as she sank. This was not the tragedy it might have been; at low tide the passengers, (even to a cat among the baggage) walked off!

The walk from the road to North Cave is easy, and takes about 15 minutes return. North Cave and the others nearby were first occupied about 8000 years ago. The floor of North Cave is composed of an Aboriginal midden, in which shells can be easily seen. A wooden walkway has been erected in the cave to protect the midden. We visited it in late spring some years ago, and was rather distracted by the birds flying in and out of the damp narrow cleft of the cave! Watch out for drips. The cave is only c. 10 metres deep.

Circular Head

Back on the highway, you will enter the district known as Circular Head. It is now 29 km to Stanley and 37 km to Smithton. Just past the Rocky Cape Store is a Visitor Information Centre and caravan park.

Cross the Detention River. Around here is an excellent view of the jetty at Port Latta, jutting out into the sea in front of The Nut. Edgecumbe Beach, with a number of shacks is on your right. The highway returns to the coast and runs alongside Hellyer Beach, past the chimneys of Port Latta and over the bridge at pretty Crayfish Creek. In late spring and early summer, this area is covered with white flowers of melaleuca. Next you come to the Savage River silo and big warehouses, and see the Savage River Mines Port Latta Pelletising Plant and Harbour Facility. Eight hundred metres on your right past this is a rest area. Cowrie Point is on your right. At the rest area are toilets and camping places, but fees need to be paid for camping.

Cross Peggs Creek. On your right is a rather sinister-looking black marsh. On your left is Route C225 to Mawbanna (14 km) and Dip Falls (26 km). Gateforth Host Farm is on your left, 2 km from the turn-off.

Dip Falls and the Big Tree. Five and a half km from Port Latta is a turn-off to the left into Route C225, the Mawbanna Road. To visit Dip Falls, follow Mawbanna Road past the railway crossing. Pine Corner Road leads to the Black River Picnic Area. Drive through myrtle and man ferns to Mawbanna, then on for another 9.5 km to a Y-fork. The left-hand fork is a no-through road, and the right-hand fork, Route C225, leads to Dip Falls. Before turning into this road, look over to your left to see the Rocky Cape National Park. Not far past this turn-off, when we visited the falls in 1988, we was rather charmed to see a huge tree stump with a young blackwood growing from it. During a 1996 visit we was delighted to find the tree still there—and growing strong.

Drive a farther 2 km to the falls. The double-tiered falls, set in temperate rainforest, are really spectacular. The walkway is quite short, but there are 152

Dip Falls, Mawbanna

The Big Tree, Dip Falls

steep steps to be negotiated to reach the foot of the falls. There is also a walking track to a point overlooking the first part of the falls. If you are careful, it is possible to climb across from the steps and stand on the ledge between the two tiers of the falls. There are toilets and good parking places available.

Leading on from the parking area at the top of the falls is a road over a bridge, leading into Newhaven Track, and on about 1 km to another parking area. Stop here and follow the signs and the walkway a short way into the bush to see the Big Tree, a massive brown top stringy bark (*Eucalyptus obliqua*). The Big Tree has a girth of over 15 m, and a diameter of 4.5 m. It's 62 m. tall and estimated to be around 360 years old. There are several other large specimens nearby—apparently their sheer bulk saved their bacon in the wood-hungry early days of the region. Men with crosscut saws and bullock waggons presumably looked at them, drooled, pictured blisters and collapsing waggons, shrugged and left them in the too-hard basket. The descendants of these settlers have extended this good work by arranging permanent protection and easy access to the giants.

After your visit to the falls, you could then return to Mawbanna, drive 5 km turn left into Corner Road, and drive 11 km to South Forest, turn right into Mengha Road and drive due north for 3 km to Forest, then 5.5 more km through North Forest to meet the Bass Highway at the Stanley turn-off. This is approximately a 60-km round trip. Alternatively, retrace your steps to the turn-off past Port Latta. The trip is then approximately 50 km.

A third possibility is to turn off into Newhaven Road on the right, drive through over the Detention River, past a sawmill, and turn left onto the Montumana Road. After a few hundred metres, turn right onto the sealed road, Route C228, to Rocky Cape. Come through Rocky Cape Siding and out onto the highway again. Having done this ourselves a few years ago, we wouldn't recommend it; the road is rough and winding, and signs are few.

Black River and the Lost Town. Shortly after the turn-off to Gateforth comes Black River, once the site of a flourishing town which rivalled Stanley in size. There is very little left of Black Wall in the Forest, but unlike most lost towns of Tasmania it was not a mining town.

Black Wall in the Forest, so named from the dense dark scrub by early sailors up the Black River, was settled in the early 1830s by William Medwin, George Anderson, (afterwards Post Master at Stanley, and one of those who helped capture bushrangers O'Connor and Bradley) and Charles T. Smith. George Anderson married a woman named Jane, and had seven children. Charles Smith must have left Black Wall quite soon, for in 1854 he was farming at Forth. It seems that these three men approached the Van Diemen's Land Company for a township reserve, and 10 acres were set aside for the purpose. several allotments were sold.

The town grew larger as indirect result of the Victorian gold rush: the demand for timber brought new settlers. As well as some thirty houses, Black Wall once had an inn—the Black River Inn, (later the Pig and Whistle)—on the west bank, licensees being Mr Whitbread, then Harry Pegg and later Thomas Smith. The inn was re-licensed in the 1890s. It was owned at some stage by William Pegg. The town also had two churches, a Methodist Church and an Anglican Church, (which was later moved to Black River, to South Forest and finally to Mawbanna), and a burying :round. The three streets were Church St, Pierce St and Woolmore St.

William Medwin (1798–1869) his wife Elizabeth Sarah (Cock) (1793–1868) and their eight children arrived at Wellington, N.Z. from Wycombe, England on the *Slains*

Elizabeth Sarah Medwin

William Medwin

Castle in 1841. Conditions were not what they had expected, so the Medwins boarded the *Ullswater* and arrived in Launceston later that same year. The family settled on the east bank at Black River, where they farmed for many years. Their five sons, Edwin, John, Matthias, William and Thomas were all farmers as well, although Thomas later became a storekeeper in Church St, Stanley, in 1871. Thomas was born in 1837 in London and died in 1904. He had seventeen children: George, Mary, David, Charlotte, Rachel, Rachel, Herbert, Allice, Annie, Minnie, Lemuel, Arthur, Eliza, Thomas, Andrew, Phillip and Leslie! Elizabeth Medwin must have been a resourceful woman: once when bushrangers Bradley and O'Connor called, planning revenge on William for having replaced Bradley's services with the more reliable ones of a ticket-of-leave man, Elizabeth calmly tied up £60 in her skirts, keeping just 2 pounds visible. Since William was not at home, the bushrangers

took food and the £2 and went away, leaving the bulk of the family's savings safe in Elizabeth's skirts. William and Elizabeth, their grandson Matthias and one of their daughters are buried at Stanley.

This Matthias bought 310 acres of land from his grandfather William, and settled with his Irish wife Mary and their ten children. One of their sons was named Luke. His property at Black River was called 'Mayura'. His wife Annie was well known for her bonnet and boots: on one occasion she walked from Flowerdale to Black River with a goose under one arm and a cow and calf behind her! Luke and Annie's son Allan (or Alan, or possibly Allen) had property at Mawbanna, where he lived with his wife Mary Ellen, ('Mollie'), and nine children. Mollie was born in Cork, Ireland, and after serving with the Women's Army in France during World War 1, she came to Tasmania with her husband to take up farming at Mawbanna, where she helped the local bush nurse.

'Gateforth', home of the Medwins

During her lifetime, she built no fewer than five houses! During the 1940s the family moved to Black River, where property had been left to Allan by Luke. He sold the property eventually to his own son Paul, who sold it to a Victorian buyer. However, it was later bought back by Rodney Medwin, who owns it today. Not a bad record of almost unbroken ownership by one family! 'Mayura' is now known as 'Gateforth', and provides colonial accommodation.

One hundred and fifty people turned up at the Medwin Reunion held at Wynyard in 1987, so the family still flourishes.

Peggs Creek, nearby, is named for another family of early settlers. William Pegg acquired his land in the mid-1860s from a John White who had had it from the Van Diemen's Land Company in 1853. William and his wife Lucy and at least one of their daughters, (Olive) were buried at the cemetery at the town. There was also a son of William named Henry, (or Harry) who bought land in the area in 1875 and who was a licensee of the Pig and Whistle inn, owned by William. Harry's wife was the Postmistress.

Black Wall in the Forest ceased to exist in the late 1880s: the last occupant was Mr Neil Swift, who lived in the old Pegg house for two years from 1955.

Close by is the railway, where you may see logs waiting to be taken to the Paper Pulp Mill. Visitor Information for the whole area is available just past Black River. Next comes Wilshire, with Myrtlebank Host Farm on your left, Route C221 to Forest and Alcomie. Wilshire Junction is where the railway crosses the road. To see the site of vanished Black Wall village, turn off at the Wilshire turn-off and then left into Murrays Road and drive back towards the river. Another early settlement in the district of which little is known was called Eastport.

Among the early settlers at Black River were John and Elizabeth (nee Stokes) Dobson. John was born in Northhampton, England c. 1815. He arrived in Tasmania in 1833 and married Elizabeth (c. 1825–1911) in Hobart in 1840. They had at least ten children. In 1866 the family leased 80 acres of land at Black River from Francis Smith of Stanley. John died at Rocky Cape, in 1904.

When you reach a junction, Route C129 leads to your left to Forest, and Route B21 to Stanley to the right. If you stop and look back to your right, you will once again see The Nut. Just past this sign is a large brown sign, indicating the many attractions of Stanley, 7 km to your right.

Stanley

Stanley is the ideal town to visit if you're looking for quality local arts and crafts, maritime and colonial history, museums, breathtaking views, fishing fleets, wind and water. You'll find a variety of galleries and craft shops, stocking everything from hand puppets to local pottery, carved and turned wood, chocolate, glassware, unique knitted garments, carved hats and boots and jewellery. Last time we were there we saw a selection of sculptures made from electronic components! The town is small enough to walk around comfortably, but it will probably take a long time if you stop off at all the intriguing shops.

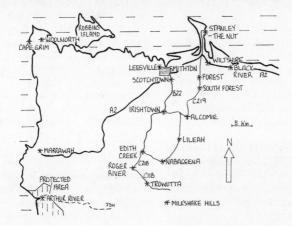

The town of Stanley is situated on a peninsula, jutting out between West Inlet and East Inlet. Halfway along the peninsula, on the eastern side, is the strange formation properly called Circular Head but always referred to as 'The Nut'. In 1854 The Nut was covered with timber, but is now grassed. Until early 1996 sheep were grazed on The Nut, but now the sheep have been removed and an attempt is being made to restore the original vegetation. The township runs right up to the base of 'The Nut'.

There is a walking track up 'The Nut', or, for the less energetic, a chairlift. From the top is a splendid—if windy—panoramic view. Stanley is a fishing village, but tourism is also important. Named after the Secretary of State for the Colonies in the early 1840s, Stanley was the headquarters of the Van Diemen's Land Company from 1825. The township was surveyed in the 1840s under the direction of James Gibson, who took over from Edward Curr as the chief agent in 1842. The town was planned by John Lee Archer. It was owing to the V.D.L. Co. that Stanley had the first school in north-west Tasmania. In 1841 they engaged Rev. Thomas Grigg from England to teach the school. Despite hitches—

mainly about fees—by 1849 thirty children were attending the Stanley Public Day School.

The port, established in 1827, is the oldest on the north-west Coast. Henry Hellyer designed a wooden wharf in 1827 for the *Tranmere*'s second voyage. A replacement was made in 1893 by contractor J.A. Austin, and a breakwater was built in around 1905.

In 1956 Stanley became the first place in Tasmania to receive television from Melbourne, when a P.M.G. technician built up a Channel 7 antenna.

It has since been the venue for an annual Circular Head Arts Festival. The population in the 1990s has hovered around the 500–600 mark.

Come into Stanley on Route B21. Halfway to the town is a scenic point, including a plaque, courtesy of the Geology Department of the University of Tasmania, describing The Nut. It seems that The Nut is the core of an ancient volcano. The inhabitants of Stanley need not worry; this volcano was active between 25 and 70 million years ago! Due to weathering, only the solidified lava of the core remains. From this paint you may look to the left to The Nut and right to part of the Rocky Cape

National Park. The water in front of you is East Arm.

Follow the road to the town and turn left into the Scenic Drive, Dove Cote Road. Follow the signs, turning right at the top of the hill. The lookout is a wooden one. From the top, you can see both the East and West Arms. If you face 'The Nut' you can see to the left the chimneys of 'Highfield' amongst the trees.

'Highfield'. To visit 'Highfield', one-time home of V.D.L. Co. Director Edward Curr, continue on the Lookout Road. At the end, there is a left-hand turn to West Beach and a right-hand turn towards the town. The house is on the right.

The V.D.L. Co. was granted the rights to the north-west corner of Van Diemen's Land in 1825, for the purpose of breeding fine wool sheep. Circular Head was chosen as the centre of operations.

'Highfield', a delightful house with many chimneys, was designed by Henry Hellyer, and was begun in 1832. Among the builders of 'Highfield' were mason John Cross, carpenters George Mann and R. Reed, and convict plasterer, John Davis (or Davies). Additions were planned by John Lee Archer and built in 1844 and 1845. The estate included many other buildings as well as the main house, many of which are

in good order. The threshing barn was built in 1828, the stables in 1836/37, the cow shed in 1839, and the cart shed in 1841. In 1857 the property was leased, and later became an historic site. The house fell into a bad state of repair, but has since been restored.

In the grounds is a large memorial to Juliana Teresa Curr, who died in June 1835 at the age of two. Just inside the existing gateway, on the left, are the remains of a well.

Drive on past 'Highfield' to reach the town. The road spirals down steeply towards The Nut, passing Godfreys Beach. As you come down from Greenhills Road, on your left is a parking area with a stone cairn, commemorating the naming of Circular Head in 1798. Up to your left is the road to The Nut track, Browns Road. Straight ahead is the old Stanley Burial Ground.

Stanley Burial Ground, one of the most charming cemeteries in the state, dates from 1828. Interesting headstones include those of Matthias Medwin, from Buckinghamshire, who died in 1898 at Burnie; surveyor and explorer Henry Hellyer (d. 1832); architect and magistrate John Lee Archer (d. 1852), his wife Sophia (d. 1863) and daughter Charlotte Lee Gibson (d. 1911).

'Highfield', Stanley

Stanley burial ground

The Nut, Stanley

Up The Nut

Enter The Nut State Reserve. For a moderate fee you may take the chairlift up (and down, if you wish). At the top is a short walk of 4 or 5 minutes to the lookout, or the scenic round trip which takes about 45 minutes. Caution: it is often very windy on top of The Nut.

From the top, it is possible to see Table Cane and part of Smithton. Look out for a compass which gives the directions and distances (in miles) to a number of landmarks including Melbourne (190 miles), Three Hummock Island (30 miles), and Woolnorth Point.

More to see in Stanley

Turn into Marshall Street and turn left. On right in Alexander Terrace is the old Plough Inn. Close by is the Touchwood Craft building, (1836), the Old Commercial Hotel, and the Town Hall. Other interesting buildings in Stanley include Bay View Hotel, opened by Joseph as the 'Shamrock Inn' in 1842, and known successively as the Shipp Inn, Stanley Hotel and the Bay View before de-licensed in 1972. Next to this is the birthplace of **Joseph Lyons**,

Australia's only Tasmanian-born Prime Minister. Two of Mr Lyons' lesser known acts are unveiling the famous 'Dog on the Tuckerbox' statue in Gundagai (1932) and the planting of the first oak tree in the Prime Ministers' Avenue of Oaks in Jackson Park, Faulconbridge, N.S.W. two years later. The 'Poets Cottage' where architect John Lee Archer lived until his death, and the childhood home of Joseph Lyons are farther along the same street and may be open to the public. On the other side of the road, look for the Bond Store, a bluestone building once used to store grain, and the old V.D.L. Co. Store, designed by the ubiquitous John Lee Archer and used as a customs house.

Take the A2 to Smithton, past Kauri Timber, which produces much of Tasmania's best timber, including pine and blackwood. Turn left into Route C217 to visit Tall Timbers, a handsome convention centre offering accommodation. Back on A2, you will see B22 leading to Irishtown.

Smithton, then and now

Smithton is a good place to stay if you plan to sample the tranquillity of the far north-west and some of the lushest pasture land

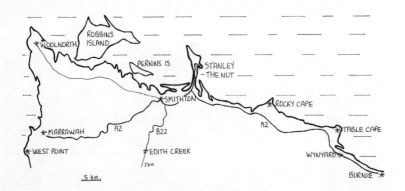

in Australia. There are drives through the Duck River Flats, day trips through the Milkshakes Reserve and the Arthur River area. Since enjoyment of drives to these areas depend on the weather, it's best to ask locally for advice on where and when to go. Trips to 'Woolnorth', the property founded in 1825 by the Van Diemen's Land Company, can be arranged for any day except Good Friday and Christmas Day.

It is 15 km by road from the Stanley turn-off to Smithton, on the Duck River. Two or three km south of the present town is Scotchtown, site of the first settlement in the area made when pioneer and former Van Diemen's Land Company employee Thomas Ollington took up land there in the early 1850s. Next came Charles Innes and finally, in 1855, policeman Peter Smith, whose selection was actually within the town boundary and for whom Smithton was probably named.

It was with the arrival of Joseph Samuel Lee, who came with his sons to set up a sawmill, that the settlement began to flourish. Their place was a kilometre or two north-west of Smithton, and became known, naturally enough, as Leesville. Encouraged by the success of the Lee's operations, more loggers and sawmillers moved in to harvest the splendid crop of

blackwoods. Smithton School opened in 1880. In the wake of the sawmillers, farmers moved in, with a large Irish family, the O'Hallorans from Tipperary, establishing the district of Irishtown 5 km south of Scotchtown. The names of the early settlers echo around the district, with O'Hallorans Hill, Ollingtons Hill, Spinks, Faheys and Connells Hills, and many others, contrasting strangely with the other place names reminiscent of the Aborigines—Nabageena, Lileah, and Trowutta.

In 1904 the Duck River Butter Factory started up in Smithton. It is no longer there, but beef, dairying and cropping are still major activities in the area: especially at Mella, (3 km from Smithton), where modern 'Lacrum' farm has been established which has a large rotary dairy, and is open for inspection between November and May each year. Other industries include vegetable dehydration and a factory processing abalone and crayfish.

Around Smithton. In Smithton, you can turn off into Route C215 to Montagu, and off that route into C213 to Marrawah. Turn off Goldie St into Smith St, and then left to Marrawah. A sign at an intersection points to Route C217 to Edith Creek on

B22, and Marrawah on the right. Turn off towards Edith Creek. Cross a creek, bypass the Irishtown turn-off, and on your right not far along is the main road leading to Allendale Gardens.

Allendale Gardens is a popular place with both locals and visitors. The gardens offer wildflower and rainforest walks, Devonshire teas, and delightful surroundings. Enter the district of Edith Creek. For a pleasant country drive through farmland, ferns and bush, continue through Edith Creek and Nabageena.

Edith Creek was named after Edith Harrisson, the wife of surveyor K.M. Harrisson. Another creek in the district is Birthday Creek, named because the surveyor first saw it on his wife's birthday. Early settlers this century included the Furphys in 1908; the Walkers and the Meaneys in 1903. The first shop was opened in 1920 by Molly Jones and Florrie Porteus. A school was opened nearby in 1916, and two others followed, finally replaced in 1954 by the current Edith Creek Primary School. Until quite recently this school was an Area School (or District High). Near the school is the old Cadbury factory, now owned by Classic Foods.

Edith Creek is in the centre of a flourishing agricultural area. Dairying and cropping are carried out in the fertile soils: even tobacco was grown for two years in 1935–36.

The Western Explorer. Past Edith Creek, you come to a sign pointing out Kanunnah Bridge, and Roger River West on Route C218. This route will lead you onto the Western Explorer, taking you west to Couta Rocks or south west to Balfour and Corinna.

Back to the Bass Highway

If you turn off to the left instead, you'll reach Nabageena. From there, follow Route C219 through Lileah, Alcomie, South Forest and Forest to rejoin the Bass Highway. Otherwise, follow the signs through Irishtown to return to Smithton.

To reach the Milkshakes Forest Reserve from Smithton, take Route B22 out of Smithton, through Edith Creek. Cross the Roger River and turn to the left to Trowutta. Follow the road round over the Arthur River at Tayatea Bridge, turn right and follow the Milkshake Road. The Reserve is about 41 ha. of virgin rain forest, with barbecues and shelters.

Arthur River, Woolnorth and Lacrum Tours. A five-hour cruise of the Arthur River is available. Contact a Tasmanian Travel Centre Office or the local tourist information point at the Smithton Council Chambers for details of this tour and other local tours to 'Lacrum', 'Woolnorth', Cape Grim etc. Near 'Lacrum', you may also visit Wombat Tarn park, where the remains of an extinct giant wombat were found in the 1980s.

Up-to-date information on tours can be obtained at any Tasmanian Travel Cents or by obtaining a copy of Travelways.

Robbins Island, near Smithton, is named after Lt Charles Robbins, R.N., who sailed through Bass Strait in the *Integrity* in 1804. Lt Robbins is remembered as the enthusiastic young man who 'kept an eye' on Commodore Nicholas Baudin, when it was suspected that the Commodore planned to claim Van Diemen's Land or King Island for the French. Robbins camped beside the French on King Island, and defiantly flew the Union Jack every day. Unfortunately, he made the mistake of flying it upside down

West of Smithton. The traveller west of Smithton has two choices: to continue on Route A2 to Marrawah, the most westerly town in Tasmania, or to take Route C215, the Montagu Road, c. 50 km out to 'Woolnorth'.

'Woolnorth'—all 22 000 hectares of it is all that remains of the V.D.L. Co's holding. Granted to the Company in 1824 or 1825, it was held until 1845 when much of the land was sold off. On 'Woolnorth', the property owned by the V.D.L. Co., stands an old cottage built in 1831 and used by many of the cooks who have worked at 'Woolnorth'. It is built of clay bricks made on the property, with wooden nails, blackwood, myrtle and eucalyptus being used in the construction. The gaol building also remains. 'Woolnorth' was first occupied by shepherds in 1829. A small jetty was erected at Woolnorth Point at around the same time.

These days, 'Woolnorth' runs beef cattle, merinos, Border Leicesters and Kashmir goats as well as cash crops and trees.

BIBLIOGRAPHY

Books
COCKER, Kathleen, *Early Houses of the North West Coast of Tasmania*, National Trust, 1972.
IRBY, Ken, *In the Beginning*.

Booklets
A Traveller's Guide to the Far North West of Tasmania.
Motor News, R.A.C.T.
Travellers' Guide to Cape Country, 1988.
'Impact '88', an *Advocate* feature.
Circular Head Local History Journal, various issues.
Sisters Creek Brag Sheet, various issues.

Pamphlets
'Let's Talk About Circular Head'
'Let's Talk About Wynyard' (Tas. Visitor Corporation)
The Western Explorer

Maps
Tasmap 1: 100 000 Land Tenure Index Series:
'Arthur River', 'Circular Head',
'Sandy Cape', 'Table Cape',
'Welcome', 'Hellyer'.

Information
Thanks to Mary Hawkes, Ken Irby, Lynn Richardson, and the people of the far north-west.

Index